ENGAGING INDIGENOUS ECONOMY

DEBATING DIVERSE APPROACHES

ENGAGING INDIGENOUS ECONOMY

DEBATING DIVERSE APPROACHES

Edited by
WILL SANDERS

Australian
National
University

PRESS

Centre for Aboriginal Economic Policy Research
College of Arts and Social Sciences
The Australian National University, Canberra

RESEARCH MONOGRAPH NO. 35
2016

ANU PRESS

Published by ANU Press
The Australian National University
Acton ACT 2601, Australia
Email: anupress@anu.edu.au
This title is also available online at press.anu.edu.au

National Library of Australia Cataloguing-in-Publication entry

Title: Engaging indigenous economy : debating diverse approaches /
                  editor William Sanders.

ISBN: 9781760460037 (paperback) 9781760460044 (ebook)

Series: Research monograph (Australian National University. Centre
                  for Aboriginal Economic Policy
                  Research) ; no. 35.

Subjects: Aboriginal Australians--Economic conditions.
                  Aboriginal Australians--Land tenure.
                  Business enterprises, Aboriginal Australian.
                  Australia--Ethnic relations--Economic aspects.

Other Creators/Contributors:
                  Sanders, Will, editor.

Dewey Number: 338.994

Cover design and layout by ANU Press.

Front cover image: Masig Island's fleet of small boats supports the island's commercial,
subsistence and ceremonial fishing activities. Dinghies such as the one shown here
provide a significant degree of economic independence and resilience to Torres Strait
Islanders across the region, in a context where other sources of income are sparse.
Photo: Annick Thomassin.

Contents

Part 4: Personal Reflections

List of figures

List of tables

Abbreviations and acronyms

4WD	Four-Wheel Drive
ABA	Aboriginals Benefit Account
ABS	Australian Bureau of Statistics
ABTA	Aboriginals Benefit Trust Account
ABTF	Aborigines Benefits Trust Fund
AEDP	Aboriginal Employment Development Policy
AHURI	Australian Housing and Urban Research Institute
AIATSIS	Australian Institute of Aboriginal and Torres Strait Islander Studies
ALRA	*Aboriginal Land Rights (Northern Territory) Act 1976* (Cwlth)
ANU	Australian National University
APY	Anangu Pitjantjatjara Yankunytjatjara
ARC	Australian Research Council
ATSIC	Aboriginal and Torres Strait Islander Commission
CAEPR	Centre for Aboriginal Economic Policy Research
CATSI Act	*Corporations (Aboriginal and Torres Strait Islander) Act 2006* (Cwlth)
CDEP	Community Development Employment Projects
CEDA	Committee for Economic Development of Australia
CLT	Community Land Trust
COAG	Council of Australian Governments
CRF	Consolidated Revenue Fund
DAA	Department of Aboriginal Affairs
EDTL	Executive Director of Township Leasing

FaHCSIA	Department of Families, Housing, Community Services and Indigenous Affairs
FIFO	Fly in/Fly out
GDP	Gross Domestic Product
GFC	Global Financial Crisis
IAS	Indigenous Advancement Strategy
IPA	Indigenous Protected Area
ITA Act	*Income Tax Assessment Act 1936* (Cwlth)
IVAIS	Indigenous Visual Arts Industry Support program
LNG	Liquefied Natural Gas
MRE	Mining Royalty Equivalent
MWT	Mining Withholding Tax
NG	Ngaanyatjarra
NGO	Non-government Organisation
NLC	Northern Land Council
NNTT	National Native Title Tribunal
NTA	*Native Title Act 1993* (Cwlth)
NTAC	Northern Territory Aboriginal Council
NTER	Northern Territory Emergency Response
NTRB	Native Title Representative Body
NWAC	Nyangumarta Warrarn Aboriginal Corporation
ORIC	Office of the Registrar of Indigenous Corporations
PBC	Prescribed Body Corporate
PZJA	Torres Strait Projected Zone Joint Authority
RJCP	Remote Jobs and Communities Program
RNTBC	Registered Native Title Body Corporate
ROCO	Register of Cultural Organisations
YMAC	Yamatji Marlpa Aboriginal Corporation

Contributors

Jon Altman is a Research Professor at the Alfred Deakin Institute for Citizenship and Globalisation at Deakin University, and an Emeritus Professor of The Australian National University located at RegNet: School of Regulation and Global Governance. From 1990 to 2010 he was foundation Director of the Centre for Aboriginal Economic Policy Research at ANU. He is an enthusiastic advocate for the power of critical and independent academic research to persuade.

PK Basu is an Associate Professor in the Faculty of Business, Charles Sturt University. His research interests include Indigenous entrepreneurship. His research has been funded by the Australian Research Council (Discovery and Linkage Grants).

Shelley Bielefeld is a Braithwaite Research Fellow at RegNet: School of Regulation and Global Governance at The Australian National University where she is undertaking scholarship on the interaction between the regulatory state and Indigenous peoples in the area of welfare reform.

Geoff Buchanan is a PhD candidate at the Centre for Aboriginal Economic Policy Research, The Australian National University. He commenced a career in policy research as Jon Altman's research assistant in 2004. He has worked at the Native Title Research Unit at the Australian Institute of Aboriginal and Torres Strait Islander Studies and currently works with the ACT Council of Social Service.

Rose Butler is a Research Associate with the Centre for Social Impact at the University of New South Wales. She undertakes Australia-based ethnographic and qualitative research on children's economic lives, family and economy, class and cultural diversity in education.

Jock Collins is Professor of Social Economics in the Management Discipline Group at the UTS Business School, Sydney, Australia. His research interests centre on an interdisciplinary study of immigration and cultural diversity and include immigrant and Indigenous entrepreneurship. His research has been funded by the Australian Research Council and the Rural Industry Research and Development Council.

Louise Crabtree is a Senior Research Fellow in the Institute for Culture and Society at Western Sydney University. She has recently led work funded by the Australian Housing and Urban Research Institute focusing on appropriate housing tenure options for Aboriginal communities in New South Wales and the Northern Territory.

Katherine Curchin is an applied political philosopher with research interests in social policy and Indigenous policy in Australia. She is a Research Fellow in the Centre for Aboriginal Economic Policy Research, The Australian National University, and holds an Australian Research Council Discovery Early Career Researcher Award. Her current research project compares Noel Pearson and Jon Altman's visions of Indigenous development.

Ben Dibley is a Research Fellow at the Institute for Culture and Society, Western Sydney University, Australia. He is co-author of *Collecting, ordering, governing: anthropology and liberal government* (Duke University Press, forthcoming).

Jacky Green is a Garawa warrior and artist from the Gulf country of the Northern Territory. He says he started painting to get his voice out: 'I want to show people what is happening to our country and to Aboriginal people. No one is listening to us. What we want. How we want to live. What we want in the future for our children. It's for these reasons that I started to paint. I want government to listen to Aboriginal people. I want people in the cities to know what's happening to us and our country.'

Chris Gregory is an Adjunct Fellow in Anthropology at The Australian National University. He is an economic anthropologist who has lived and worked in Papua New Guinea, India and Fiji. He is the author of *Observing the economy* (Routledge, 1989, with Jon Altman). A second edition of his book, *Gifts and commodities*, has just been published by HAU books.

Seán Kerins is a Research Fellow at the Centre for Aboriginal Economic Policy Research, The Australian National University. Over the past 25 years he has worked with Indigenous peoples and local communities on cultural and natural resource management issues in Aotearoa/New Zealand, the Faroe Islands, Norway and Australia.

Emma Kowal is Professor of Anthropology in the Alfred Deakin Institute for Citizenship and Globalisation and the School of Humanities and Social Sciences at Deakin University. She is the author of *Trapped in the gap: doing good in Indigenous Australia* (Berghahn, 2015).

Branka Krivokapic-Skoko is an Associate Professor in the Faculty of Business, Charles Sturt University. Her research interests include the revitalisation of regional and rural Australia through ethnic business and immigration. Her research has been funded by the Australian Research Council and the Rural Industry Research and Development Council.

Richard Martin is a Research Fellow and Consultant Anthropologist at the University of Queensland. His research is focused on the politics of land and identity in Australia. He has undertaken numerous applied projects, including research on multiple native title claims and cultural heritage matters around Queensland. He was co-editor (with Cameo Dalley) of *Dichotomous identities? Indigenous and non-Indigenous people and the intercultural in Australia*, *The Australian Journal of Anthropology*, Volume 26, Issue 1 (2015).

Kerry McCallum is Senior Research Fellow in the News and Media Research Centre, Faculty of Arts and Design, University of Canberra. Her research in political communication examines the relationships between changing media, political participation and the development of social policy, with a particular focus on Australian Indigenous affairs.

Pamela McGrath is currently Research Director with the National Native Title Tribunal. Her research interests include the social impacts of native title, Indigenous heritage management, information management and archiving. She has worked in the native title sector for over 15 years and in 2010 co-founded the Centre for Native Title Anthropology at The Australian National University.

Mark Morrison is Sub-Dean Research in the Faculty of Business, Charles Sturt University. His research has been funded by the Australian Research Council (Discovery and Linkage Grants), the US Environmental Protection Agency and National Science Foundation, NSW Environmental Trust, Land and Water Australia, Country Energy, IPART and the US Forest Service.

Stephen Muecke is Professor of Ethnography in the Environmental Humanities Program at the University of New South Wales. His book *The Mother's Day protest and other fictocritical essays* will be published by Rowman and Littlefield International in June 2016.

John Nieuwenhuysen is a Fellow of the Academy of Social Sciences in Australia, and is currently Emeritus Professor, Monash University. In 2003 he received an award (AM) in the Order of Australia for services to independent research on immigration, multicultural, equity, indigenous, taxation, labour and industry issues, and to reform of the liquor laws of Victoria.

Nicolas Peterson is Professor of Anthropology at The Australian National University. He has a long-standing interest in Australian Aboriginal anthropology, land and sea tenure, economic anthropology, and fourth-world peoples and the state. His most recent book is *Experiments in self-determination: histories of the outstation movement in Australia* (coedited with Fred Myers, ANU Press, 2016).

David P Pollack is a former adviser in the Australian Government specialising in land rights, native title and royalty management. He has a special interest in the Aboriginals Benefit Account and worked closely with Jon Altman in researching the financial aspects of the *Aboriginal Land Rights (Northern Territory) Act 1976* during the period of the Reeves Review in the late 1990s.

Kim de Rijke is Lecturer in Anthropology at the University of Queensland. His current research is focused on the sociocultural dimensions of unconventional gas developments in Australia, Europe and the US. For the past 13 years he has also carried out applied research on native title and Indigenous cultural heritage, and was managing and senior anthropologist at the Kimberley and Central Queensland Aboriginal Land Councils from 2003 to 2008.

Marianne Riphagen is a Visiting Fellow at the School of Archaeology and Anthropology, The Australian National University. She also teaches anthropology at the Radboud University Nijmegen, the Netherlands. Her research has focused on art created by urban-based Indigenous Australians, Indigenous cosmopolitanism and the economic value of Aboriginal cultural heritage in Australia's Western Desert.

Will Sanders joined the staff of the Centre for Aboriginal Economic Policy Research (CAEPR) as a Research Fellow in 1993, having previously been a CAEPR Associate and co-author with Jon Altman of CAEPR's Discussion Paper No. 1. He works on policy issues relating to housing, local government and social security. His political science training has also led to a research interest in Indigenous people and elections. Will was Deputy Director of CAEPR from 2010 to 2014.

Benedict Scambary is an anthropologist with 20 years' experience working with Aboriginal people in the Northern Territory. He completed his PhD at the Centre for Aboriginal Economic Policy Research under the supervision of Jon Altman in 2007. He is currently the Chief Executive Officer of the Aboriginal Areas Protection Authority.

Leon Terrill is a lecturer in the University of New South Wales Law School and a Research Director at the Indigenous Law Centre. He is the author of *Beyond communal and individual ownership: Indigenous land reform in Australia* (Routledge, 2015) and teaches land law, contract law and Indigenous legal issues.

Annick Thomassin is an anthropology PhD candidate at McGill University (Canada). Her thesis examines the politics underpinning fisheries co-management strategies in Torres Strait. She is also a Research Officer at the Centre for Aboriginal Economic Policy Research, The Australian National University, where her research focus is largely on the political ecology of coastal and marine resources management.

David Trigger is Professor of Anthropology at the University of Queensland. His research interests encompass the different meanings attributed to land and nature across diverse sectors of society. He has carried out more than 35 years of anthropological study on Indigenous Australian systems of land tenure, including applied research on resource development negotiations and native title. He is the author of *Whitefella comin': Aboriginal responses to colonialism in northern Australia* (CUP, 1992).

Lisa Waller is a Senior Lecturer in the School of Communication and Creative Arts, Deakin University. Her research is concerned with how news media shape society, from Indigenous Affairs policy, to their role in regional and rural identity formation and the administration of justice.

Ed Wensing is a Fellow of the Planning Institute of Australia and of the Higher Education Academy. He is currently a PhD Scholar at the National Centre for Indigenous Studies, The Australian National University, and Adjunct Associate Professor in the College of Marine and Environmental Sciences at James Cook University. He has over 40 years' experience as an urban and regional planner and policy analyst and has worked extensively with Aboriginal and Torres Strait Islander people on a wide range of land administration and land use planning matters.

Kaely Woods has had a long career as a senior bureaucrat in Indigenous affairs. She is now a PhD candidate at The Australian National University, researching the role and value of Indigenous culture in economic development, particularly in remote Australia. Her other research interests include Indigenous control, governance, and participation in enterprises and services across cultural and other industries.

1

Taking difference seriously: Life, income and work for Jon Altman and friends

Will Sanders

The engagement of Indigenous Australians in economic activity is a matter of long-standing public concern and debate. Jon Altman has made it the focus of an academic and public career spanning almost 40 years. First as an economist at Melbourne University and then as an anthropologist at The Australian National University (ANU), Jon explored issues of life, income and work among Indigenous Australians at geographic scales from the local to the national (Altman & Nieuwenhuysen 1979, Altman 1987). He tussled early with policy questions around mining, tourism, arts and homelands (Altman 1983, 1988; Altman & Taylor 1987, Altman et al. 1989) and with the research methods of economic anthropology (Gregory & Altman 1989). All this was done before Jon established the ANU Centre for Aboriginal Economic Policy Research (CAEPR) in 1990, of which he became the foundation Director. Jon's output over the next 20 years, often in conjunction with his CAEPR colleagues, was sustained and prolific (Thomassin & Butler 2014). At the 10-year mark, Jon engaged Tim Rowse to review 'the CAEPR corpus', which resulted in the book *Indigenous futures: choice and development for Aboriginal and Islander Australians* (Rowse 2002a). Launching book, Hal Wootten wondered whether Tim's focus on the ideas of choice and 'the Indigenous sector' was what Jon expected. For Wootten (2002: 79), this was a worryingly positive 'lens' on developments and achievements about which he was 'much less sanguine'. He saw 'prison camps' with walls only partly torn down, or in the jocular metaphor of Aboriginal people, a 'yabbie bucket' out of which it was still very hard to jump. Rowse's response to Wootten was that he was 'taking choice seriously' among Indigenous Australians, as he argued CAEPR research had done over the previous decade (Rowse 2002b: 82).

My impressions of Jon's work over 35 years are that he has always taken Indigenous choice and difference very seriously. He has seen past Indigenous agency contributing to current social and economic circumstances and current Indigenous agency contributing to future possibilities. This is not to deny that the economic structures surrounding Indigenous people can be powerfully constraining, but it respects Indigenous people as competent judges of the possibilities and opportunities they face. Jon's hybrid economy approach suggests that Indigenous people are competently exploring their comparative advantage drawn from the customary sector, while also exploring the opportunities and constraints they face in the market and state sectors. These exploratory choices both reflect and lead to differences, among Indigenous Australians and between Indigenous and settler Australians. Differences in socioeconomic status cannot simply be reduced to ideas of disadvantage and structural lack of opportunity. These are contentious ideas, but ones worth thinking about hard and taking seriously.

The following collection of papers is drawn from a conference held in September 2014 to coincide with Jon's 60th birthday and his retirement from CAEPR and ANU as a member of staff. It includes contributions from some of Jon's most long-standing colleagues: his economist colleague from the University of Melbourne John Nieuwenhuysen; his anthropology PhD supervisor from ANU Nicolas Peterson; and his postdoctoral collaborator on the methods of economic anthropology Chris Gregory. It also includes numerous contributions from younger scholars who have found Jon's work stimulating or useful in shaping their own. What is missing, quite notably, is papers by Jon's CAEPR colleagues of the last 25 years. This is explained in part by the interest expressed by over 50 people in giving papers at the conference. The program committee of Tim Rowse, Kirrily Jordan and myself chose 35 and in the process cut out a number of offerings by CAEPR staff.

This was not intentional, but it seemed reasonable. Long-standing staff could contribute to the conference and the CAEPR publication program in other ways, while for those beyond CAEPR the conference was a rare opportunity to engage directly with Jon and his work.

Part 1 of this collection focuses on Jon's core concept of the hybrid economy, in theory, practice and policy. In Chapter 2, one of Jon's PhD students, Geoff Buchanan, provides a 'genealogy' of Jon's work, going right back to a Master's thesis on export instability in Samoa. Jon was already interested in the idea of 'subsistence affluence' as an alternative to exposure to the vagaries of the capitalist market economy. Jon's academic journey was 'circuitous', argues Buchanan, taking in 'articulation of modes of production' and 'relative autonomy' before settling on the idea of 'economic hybridity'. At the other end of the collection (Chapter 21), another one of Jon's PhD students, Ben Scambary, argues that Jon has used his privileged position in academia over many years to 'speak truth to power' in a 'frank and fearless' way. Ben's PhD was part of a CAEPR research project on relations between Aboriginal communities and mining companies. He notes acknowledgement that CAEPR's research was 'a key influence on Rio Tinto's $2 billion mining agreement in the Pilbara', speaking truth to corporate power (see also Scambary 2013).

Two other contributions in Part 1 are from PhD students who have been influenced, though not supervised, by Jon Altman. Kaely Woods is a former senior Indigenous affairs bureaucrat who engaged with Jon and CAEPR during the 1990s and 2000s. Having left the public service, she is now trying to push further Jon's methods of measuring and valuing non-market aspects of Indigenous activity. Woods is using 'choice modelling' to test and value 'the tension and trade-offs between paid employment and cultural activity' for Indigenous people (Chapter 7). In Chapter 8, Annick Thomassin provides a classic account of hybridity in the 'life projects' of Masig Islanders in the Torres Strait. Being a 'fisher' on Masig is, she argues, not a 'job' or a 'profession' but a 'way of life'. While fishing is a useful way to feed the family, it can be seasonal and unreliable, as too can be the income derived from it. So land-based activities under the long-running state sector Community Development Employment Projects (CDEP) scheme have provided fishers with a steady base income on which to build.

Although a McGill University PhD scholar, Thomassin has chosen to sit at CAEPR for the last five years, clearly influenced and inspired by Jon's work.

While this volume is a festschrift for Jon Altman, it also attempts to be critical. Jon often gives 'robust' critiques of other people's work and he asks for nothing less in return. In Chapter 3, Chris Gregory picks at the logic of Jon's three-sector model of economic engagement and income generation. In strict binary terms, the model leads to eight segments, not seven, and the sectors themselves must also be separately considered. There are thus 11 distinct spaces to be logically considered in the hybrid generation of work, life and income, not just seven. Chris also points out that Jon's empirical work on the changing relative importance of the three sectors over time is not represented in his Venn diagram. This, Gregory argues, would lead to a consideration of 'changing relations of domination and subordination', as much as hybridity.

Chapters 4–6 continue in this critical vein. De Rijke, Martin and Trigger raise questions about the idea of 'customary environmentalism' which they discern at the heart of Jon's recent research project with others entitled People on Country. Despite aspirations of 'two way' knowledge exchange, they argue that contemporary Indigenous environmental work is often a more prosaic form of low-waged employment, continuing more than transforming past economic relations. Nicolas Peterson sees Jon's hybrid economy model as only relevant to a small proportion of Indigenous people, even in remote areas. He suggests that for the 'difficulties the majority of the remote area populations are facing', the model is not 'a coherent basis for policy'. Katherine Curchin offers the idea of 'partial commodification' as a way of thinking more clearly about the 'livelihood activities which typify the hybrid economy' and she notes that there are also many non-Indigenous people, like academics, whose livelihoods 'mediate market and non-market norms'.

The later chapters in Part 1 all focus on the practice of the hybrid economy in particular regions, although at times they are also oriented to theory or policy. In Chapter 9, Seán Kerins and Jacky Green show how they have worked together on alternative development strategies in the Gulf country. This has occurred under the auspices of the People on Country project, combining the labours of an Indigenous land owner and artist with those of an academic collaborator. Green's paintings are both striking and powerfully evocative of ideas of hybrid land-based development. His words of explanation, carefully recorded by Kerins, suggest how these images draw on adverse Indigenous experiences of imposed economic development. The case for difference and alternative development strategies on country could not be more strongly put.

In Chapter 10, Marianne Riphagen revisits Altman's work in the 1980s on tourism and art at Mutitjulu, adjacent to Uluru. She reflects on more recent developments at Maruku Arts. With the commercial success of wooden artefacts, known as punu, declining since 2007, Maruku has experimented with art markets and dot painting workshops for tourists in Yulara since 2012. Riphagen notes that these initiatives have provided additional income for Indigenous artists resident at Mutitjulu, but that punu production has largely been based in other communities some distance away. While the local Mutitjulu artists have benefited from Maruku's recent experiments, the broader 'regional economy' of art production has had attention drawn away from it and possibly fallen further into decline. Maintaining comparative advantage in the hybrid economy can require changing explorations of possibilities with unintended adverse consequences as well as successes.

In Chapter 11, via a slightly obscure reference to Karl Marx's 11 theses on Feuerbach (Tucker 1972: 107–9), Stephen Muecke and Ben Dibley offer us 'five theses for reinstituting economics' developed from their observations of Broome during conflict over the proposed gas plant at James Price Point. They see the proponents of the gas plant, Woodside and the Western Australian government, as using a 'modern' language of 'the Economy' from which all supposedly benefit. As environmental humanists, Muecke and Dibley want to reinstitute a more grounded, ethnographic language of 'economies' that have local 'contingencies' and do not 'determine all values'. Their economies are 'earthbound' and variable, have 'non-human stakeholders' and are all 'hybrid', just 'especially in Aboriginal Australia'. They see Altman's work as contributing to this 'deflation of the Economy' into 'a diversity of economic activities and livelihood sources which evidence creative postcolonial adaptation'.

Part 2 of the collection focuses on the somewhat unlikely twin ideas of neoliberalism and guardianship in recent debates about Indigenous policy. Shelley Bielefeld shows how there is a return to state paternalism, as well as market liberalism, in recent policies of income management within the social security system. She sees this as a continuation of the unfinished 'colonial project' of reforming Indigenous norms (Chapter 12).

Kerry McCallum and Lisa Waller (Chapter 13) provide an analysis of the media and Indigenous policy over a 20-year period. They focus on *The Australian* newspaper as a self-conscious 'keystone' of Australian Indigenous affairs reporting promoting 'neoliberal policy agendas'. They also note the 'singular influence' of Noel Pearson as a regular commentator columnist in *The Australian*. Jon Altman, by way of contrast, has been a regular commentator columnist in *The National Indigenous Times* and *Tracker,* two somewhat more marginal parts of the Australian media landscape.

Emma Kowal (Chapter 14) offers a more personalised account of how, as a young medical and arts graduate, she enthusiastically stepped into the public health gap between Indigenous and other Australians. A few years later, disillusioned and sensitised to the 'moral politics of race and identity', she developed an analysis of the 'intense identity work that consumes so much effort in Indigenous affairs'. She sees Jon, like herself, as 'trapped in the gap' between 'two equal and opposing fears', which she labels 'remedialism' in one direction and 'orientalism' in the other. This is a sophisticated analytic version of a central question that has always hung over CAEPR's and Jon's work: when is socioeconomic difference to be judged adversely as structural disadvantage and lack of opportunity and when supportively as reflecting autonomy, informed choice and cultural difference (see for example Altman and Rowse 2005)?

In Chapter 15, Leon Terrill uses the idea of renewed state paternalism in his account of the recent push for 'township leases' on Aboriginal land in the Northern Territory. He sees 'neoliberal paternalism' as a two-step process in which the state first imposes higher levels of 'discipline' on poor individuals and households through requirements like standardised rent and tenancy agreements. The more distant and long-term second step is to produce responsible and competent actors in private housing markets. Having identified the first step as a form of guardianship, Terrill asks whether there are others, besides government, who could exercise this 'control'. Jon would argue that in the 'massive change in land titling in Australia' since 1977, it has been Aboriginal land councils and groups of traditional owners who have exercised such control, but that recent governments have not respected their different choices.

Terrill's contribution leads in well to Part 3 of the collection focusing on applications of Altman's ideas in land, housing and entrepreneurship.

Ed Wensing (Chapter 16) examines both native title and 23 statutory forms of Aboriginal land rights developed in Australia in the last half century. His focus is on the inability of native title holders to use their interests in land as part of the 'modern economy'. He argues that it is appropriate that Aboriginal land cannot simply be sold, but that it ought to be able to be leased and used to secure a mortgage. Some of the statutory land rights regimes show how this can be done, but they too can be restrictive and ultimately are also subject to the restrictions of native title. As a land use planner, Wensing wants to break through some of these 'legal orthodoxies' and think differently.

In Chapter 17, Louise Crabtree takes inspiration from the idea of hybridity in exploring possible alternative affordable housing tenures beyond the existing polarised options of mortgagee home ownership and public housing. Through ideas of community land trusts, she opens up a spectrum of variable equity housing tenure possibilities between these polarities. Her empirical inspiration comes from outside Australia, but is clearly reinforced by Altman's determination to take difference seriously.

David Pollack's political economy of the Aboriginals Benefit Account in the Northern Territory in Chapter 18 is more historical in its inspiration. Rich in legislative and policy detail, it revisits ideas about the use of mining royalty equivalents (MREs) derived from Aboriginal land which Altman explored in an official review in 1985. Pollack asks why the ambiguous policy foundations noted by Altman have continued since with their shortcomings and inconsistencies.

Pamela McGrath (Chapter 19) reports on a study of how much labour, or work, has gone into native title processes for the Nyangumarta people over the last 15 years. McGrath finds that more than 140 Nyangumarta have allocated over 2,700 days to native title business, but that they have only derived possibly $250,000 income, as their predominant mode of involvement is as unpaid volunteers. It is the 300 non-Nyangumarta—lawyers, mining executives, bureaucrats, anthropologists, etc.—who have derived significant income from these activities. Jon Altman will not be surprised by these findings, either as a well-paid ANU academic or from his own time allocation studies of Indigenous groups. Indigenous income from activities related to custom is more imputed than monetary, while settlers are well paid for their engagements.

Jock Collins and his co-authors (Chapter 20) report on a recent survey of over 300 Indigenous entrepreneurs, plus 38 more in-depth interviews. Through the idea of the 'community contribution' of Indigenous businesses they discern a large hybrid economy, while also arguing that it is the market that sets basic business constraints.

Part 4 of the collection comprises personal reflections, by PhD student Ben Scambary (as already discussed), by senior colleague John Nieuwenhuysen and by Jon Altman himself. John Nieuwenhuysen clearly takes considerable pride in having lured Altman from New Zealand to Australia with the offer of a job at Melbourne University in 1976. Thus began an association of almost 40 years in which, Nieuwenhuysen argues, Jon Altman has kept the 'faith for independent, fearless scholarly research' that is 'directly related to policy' and 'exposed to public debate'. Jon Altman's own reflections reinforce this idea when he notes that the 'social justice fire' that he shared with a young Aboriginal man in Melbourne in the late 1970s has not 'abated'. Jon clearly takes great pride in advocating forcefully for his friends of 35 years at Mumeka and for other Indigenous groups across Australia. Indeed, in retrospect, forceful outspoken advocacy is perhaps Jon's default setting, which was perhaps just slightly tempered during his first 17 years as the Director of CAEPR.

Nic Peterson identifies 2007 and the Northern Territory Emergency Response (NTER) as a turning point at which Jon Altman became the outspoken critic of 'the government's approach in Indigenous affairs' and was no longer interested in the measured, insider-speak of policy targets and reform. Jon agrees, saying that he took a 'decisive stance' against the NTER and that he no longer felt it was 'possible to produce research in good faith that would be genuinely received by government at face value'. This was a difficult stance to take as the Director of a university centre receiving significant government funding and, no doubt, it contributed greatly to Jon's decision to stand down from the CAEPR directorship just three years later. These were difficult years at CAEPR, as they were in Indigenous affairs more generally. Collegiality and friendship forged over the previous two decades was tested to the limits, as some wanted to become outsider critics of government with Jon and some to continue to play the measured, insider game.

The tensions within CAEPR during these years were not so much disciplinary as strategic. If, following Altman and Rowse 2005, this was economics and equality versus anthropology and difference, where did John Taylor and I fit in the mix? John Taylor's measured population geographies and demographies were the very centre of the CAEPR corpus, producing powerful numbers with which public servants, politicians and Indigenous communities all wanted to engage. My own contributions from a political science background sometimes included numbers but were more distinctive for their focus on the internal dynamics of the state sector. I am not sure that my contributions were so well appreciated within government and they certainly had little to do with differences between anthropology and economics. But Jon Altman always defended both the independence and the wide interdisciplinary nature of CAEPR, which enabled my own work (and income) to be sustained over many years. For this I will be forever grateful.

It is with sadness that I note the absence of any contribution to this conference or volume from John Taylor. Indigenous affairs is, in many ways, a hard school. John Taylor took over as CAEPR Director in 2010 and continued, with other staff members, to produce those powerful numbers. Jon Altman tells us in his reflections that he had by then abandoned the 'path to parity' with its 'imagined homo-topia' and its 'hegemonic deficit-focused indicators of success, failure and accountability'. This forthright outsider stance meant that Jon Altman was not easy to have on staff at CAEPR over the next four years, but his presence was always worthwhile.

The economic activities of Indigenous Australians are challenging to engage with, conceptually, empirically and strategically. Like Jon, I was drawn into this field as a young postgraduate over three decades ago. Jon's work displayed a clarity of thought and method which is its hallmark to this day. It also displayed that fire of commitment to social justice and advocacy for modern hunter-gatherers, which is still evident in all that Jon says and does. Just to think that some Indigenous Australians can be modern hunter-gatherers is to take difference very seriously. We need more serious theorists of difference in Australia, like Jon Altman, to continue exploring Indigenous peoples' postcolonial economic possibilities. Otherwise we may indeed lapse into some lazy, unintellectual 'homo-topia'.

References

Altman J (1983). *Aborigines and mining royalties in the Northern Territory*, Australian Institute of Aboriginal Studies, Canberra.

Altman J (1987). *Hunter-gatherers today: an Aboriginal economy in north Australia*, Australian Institute of Aboriginal Studies, Canberra.

Altman J (1988). *Aborigines, tourism and development: the Northern Territory experience*, Monograph, Australian National University North Australia Research Unit, Darwin.

Altman J, McGuigan C & Yu P (1989). *The Aboriginal arts and crafts industry: report of the review committee*, Department of Aboriginal Affairs, Australian Government Publishing Service, Canberra.

Altman J & Nieuwenhuysen J (1979). *The economic status of Australian Aborigines*, Cambridge University Press, Cambridge.

Altman J & Rowse T (2005). Indigenous affairs. In Saunders P & Walter J (eds), *Ideas and influence: social science and public policy in Australia,* University of New South Wales Press, Sydney.

Altman J & Taylor L (1987). *The economic viability of Aboriginal outstations: a report to the Australian Council for Employment and Training*, Australian Government Publishing Service, Canberra.

Gregory C & Altman J (1989). *Observing the economy*, Routledge, London & New York.

Rowse T (2002a). *Indigenous futures: choice and development for Aboriginal and Islander Australians*, University of New South Wales Press, Sydney.

Rowse T (2002b). Taking choice seriously: reply to Hal Wootten. *Australian Aboriginal Studies* 2:82–3.

Scambary B (2013). *My country, mine country: Indigenous people, mining and development contestation in remote Australia*, CAEPR Research Monograph No. 33, ANU E Press, Canberra.

Thomassin A & Butler R (2014). *Engaging Indigenous economy: a selected annotated bibliography of Jon Altman's writings 1979– 2014*, Working Paper 96, Centre for Aboriginal Economic Policy Research, The Australian National University, Canberra.

Tucker R (ed.) (1972). *The Marx-Engels reader*, Norton & Company, New York.

Wootten H (2002). Review article—Indigenous futures: choice and development for Aboriginal and Islander Australians. *Australian Aboriginal Studies* 2:78–82.

Part 1: The Hybrid Economy: Theory, Practice and Policy

2

From Samoa to CAEPR via Mumeka: The hybrid economy comes of age

Geoff Buchanan

Introduction

In 2001, Jon Altman introduced the hybrid economy framework as a means of addressing the economic development problem faced by Indigenous people living on Aboriginal land in remote and regional Australia. For Altman, the distinctive economies in these locations—made up of market, state and customary components—were poorly understood 'by politicians, policy makers and Indigenous people and their representative organisations alike' (2001: v). The hybrid economy framework was subsequently depicted as a Venn diagram emphasising the linkages and interdependencies of the three overlapping sectors (see Fig. 2.1).

Altman argued that to understand the hybrid economy required 'a hybrid analytical framework that combines science, social sciences and Indigenous knowledge systems' (2001: v). The framework was developed at a time when, as a social scientist, Altman was collaborating with biological scientists at the Key Centre for Tropical Wildlife Management and with Bawinanga Aboriginal Corporation in Maningrida, central Arnhem Land. Emphasis was placed on the role such a framework might play in achieving 'sustainable development on Aboriginal land in the twenty-first century' (Altman 2001: v), particularly through the customary and commercial use of wild resources. For Altman, the fundamental development dilemma was how to grow the hybrid economy—primarily through the expansion of the customary and market sectors—given that state intervention was thought to have peaked.

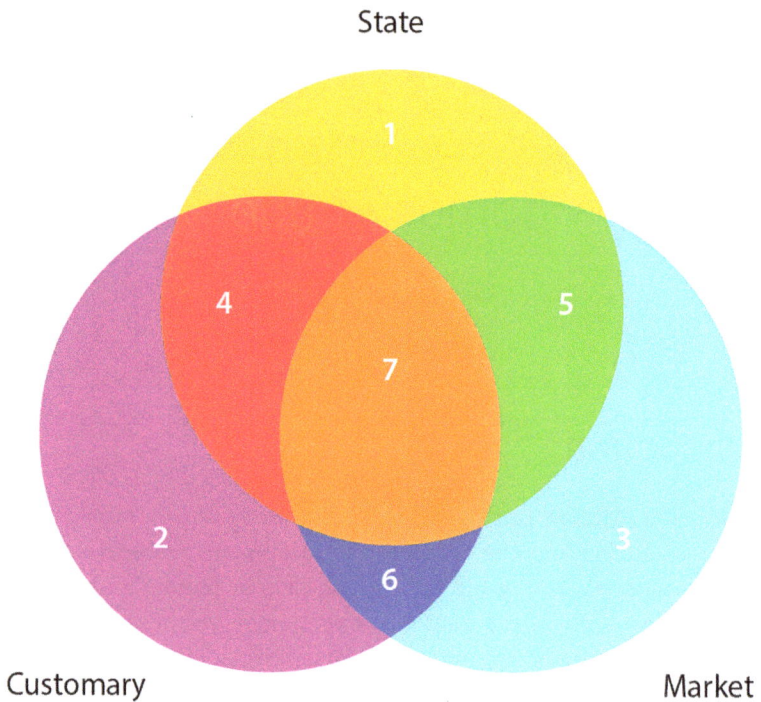

Fig. 2.1 The hybrid economy model
Source: Altman (2005)

In this chapter, I provide a truncated genealogy of the hybrid economy. I dig among Altman's earliest research to expose some of the roots of the hybrid economy. One of these roots can be traced back to Samoa. Another can be traced along a circuitous route from remote Australia to rural China and back. These roots reveal that hybridity has long been at the heart of Altman's engagement with Indigenous economy— an engagement that has sought to illuminate and appreciate economic difference via an anthropological consciousness.

A brief genealogy of the hybrid economy

A detailed genealogy of the hybrid economy might start with linguistic roots. According to the Oxford English Dictionary, the word 'hybrid' has its roots in the realm of animal husbandry, deriving from the Latin *hybrida*: the offspring of a tame sow and wild boar. The ancient Greek roots of 'economy' also relate to husbandry, but in the sense of 'the administration and management of a household; domestic economy'. This etymology provides rich ground for a lengthy discussion, but lacking that luxury, the starting point of this genealogy is neither Greece nor Rome, but the islands of Samoa. Samoa is a place with which Jon and I share a connection. For both of us it represents a site of our early engagement with Indigenous economy. Western Samoa, as it was then called, was a key case study site for Altman's MA (Hons) in Economics undertaken at the University of Auckland between 1974 and 1976. Altman's Master's thesis examined export instability and economic growth in Pacific Island economies, including Samoa. I had lived in Samoa in 2003 and worked as a volunteer with an environmental non-government organisation there. This perhaps stood me in good stead when I applied for a position as Altman's research assistant at the Centre for Aboriginal Economic Policy Research (CAEPR) in 2004. I recall a tropical Samoan vibe at my job interview where Professor Altman was dressed in his formal summer attire of t-shirt, shorts and sandals.

Subsistence affluence and Fred Fisk's influence: Opportunity and response

Samoa saw Altman's formal engagement with development dilemmas in an Indigenous economy characterised by both a subsistence and market sector. In an article published in 1978, he stated that the Samoan economy was 'in a state of transition from being a predominantly primitive subsistence-based economy to a market economy' (1978: 39). At the same time, he noted that subsistence affluence remained a real alternative for Samoan agricultural producers and acted as a disincentive to engage with a market economy characterised by export instability. Altman's view here was influenced by Fred Fisk's model of development based on the rural sector of Papua New Guinea.

Fisk's theoretical influence related to his contributions to the 'opportunity and response' school of thought. At the core of opportunity and response theory was the view 'that contact between capitalist and non-capitalist economic systems results in the former providing opportunities to which the latter respond in varying degrees' (Altman 1987: 7). Under Fisk's own model, contact with capitalism saw the virtual disappearance of the pure subsistence unit while groups' engagement in cash production was based on their response to the force of incentives. For Fisk, this 'response factor' was 'determined by internal factors: the cultural, economic and political characteristics of the group modified by external factors' (Altman 1978: 39). Moving his focus from Samoa to Australia, Altman's early research on outstation economies reveals Fisk's ongoing influence.

In 1977 Altman took part in a study at the Economics Department at the University of Melbourne exploring the economic status of Australian Aborigines. The study resulted in a landmark book co-authored by Altman and John Nieuwenhuysen (1979). The book's authors drew on Fisk's work to produce a formal economic model of outstation economies based on three scenarios: pre-contact, contemporary, and prospective (Altman & Nieuwenhuysen 1979: 208–10) (see Fig. 2.2). This modelling suggested that contemporary—or 'neo-traditional'— hunting and gathering, aided by Western technology and production techniques and access to the market for basic needs, resulted in a drop in demand for subsistence goods and a labour surplus available for cash income earning activities. While the contemporary scenario suggested a form of subsistence affluence, the prospective model raised concerns about sustainability in a context of permanent settlements, population growth and resource depletion.

Fig. 2.2 Decentralised communities: A model

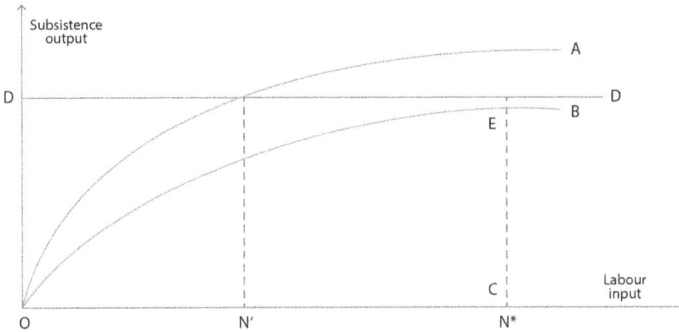

2.2.1 Traditional (pre-contact) household production scenario
Source: Altman & Nieuwenhuysen (1979: 208–10)

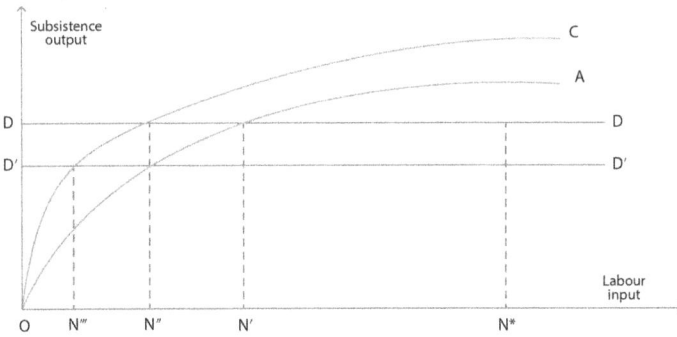

2.2.2 Neo-traditional (post-contact) household production scenario
Source: Altman & Nieuwenhuysen (1979: 208–10)

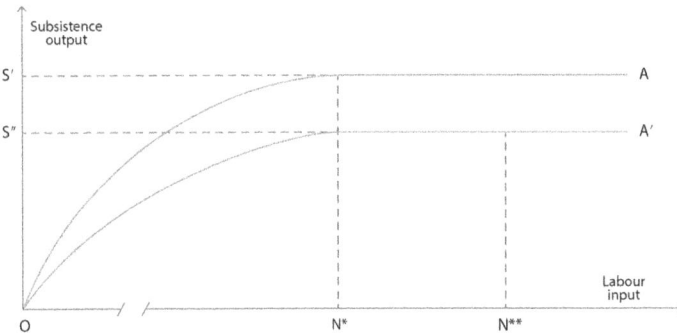

2.2.3 Prospective household production scenario
Source: Altman & Nieuwenhuysen (1979: 208–10)

Altman and Nieuwenhuysen described decentralised community economies not as a hybrid, but as 'an amalgam of traditional and market-oriented economic activities' (1979: 96). It was while working on this study that Altman realised, as an economist, the 'need to transcend the disciplinary boundaries between economics and anthropology' (Altman 1987: xii). In these early publications we see the emergence of two fundamental elements of Altman's hybrid economy. First is his focus on the subsistence or customary sector and its relationship with the capitalist economy. Second is his emphasis on the need for an interdisciplinary analytical and intellectual framework. My focus in this chapter is on the first element, though in a sense it cannot be separated from the second.

In 1978 Altman transitioned from Melbourne to Canberra, from economics to anthropology, and from macro-level to micro-level analysis. As a doctoral candidate at the Department of Prehistory and Anthropology at The Australian National University, Altman undertook ethnographic fieldwork in 1979–80. He participated in and observed in great detail the outstation economy of Kuninjku people at Mumeka in the Maningrida region of central Arnhem Land. Fisk's influence is acknowledged in Altman's adaptation of the formal economic tool of social accounting to attribute an imputed income value to subsistence production alongside cash income from art and craft production and social security payments (Altman 1982, 1987). Fisk was one of Altman's examiners and he subsequently drew on Altman's research to estimate the contribution of the customary sector to outstation economies as part of his survey of the contemporary Aboriginal economy in town and country (see Fisk 1985).

In Altman's view, the failure of formal economics to measure non-monetary productive activities was due to their being seen as 'antithetical to the capitalist or market ideology' (Altman 1987: 47). This view persists in his work and underpins the hybrid economy as a challenge to neoliberal normalisation under late capitalism. Altman has long argued for the formal measurement of the subsistence, informal or customary sector and the recognition of the sector's significance by policy makers. His persistence has at the very least resulted in the inclusion of questions around people's participation in the customary sector in the Australian Bureau of Statistics' National Aboriginal and Torres Strait Islander Social Survey—though not yet to Altman's satisfaction (Altman & Allen 1992; Altman et al. 2006, 2012).

A circuitous root: Articulation theory and economic hybridity

Altman's PhD thesis critically engaged with the development and underdevelopment paradigms as a means of explaining the economic changes experienced by the Kuninjku residents of Mumeka (Altman 1982, 1987). Fisk's opportunity and response school of thought fits within the development paradigm. From the underdevelopment paradigm Altman drew on the Marxist framework known as 'articulation of modes of production' or 'articulation theory' (Altman 1987: 8–9). For Altman, a key limitation of both paradigms was their failure to recognise people's agency or autonomy in the face of capitalism. His approach sought to combine elements of both paradigms to examine 'the possibilities that the positive benefits of capitalism may be utilised, or that indigenous minorities may regard themselves as exploiters of the capitalist system' (Altman 1987: 9).

Altman's conclusion emphasised the resilience of the customary economy and the relative autonomy of Kuninjku people:

> [The Mumeka economy] has demonstrated remarkable resilience in adapting to changed circumstances after colonisation. ... Eastern Gunwinggu [Kuninjku] people have adapted their economy to incorporate some elements of the alien system, while maintaining many of their own cultural and economic practices. Rather than just responding to changed circumstances these people have continued to create their own social and economic environment within the new structural limitations placed on their lifestyle by the wider Australian society. With this autonomy, eastern Gunwinggu people have chosen to maintain their hunter-gatherer economy in modern Australia (1987: 236).

This conclusion is echoed in Frances and Howard Morphy's recent observation that Yolngu engagement with the three sectors of Altman's hybrid economy 'comes from a relatively autonomous position'— 'enabling them to create an economy in place that articulates with the overall sociocultural trajectory of their society' (Morphy & Morphy 2013: 180). Morphy and Morphy caution that, by being nested in the notion of 'the intercultural', the hybrid economy concept may draw attention away from people's agency and effectively separate the economic from the sociocultural context. They put forward the notion of relative autonomy—adapted from structural Marxism—as an important corrective to theories of the intercultural and hybridity. Looking back we see that as a doctoral student whose supervisory panel included Howard Morphy, Altman saw relative autonomy as an important corrective to structural Marxism in the form of articulation theory, emphasising Kuninjku people's choice to live a 'relatively autonomous lifestyle' at Mumeka (1982: 32). In Altman's own words, 'things go round' (JC Altman, pers. comm., 1 November 2014).

Fig. 2.3 Jon Altman at work, Gurror outstation, Maningrida region, north-central Arnhem Land, Northern Territory, May 1980
Photo: Jon Altman Collection, courtesy of AIATSIS

A similar corrective to articulation theory lies at the heart of the notion of economic hybridity from which the hybrid economy got its name. Altman (2009) cites a paper by Mayfair Yang on economic hybridity in Wenzhou in rural China as the inspiration for the term 'the hybrid economy'. In that paper, Yang (2000) puts forward the notion of 'economic hybridity' as an alternative to articulation theory. For Yang, 'the integration and fusion within organic structure which is encapsulated in the notion of hybridity' recommended itself over articulation theory 'wherein modes are presented as more or less intact, distinct, and separate' (Yang 2000: 478). Yang's paper was inspired by Gibson-Graham's 'call for a theoretical move away from a model of monolithic global capitalism and notions of one-way "penetration" of capitalism' (Yang 2000: 477). As had Altman before them, Yang (2000) and Gibson-Graham (2006) acknowledged the positive role articulation theory played in capturing the heterogeneity of economies while rejecting its view 'that capitalism has inevitable penetrative powers' and that 'pre-capitalist relations of production are always transformed on contact with capitalism' (Altman 1987: 225).

For Yang, the logic of economic hybridity is subversive of capitalist principles—contesting and rechannelling capitalism toward alternative ends. Yang draws on Baudrillard's critique of historical materialism and the failure of Marxism 'to achieve a radical break from capitalist epistemology' (Yang 2000: 482). For Baudrillard, this included a failure to recognise the articulation between economics and other social relations in pre-capitalist societies—ultimately doing violence to these societies where 'the point of life and structural order are predicated not on production but on symbolic exchange with humans, spirits, and ancestors' (Yang 2000: 482). In line with the notion of relative autonomy, economic hybridity is based on the view that local sociocultural structures and mechanisms inform economic practice. For Yang it is these structures that 'ensure local autonomy from external forces such as the centralized state and capitalism' (2000: 493). And so, in Yang's discussion of economic hybridity in rural Wenzhou's ritual economy we hear echoes of Altman's discussion of relative autonomy in remote Mumeka's hybrid economy.

Conclusion: Illuminating Indigenous economy through hybridity

In his earliest engagements with Indigenous economy in Samoa and Australia, Altman applied formal economic techniques to analyse the informal economy following Fred Fisk's example. In the production of social accounts of state, market and customary contributions to the Mumeka economy we clearly see the methodological and empirical foundations of the hybrid economy in Altman's doctoral research. We also find the notion of relative autonomy being used as a critical corrective to the Marxist framework of articulation of modes of production. In turn, we find a clear theoretical link with the notion of economic hybridity as an alternative to articulation theory.

Yang's notion of economic hybridity was derived from Mikhail Bakhtin's notion of linguistic hybridity. Bakhtin's notion refers to the ability of language to be double-voiced. As Young puts it: 'Hybridity is itself an example of hybridity, of a doubleness that both brings together, fuses, but also maintains separation' (1995: 22). Bakhtin made a distinction between unconscious, organic hybridisation and conscious, intentional hybridity: while organic hybridity gives birth to an amalgamation, intentional hybridity creates division and separation through contestation (Young 1995). We might then read Altman's writing on the hybrid economy as a form of linguistic hybridity wherein there is an amalgamation that stresses separation. In these terms, the hybrid economy gives birth to an economic amalgamation in order to argue for an alternate development trajectory on the Indigenous estate.

To borrow from Bakhtin, the hybrid economy can be seen as a mixture of two social science languages within the limits of a single concept, an encounter of two different disciplinary consciousnesses—anthropological and economic—separated from one another by disciplinary boundaries (see Bakhtin 1981: 358). We might also describe Altman's hybrid analytical framework as an epistemic hybrid: an organised system for bringing different knowledges in contact with one another; a system having as its goal the illumination of Indigenous economies by means of various knowledges, and the carving out of livelihoods through alternate development (see Bakhtin 1981: 361).

Evidently, hybridity has long been at the heart of Jon Altman's engagement with Indigenous economy. The hybrid economy is the result (and continuation) of a long-term anthropological engagement with development dilemmas in Indigenous Australia and with policy discourse in Indigenous affairs. Throughout this engagement Altman has untiringly argued for alternate development based on an appreciation of economic difference. He has transcended disciplinary boundaries, combined paradigms, synthesised theories, established and led a multidisciplinary research centre, and brought together social sciences, biophysical sciences and Indigenous knowledge systems to explore hybrid economic futures on the Indigenous estate. Hybrid research has been part and parcel of Altman's engagement and has been fundamental to the development of the hybrid economy (Altman 2001, Altman & Cochrane 2005, Altman & Kerins 2012).

Digging among the roots of the hybrid economy reveals continuity amidst change in a career dedicated to illuminating Indigenous economy by embracing hybridity.

Fig. 2.4 Jon Altman digging for white pigment at Gudjangal, Maningrida region, north-central Arnhem Land, Northern Territory, September 1980

Photo: Jon Altman Collection, courtesy of AIATSIS

References

Altman JC (1978). Export instability and its consequences for economic growth and development: Western Samoa. *Pacific Viewpoint* 19(1):26–46.

Altman JC (1982). Hunter-gatherers and the state: the economic anthropology of the Gunwinggu of north Australia, PhD thesis, The Australian National University, Canberra.

Altman JC (1987). *Hunter-gatherers today: an Aboriginal economy in north Australia*, Australian Institute of Aboriginal Studies, Canberra.

Altman JC (2001). *Sustainable development options on Aboriginal land: the hybrid economy in the 21st century*, Discussion Paper 226, Centre for Aboriginal Economic Policy Research, The Australian National University, Canberra.

Altman JC (2005). Economic futures on Aboriginal land in remote and very remote Australia: hybrid economies and joint ventures. In Austin-Broos D & Macdonald G (eds), *Culture, economy and governance in Aboriginal Australia*, University of Sydney Press, Sydney.

Altman JC (2009). The hybrid economy and anthropological engagements with policy discourse: a brief reflection. *The Australian Journal of Anthropology* 20(3):318–29.

Altman JC & Allen LM (1992). Aboriginal and Torres Strait Islander participation in the informal economy: statistical and policy implications. In Altman JC (ed.), *A national survey of Indigenous Australians: options and implications*, CAEPR Research Monograph No. 3, Centre for Aboriginal Economic Policy Research, The Australian National University, Canberra.

Altman JC, Biddle N & Buchanan G (2012). The Indigenous hybrid economy: can the NATSISS adequately recognise difference? In Hunter B & Biddle N (eds), *Survey analysis for Indigenous policy in Australia: social science perspectives*, CAEPR Research Monograph No. 32, ANU E Press, Canberra.

Altman JC, Buchanan G & Biddle N (2006). Measuring the 'real' Indigenous economy in remote Australia using NATSISS 2002. *Australian Journal of Labour Economics* 9(1):17–31.

Altman JC & Cochrane M (2005). Sustainable development in the indigenous-owned savanna: innovative institutional design for cooperative wildlife management. *Wildlife Research* 32:473–80.

Altman JC & Kerins S (eds) (2012). *People on country: vital landscapes, Indigenous futures*, The Federation Press, Sydney.

Altman JC & Nieuwenhuysen JP (1979). *The economic status of Australian Aborigines*, Cambridge University Press, Cambridge.

Bakhtin MM (1981). *The dialogic imagination*, University of Texas Press, Austin.

Fisk EK (1985). *The Aboriginal economy in town and country*, George Allen & Unwin, Sydney & Australian Institute of Aboriginal Studies, Canberra.

Gibson-Graham JK (2006). *The end of capitalism (as we know it): a feminist critique of political economy*, 2nd edn, University of Minnesota Press, Minneapolis.

Morphy F & Morphy H (2013). Anthropological theory and government policy in Australia's Northern Territory: the hegemony of the 'mainstream'. *American Anthropologist* 115(2):174–87.

Oxford English Dictionary (OED) Online (2014). Oxford University Press, Oxford.

Yang MM (2000). Putting global capitalism in its place: economic hybridity, Bataille, and ritual expenditure. *Current Anthropology*, 41(4):477–509.

Young RJC (1995). *Colonial desire: hybridity in theory, culture, and race*, Routledge, London.

3

From public policy to pure anthropology: A genealogy of the idea of the hybrid economy

Chris Gregory

The argument

I have carried out fieldwork with Aboriginal people in Papua New Guinea, Fiji and India and it is from this comparative perspective that I cast my critical eye over Jon Altman's concept of the hybrid economy. My title is a double twist on a critique Jon wrote of Nic Peterson's notion of demand sharing (Altman 2011a). My critique is offered in the same spirit: to critique Jon's ideas, not to celebrate or denigrate him as a person. I make three points.

First, pure anthropology must precede public policy, description must precede prescription. When the issue concerns an economic policy, this means that study of comparative ethnography, economy history, and historical geography must come first. Such is the approach of 19th-century political economy and 20th-century economic anthropology. Mainstream economics does not share this assumption. Their free market policies come first; their abstract ahistorical theories provide the justification for policies of this kind. Jon is actively engaged in policy whereas I am not but we are in agreement when it comes to the primacy of pure anthropology. We both agree that pure economic anthropology provides a radical empirical critique of the conventional wisdom that informs mainstream economics.

Second, pure anthropology must be theoretically informed. Again, we agree, but it is the specificity of Jon's notion of the hybrid economy that I question. Jon's theory was inspired by Yang's (Yang 2000) but Jon claims (Altman 2009: 319) that his theory is 'radically different' to Yang's because fiscal transfers from the state loom large in Australia. This argument was true prior to 1996 but it is no longer true today. Development policy has undergone a revolution: incentives in the form of fiscal transfers have become the norm (Ballard 2012). Jon's conceptual framework is, therefore, completely general and is one offspring in a long line of thinking about the idea of the economy. Yang's 2000 theory of economic hybridity is a critique of 1970s articulation theory; articulation theory, in turn, was a critique of 1960s tribal economy which abstracted from the historical fact of colonisation; tribal economy, in turn, was a critique of earlier political economy, a Eurocentric theory that universalised commodity exchange, and so on up the intellectual lineage and back in time. If fiscal transfers no longer define the specificity of economic hybridity in Australia then what are the defining characteristics of the Australian case? This is an extremely difficult empirical question which I will not attempt to address in this short essay.

This brings me to my third point. Jon, like most anthropologists, is wary of binary thinking. Indeed, he sees his conception of economic hybridity as a means of transcending 'false binaries'. But binary thinking is absolutely essential to good conceptual thought. The binaries in Jon's conception of hybridity are loose and incomplete. Logical errors can sometimes be fatal for a theory but in this happy case, they are not. My critique of Jon's conceptual framework makes it more rigorous. This essay, then, will endeavour to tighten Jon's binaries and to identify an important missing category in his analysis.

A critique of Altman's concept of economic hybridity

Jon's (Altman 2001) theory began with a simple list. He distinguishes three 'conceptual sectors'—state, customary, market—and four 'cross-cutting cleavages' between these three sectors whose 'linkages and interdependencies' define the 'nature of hybridity'. Thus we have seven items in the list:

1. State
2. Customary
3. Market
4. State and customary
5. State and market
6. Customary and market
7. State and customary and market.

In 2005 the seven items in the list is reformulated as a Venn diagram (Altman 2005). This is shown as V1 in Fig. 3.1. This Venn diagram goes through another eight variations over the next six years. These are shown as V2 to V9 in Fig. 3.1. All nine variations contain minor logical and conceptual problems of one kind or another. The only constant is the numbering from 1 to 7 but to the extent that this numbering refers to the seven items in the list it is a mis-specification. From the point of view of strict binary logic, there are three sectors and eight segments, 11 categories in total. This poses the crucial question of the socioeconomic interpretation of the 11 categories and, in particular, of the eighth segment shown in V1 as mere decorative background. V1 poses other questions: Does the larger relative size of the state circle have any significance? Is it supposed to represent the idea that this sector is dominant in some sense? Before we try to answer these questions it is necessary to look at the other variations.

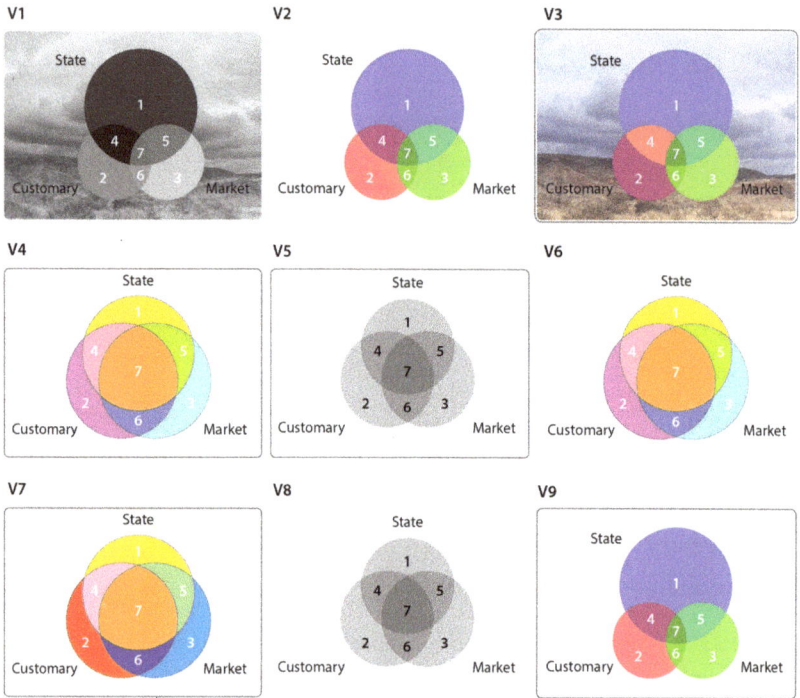

Fig. 3.1 Nine variant forms (V1–9) of the visual representation of the hybrid economy

Various sources: listed in accompanying text

V2 (Altman et al. 2006) is a minor variation on V1. It is in colour rather than greyscale and the decorative background has been removed. Note that the colouring does not conform to the logic of hybrid colour. For example, blue and red gives purple not dark red. V3 (Altman 2006) is a colour version of V1 but with one crucial difference of great logical significance: the decorative background has a border. This poses, once again, the central question of the socioeconomic significance of the bounded space outside the circles. V4 (Altman & Branchut 2008) is a new variant. The border is preserved but the size of the circles, the sizes of the segments and the colouring has changed. The three sectors are of equal size but the central overlapping segment has grown in importance. The colours of the hybrid segments, while different, still do not conform to the logic of hybrid colour. The removal of the decorative background poses the question, again, of the significance of the bounded white space?

V5 (Altman 2009) is another significant variation. Segment 7 loses its dominant relative size and the greyscale colouring harmonises with the logic of hybridity: the greater the mix, the darker the grey. But grey is a hybrid mixture of black and white. What interpretation should we give to the unnumbered white segment? Where is the black? V6 (Altman, Biddle et al. 2009) is V4 without the boundary. V7 (Altman, Jordan et al. 2009) is the only one that uses primary colours for the three primary sectors. This is an important innovation. Blue plus yellow is green as shown but thereafter things go wrong. Red plus yellow is orange, not pink. V8 (Altman & May 2010) is a greyscale version of V5 with the boundary removed and along with it the unnumbered white segment. V9 (Altman 2011b) returns us to V3 without the decorative filler. The restoration of the boundary reposes the central question of the interpretative significance of the bounded outside segment.

When the nine variations are considered as a whole it can be seen that the only constant is the numbering of the segments from 1 to 7. The shape and colouring of the segments varies as the diameter and relative positioning of the circles changes. Note, too, that the diagrams are either in colour or greyscale—none are in straight black and white.

The pure logic of hybridity: Binary logic versus colourful logic

What interpretations should we give to these variations? Strict binary logic can help us answer this. Our authority should be none other than John Venn (1894) of Venn diagram fame. He developed his diagrams to give geometrical form to Boole's (1854) binary logic which was expressed in difficult-to-grasp algebraic form.

My V10 (see Fig. 3.2) gets to the heart of the matter in black and white: three sectors, X, Y, Z, and eight segments. This is the logic of hybridity in its pure Boolean form.

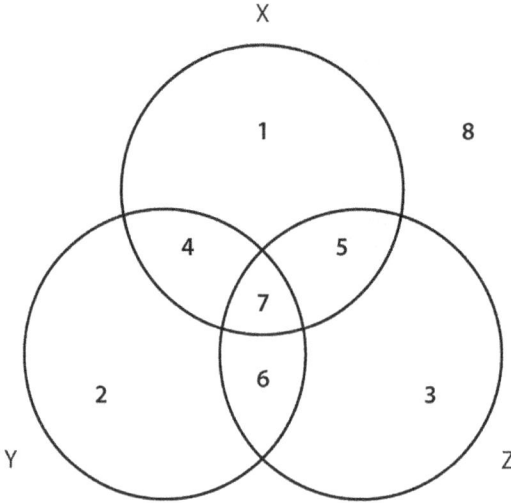

Fig. 3.2 The 'true' binary logic of the hybrid economy in black and white (V10)
Source: Author's depiction

We can use coloured circles to represent the three sectors as shown in V11 (in Fig. 3.3) but this clearly does not change the fact that three overlapping circles create eight logical segments. The three coloured circles and the eight segments remind us that 11 interpretable categories are at stake here.

Filling in the three circles with the three primary colours introduces the logic of colour. This complicates things because it introduces more interpretative possibilities. It has the advantage that it provides a logically rigorous non-biological conception of hybridity. When a yellow pigment is mixed, firstly, with blue it gives green (segment 4) and, secondly, with red it gives orange (segment 5). When blue is mixed with red it gives purple (segment 6). When all three colours are mixed they give black (segment 7) which represents the presence of colour; white, the absence of colour, defines segment 8. The non-overlapping primary colours give the segments 1, 2 and 3 as shown in Fig. 3.4.

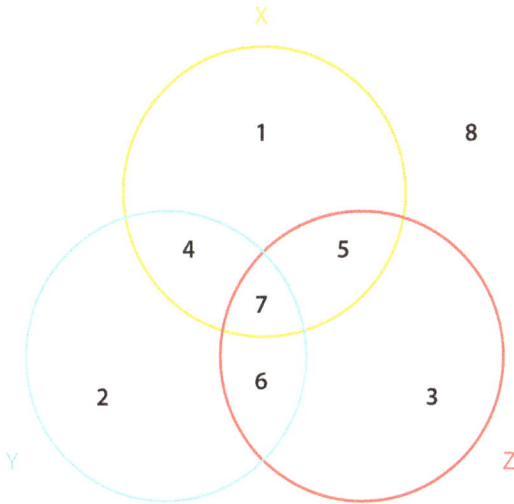

Fig. 3.3 The 'true' binary logic of the hybrid economy showing distinction between the eight bounded white segments and the three coloured sectors (V11)

Source: Author's depiction

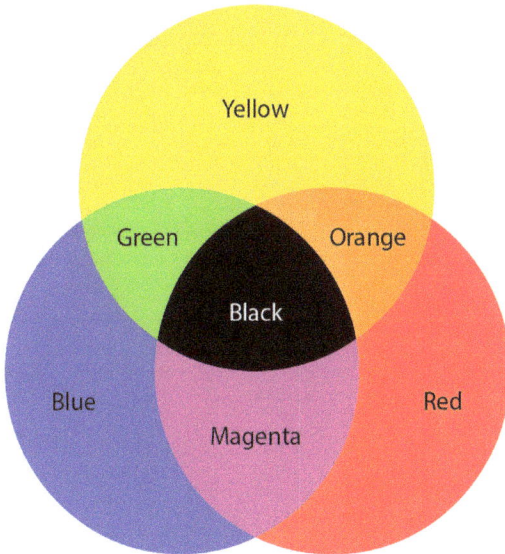

Fig. 3.4 The 'true' binary logic of the hybrid economy showing how the 'true' logic of primary colours creates eight coloured segments

Source: Author's depiction

Two questions are posed: (a) What interpretation can be given to the segments and the 'missing' eighth segment in particular? (b) How should we interpret the relationship between the three sectors in their own right? What additional interpretative possibilities does the logic of colour introduce? For example, hybrid colour presupposes the simultaneous mixing of colours but when the circles are filled in at different points of time there is no mixing; the latest one applied dominates.

Interpretation of the binary logic of the eight segments

We can now come to the interpretation of the unnamed eighth segment using Jon's definitions of the three primary sectors as means of livelihood: X refers to income received from the state, Y to income from the customary sector, and Z to income received from the market. Boole's zero/one binary logic defines eight segments as shown in colour and in binary numbers as shown in Fig. 3.5.

Segment	X	Y	Z	Interpretation
1	1	0	0	livelihood from X but not Y or Z
2	0	1	0	livelihood from Y but not X or Z
3	0	0	1	livelihood from Z but not Y or Z
4	1	1	0	livelihood from X and Y but not Z
5	0	1	1	livelihood from Y and Z but not X
6	1	0	1	livelihood from X and Z but not Y
7	1	1	1	livelihood from X and Y and Z
8	0	0	0	does not receive income from any sector

Fig. 3.5 Interpretation of the eight segments defined by Boole's zero/one binary logic

Source: Author's depiction

The yellow 100 segment refers to someone who gets income from the state sector but not the other two sectors. The blue 010 segment refers to someone who gets income from the customary sector but not the other two and so on. Thus the black 111 segment refers to someone who gets income, or 'works in', all three sectors.

Most of Jon's ethnographic examples (Altman 2009: 323) are of people who earn income from *all* sectors. One example is of a renowned bark painter and respected hunter who, because of his success, receives no income from the state. His interpretation of his own data is that the former work in all seven numbered *segments* while the latter works in all segments except 1 and 4.

It follows that the eighth segment refers to someone who does not receive income from any sector. Such people might include young children, the elderly, unemployed young people who do not qualify for unemployment, the homeless, and so on. These people are the ones who must 'beg, borrow or steal', as the saying goes.

It hardly needs to be said that this missing category from Jon's analysis is of profound importance. Their existence raises the question of how they survive. For Nic Peterson the answer is to be found in the phenomenon of 'demand sharing' (Peterson 1993) within the domestic moral economy where marriages of both intra-cultural and inter-cultural kinds are of great importance (Peterson & Taylor 2003).

If Jon's Venn diagram representation of the concept of the hybrid economy leaves him open to the charge that he focuses on production to the exclusion of exchange and distribution, then Peterson's notion of the domestic moral economy leaves him open to the charge that he focuses on exchange to the exclusion of production. Clearly both perspectives are needed. We also need to add consumption to the mix.

Jon knows this very well of course. His book (Altman 1987) carefully and meticulously articulates the empirical interrelationships between the spheres of production, consumption, distribution and exchange; the chapters in our joint book on methods (Gregory & Altman 1989) does the same, thanks, I must say, to Jon's rightful insistence.

Some people call people in the eighth segment 'bludgers'. Guy Standing (2014) calls these people, and others like them whose income is insecure, members of the precariat. His recent book, *The precariat: the new dangerous class*, does not refer to Jon's work but it could have because Standing's sectoral analysis can be seen as the latest offspring in a lineage of which hybridity is a part. Standing distinguishes six sectors which can be reduced to Altman's three sectors.[1] Given that the family, the market and the state are the three major institutions of modern economic life, this is hardly surprising. Altman's 'customary sector' is just another name for 'family' considered in its broadest sense. Gleaning, another word for foraging, has long been a 'customary' feature of marginal families in hybrid economies in Europe.

Interpretation of the three sectors

Jon, as we have noted, sometimes conflates the three primary sectors with the three non-overlapping segments numbered 1, 2 and 3. But, as the coloured circles in V11 show (see Fig. 3.3), the three sectors each consists of four segments: sector X, for example, is the sum of segments 1, 4, 5 and 7. In other words, when talking of the three primary sectors we must refer to the areas of the three circles. When these are represented by the primary colours two things can happen. First, the colours can mix and we have the binary logic of hybridity. Another interpretative possibility is that they don't mix, that one or the other of the colours dominates the rest and comes out on top as it were. This analogy takes us from the logic of economic hybridity to that of the general logic of political power—the relations of domination and subordination—and of historically contingent relations between coercion/resistance and persuasion/collaboration. Guha has creatively used colourful logic of this kind in his analysis of peasant insurgency in colonial India (Guha 1983, 1989).

Let us see how it might apply to data Jon has collected on the relative importance of the three sectors over time. Jon's PhD fieldwork has enabled him to present a 'snapshot' picture of the Mumeka economy as he observed that the customary sector was dominant in 1979–80, accounting for 64 per cent of total income earned in the community compared with 26 per cent for the state and 10 per cent for the market

---

1   'The composition of social income can be broken into six elements. The first is self-production, the food, goods and services produced directly, whether consumed, bartered or sold, including what one might grow in a garden or household plot. Second, there is the money wage or the money income received from labour. Third, there is the value of support provided by the family or local community, often by way of informal mutual insurance claims. Fourth, there are enterprise benefits that are provided to many groups of employees. Fifth, there are state benefits, including social insurance benefits, social assistance, discretionary transfers, subsidies paid directly or through employers, and subsidised social services. Finally, there are private benefits derived from savings and investments. Each of these can be subdivided into forms that are more or less secure or assured, and which determine their full value' (Standing 2014: 11).

sector. Subsequent fieldwork in 2003, albeit from a much shorter time, revealed that the state sector had become dominant providing 57 per cent of all income; the relative importance of the customary sector fell by half to 32 per cent while the market sector remained virtually unchanged at 11 per cent (Altman 2009: 323). Jon does not express this in Venn diagram form for the simple reason that we move from a concern with economic hybridity of segments at a point in time to the relative politico-economic dominance of the three sectors over time. Fig. 3.6 gives a visual representation of these historical changes.

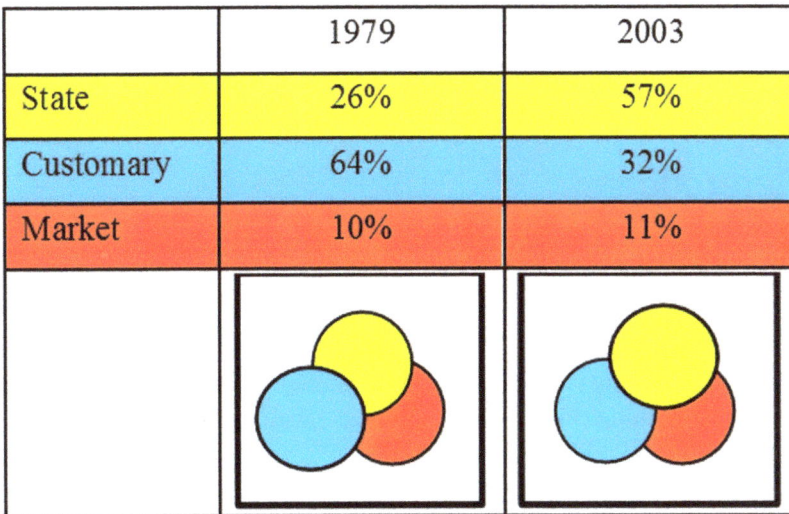

	1979	2003
State	26%	57%
Customary	64%	32%
Market	10%	11%

Fig. 3.6 Interpretation of the three sectors using data on their changing relative importance over time

Source: Author's depiction

Fig. 3.6 looks like a Venn diagram but it is not a 'true' Boolean binary version. It is not a 'false' binary model either. It is a visual representation of political power, of relative domination and subordination. This is an altogether different mongrel.

Conclusion

Jon's model of the hybrid economy is a completely general one in the non-mainstream tradition of political economy. It is a conceptual framework rather a theory in the sense that it generates questions to guide data collection during fieldwork. It is empirical data of this kind, when seen in comparative context, which reveals the specificity of the Australian case. Hybridity is a notion that can be seen in biological or purely logical terms. Jon's notion of hybridity is logical rather than biological but it contains a number of minor logical errors. Venn diagrams are visual representations of Boole's zero/one binary logic. The strict application of this logic defines eight logical spaces, not seven as Jon's diagram shows. Hybridity is best represented by the logic of colour but Jon's use of colour obscures rather than clarifies the logic of hybridity. My identification of these logical errors in his model are not fatal; to the contrary, they improve the model and reveal how the logic of primary and secondary colours can help us think about changing relations of domination and subordination over time.

References

Altman JC (1987). *Hunter-gatherers today: an Aboriginal economy in north Australia*, Australian Institute of Aboriginal Studies, Canberra.

Altman JC (2001). Aboriginal economy and social process: the Indigenous hybrid economy and its sustainable development potential. *Arena Magazine* 56:38–9.

Altman JC (2005). Economic futures on Aboriginal land in remote and very remote Australia: hybrid economies and joint ventures. In Austin-Broos D & Macdonald G (eds), *Culture, economy and governance in Aboriginal Australia*, University of Sydney Press, Sydney.

Altman JC (2006). *The Indigenous hybrid economy: a realistic sustainable option for remote communities?* Topical Issue 2, Centre for Aboriginal Economic Policy Research, The Australian National University, Canberra.

Altman JC (2009). The hybrid economy and anthropological engagements with policy discourse: a brief reflection. *The Australian Journal of Anthropology* 20:318–29.

Altman JC (2011a). A genealogy of 'demand sharing': from pure anthropology to public policy. In Musharbash Y & Barber M (eds), *Ethnography and the production of anthropological knowledge: essays in honour of Nicolas Peterson*, ANU E Press, Canberra.

Altman JC (2011b). Alleviating poverty in remote Indigenous Australia: the hybrid economy. In Argyrous G & Stilwell FF (eds), *Readings in political economy: economics as a social science*, Tilde University Press, Prahran, Victoria.

Altman JC, Biddle N, Buchanan G, Ens E, Jordan K, Kerins S & May K (2009). Indigenous interests in land and water. In Stone P (ed.), *Northern Australia Land and Water Science Review*, Australian Government Department of Infrastructure, Transport, Regional Development & Local Government, Canberra.

Altman JC & Branchut V (2008). *Fresh water in the Maningrida region's hybrid economy: intercultural contestation over values and property rights*, Working Paper 46, Centre for Aboriginal Economic Policy Research, The Australian National University, Canberra.

Altman JC, Buchanan G & Biddle N (2006). The real 'real' economy in remote Australia. In Hunter B (ed.), *Recent evidence on Indigenous socioeconomic outcomes: a focus on the 2002 NATSISS*, ANU E Press, Canberra.

Altman JC, Jordan K, Munro I, Ryan M & Mirikul M (2009). Maningrida region, Arnhem Land, Northern Territory. In Green D, Jackson S, & Morrison J (eds), *Risks from climate change to Indigenous communities in the tropical north of Australia*, Australian Government Department of Climate Change, Canberra.

Altman JC & May K (2010). Poverty alleviation in remote Indigenous Australia. In Minnerup G & Solberg PP (eds), *First world, First Nations: internal colonialism and Indigenous self-determination in northern Europe and Australia*, Sussex Academic Press, Eastbourne, UK.

Ballard R (2012). Geographies of development II: cash transfers and the reinvention of development for the poor. *Progress in Human Geography* 37(6):811–21.

Boole G (1854). *An investigation of the laws of thought, on which are founded the mathematical theories of logic and probabilities*, Dover Publications Inc., New York.

Gregory CA & Altman JC (1989). *Observing the economy*, Routledge, London.

Guha R (1983). *Elementary aspects of peasant insurgency in colonial India*, Oxford University Press, Delhi.

Guha R (1989). Dominance without hegemony and its historiography. In Guha R (ed.), *Subaltern studies VI: writings on South Asian history and society*, Oxford University Press, Delhi.

Peterson N (1993). Demand sharing: reciprocity and the pressure for generosity among foragers. *American Anthropologist* 95(4):860–74.

Peterson N & Taylor J (2003). The modernising of the Indigenous domestic moral economy: kinship, accumulation and household composition. *The Asia Pacific Journal of Anthropology* 4(1):105–22.

Standing G (2014). *The precariat: the new dangerous class*. Bloomsbury, London.

Venn J (1894). *Symbolic logic*. Chelsea Publishing, New York.

Yang MM (2000). Putting global capitalism in its place: economic hybridity, Bataille, and ritual expenditure. *Current Anthropology* 41(4):477–509.

4

Cultural domains and the theory of customary environmentalism in Indigenous Australia

Kim de Rijke, Richard Martin and David Trigger

Introduction

Under the long-term leadership of Professor Jon Altman, the Centre for Aboriginal Economic Policy Research (CAEPR) at The Australian National University has had an impressive publication output. The Centre has consistently focused on the important but challenging intersection of academic research and policy development relevant to Indigenous people in Australia. This paper engages with some of the intellectual concepts employed in the Centre's recent work, concentrating particularly on the volume edited by Jon Altman and Seán Kerins (2012) *People on country: vital landscapes, Indigenous futures.* The book promotes one of CAEPR's key pieces of recent policy advice: that Indigenous involvement in environmental work through ranger programs promotes improved environmental health as well as healthier human lifestyles, while bringing alternate forms of economic development for regional- and remote-living Indigenous people.

We offer some points of discussion to inform a respectful but robust debate about this proposition. Firstly, we focus on the scope of the research upon which some of the conclusions by Altman, Kerins, and others are based. Secondly, we pay attention to the two-way approach between Western science and Indigenous knowledge as it is promulgated by the authors, drawing on de Rijke's (2013) and Martin's (2013a) previously published reviews of *People on country*. We follow these discussions with a number of observations resulting from our own academic and applied work with Aboriginal people in the Gulf Country and southern Queensland.

While cognizant of the polemical nature of the debate about futures for Indigenous people in regional and remote Australia, we maintain the importance of a critical engagement with the literature and continued empirical research in this field. We come to the conclusion that the rigour of the Centre's current 'direct-action research' may be undermined by a political engagement that avoids critical discussion of fundamental concepts such as cultural domains, traditional knowledge and customary environmentalism, and call for further research into localised environmental knowledge and alternative development aspirations around Australia.

Customary environmentalism in Aboriginal communities

In *People on country*, a strong argument is made about the importance of Indigenous environmentalism and the customary economy across Australia. Such generalisations are particularly based on research in northern Australia (at Maningrida, Nhulunbuy, Yirrkala, Ngukurr and Kabulwarnamyo in Arnhem Land, and Borroloola in the Gulf Country) where classical Indigenous traditions have been retained the most (a counter-example from Guyra in northern New South Wales is also discussed).[1] However, generalisations about the role of customary environmentalism and the customary economy more broadly are unconvincing in the absence of supporting empirical data obtained from a sufficiently broad range of locations across the country. It is problematic to use research findings based primarily on northern Australia as the basis for nation-wide generalisations and/or policy

---

1   Classical Indigenous traditions should not be regarded as unchanged, static practices and beliefs. Rather, the term is employed, where relevant, to indicate a significant degree of continuity in Indigenous traditions since colonisation.

advice. Indeed, even in regions where classical Indigenous cultures appear strongest such as northern Australia, an adequate account of people's lives cannot neglect to describe the challenges to the reproduction of customary knowledge and practices. These include material and cultural attractions of the wider Australian society as well as the realities of socioeconomic inequality, structural discrimination, interpersonal violence, and related social crises (Sutton 2009).

An argument often posited in these discussions is the significance of bush foods for impoverished Indigenous people's diets. While such significance may well be found in some regions (e.g. O'Dea 1984, Scelza et al. 2014), it is important that relevant quantitative data across Australia is obtained. We realise the numerous difficulties associated with such a research project, but such empirical data is important if we wish to distinguish between the symbolic and dietary significance of bush foods in all regions of Australia. It is possible to elicit supportive commentary from Indigenous people in many settings regarding the significance of bush foods as 'income', country as a 'supermarket', and so on. But based on our own observations and discussions with anthropologists working across the country, we find in 2014 a strong reliance on store-bought consumer goods, and little evidence to attribute significant dietary contributions of bush foods in many locations, particularly those away from the resource-rich coastal regions.

Relatedly, we suggest that in discussions about customary practices, researchers should take seriously matters of intergenerational cultural change, as well as assertions about continuity. While senior generations in regions like Arnhem Land may well assert the relevance of customary practices in contemporary life, and indeed maintain such bush-oriented activities, we find little acknowledgement of the socioeconomic realities and cultural transformations occurring across generations in *People on country* and related publications.

Further, with regard to environmental work in northern Australia, we note Merlan's view that ranger programs 'in providing desirable kinds of work, draw on Indigenous interest and capacity but also deliberately undertake to transform consciousness and practice with respect to the environment' (Merlan 2013: 638). The nature of such transformation has been underexplored in the literature, which has tended to present a traditionalist interpretation of ranger activities. This is particularly accomplished through the pervasive dichotomisation of Western science and Indigenous knowledge within discussions about Indigenous involvement in environmental management activities. We now turn to an examination of this heuristic.

Western science, Indigenous knowledge, and the intercultural

Alongside the empirical question of Indigenous people's continuing reliance upon customary activity in the bush and the environmental impact of such activities, a key concept raised by many contributors to *People on country* which requires further analysis is the two-way concept. It is distinguished in the book and in much related literature as Western science and Indigenous knowledge, said to combine in environmental work in such a way as to 'contribute to the development of shared aspirations, approaches and outcomes' (Ens 2012: 45). This poses the issue of differentiating between these different ways. As Ens puts it in the book:

> [I]dentification of each part is becoming increasingly important to legitimise work as two-way and not simply dominated by western ideology and approaches, with tokenistic Indigenous involvement and labour (2012: 47).

We endorse Ens's scepticism, and further ask: is the two-way concept meaningful theoretically, as well as practically? Does it not posit reified and/or valorised cultural domains in which tradition becomes a storehouse of customary knowledge, rather than an arena of Aboriginal sociality that is adapted and negotiated through interaction with the proximal people and institutions of Australian society (Trigger 1986, 1997)? How does it deal with intercultural interaction, change, creativity and improvisation? We caution here against confounding research with an ideology of traditionalism that explicitly or implicitly endorses strategic essentialism and an uncritical support for a politics of separatism.

While Altman's hybrid economy model can in principle be understood as a useful heuristic device to analyse a thoroughly interactive social world, the two-way approach can be seen to pitch an essentialised

Aboriginal *Gemeinschaft* against a modern Australian *Gesellschaft* (concepts coined by the sociologist Tönnies in 1887, see Gelder 2005). In contrast to such an approach, we call for the examination of an intercultural relationality in which Indigenous social relations with the wider society are constrained yet pervasive in day-to-day life (Merlan 1998, 2013). We seek to avoid any unexamined 'postcolonial logic' (Kowal 2008) that, in the area of environmental work, may risk promoting a romanticisation of Aboriginal people as the 'new noble savages' (Langton 2013: 63).

Without dismissing the influence of Indigenous laws and customs on contemporary activities, we observe little empirical research on the actual role of what may be considered traditional knowledge in environmental work being undertaken among Indigenous people today. How do weed eradication programs, marine debris collection and burning practices with aerial incendiary devices draw on such traditional knowledge? Is the trope of customary knowledge meaningful or informative in describing the early dry season drops of incendiary devices from helicopters to create fire breaks on pastoral properties in return for carbon emission reduction funds? What ideological work do the words 'customary' or 'traditional' accomplish here?

A related issue is the question: Who or what drives such programs and environment-oriented activities? We note here the structural division of *People on country* into one part written by academics and another by Indigenous partners as facilitated by academics and other advisors. What is the nature of such whitefella facilitation? One chapter which specifically addresses this is provided in *People on country* by ecologist Emilie Ens, who points to 'differing perceptions of what work is and how it should be conducted' in Arnhem Land with reference to the failure of Indigenous rangers to follow through with projects in the absence of the ecologist (Ens 2012: 62). We are unsure where such 'differing perceptions' leave the conceptual proposition of 'dialectical interdependence' as advanced by Altman (2012: xix). In this case, whitefella supervisors were clearly central to the success of two-way activities. Where does this leave the concept of shared environmentalist sentiments? Is it not more accurate to understand such activities as little different from long-established patterns of Aboriginal engagement in sectors of the workforce via employment that becomes available through enterprises driven by Euro-Australian agencies?

We also ask whether the two-way approach is meaningful and effectual politically. Is there a realistic expectation of continued state funding for environmental work in Indigenous communities? What assumptions is the expectation of such support premised on? Does the two-way approach risk marginalising or trivialising Indigenous contributions that are not strictly traditional, effectively positioning Working on Country as a form of positive discrimination, possibly even a romanticised kind of work-creation program? We note the homologies here with the historical employment of Indigenous people in low-waged work arising in aspects of environmental management, such as the handling of dangerous chemicals, tackling of invasive species, and so on. With the idea of two-way customary environmentalism are we observing a shift of substance or rhetoric?

The two-way concept leaves us with questions about epistemology and the intellectual examination of intercultural identities, and about the meaning of keywords such as 'partners', 'participation', and 'interdependence'. In our view, it also risks leaving unaddressed how we might envisage the road to economic self-reliance based on environmental work for Indigenous people in rural and remote regions across Australia.

Our observations

During our ethnographic work in the Gulf Country (Trigger & Martin), the Kimberley and southern Queensland (de Rijke), we have observed in all these locations a strongly articulated desire among Indigenous people to (re)connect and be involved with their country.

The idea of tradition figures sociopolitically and as a form of advocacy across all these settings, particularly in Indigenous engagements with the state. One example is the use of 'tradition' in grant applications and policy documents directed toward priorities such as the registration of Indigenous Protected Areas (IPAs). Such applications characteristically include information about clan estate organisation and Dreamings without specifying how such information relates to the pursuit of the priorities of an IPA. Indeed, it is hard to envisage how local clan estate organisation (in regions with this customary tenure system) or principles affiliating particular families of polity with specific areas (Sutton 2003: 206–31) could be meaningfully deployed towards contemporary land management priorities which typically require landscape-level solutions, for example directed towards the control of invasive species like rubber vine. It is even more difficult to envisage how Dreaming information and other esoteric religious knowledge might be relevant to this encounter with the state. This is not to suggest there is no addressing of land management in IPA discourses, but the reference to classical forms of land tenure and religious knowledge to leverage funding raises the question again of what ideological work the idea of 'tradition' is really doing here, as much for the state's policies and conceptions of the locus of Aboriginal culture in Australian society, as for self-conscious traditionalism among relevant Aboriginal individuals, families and organisations.

Likewise, across all these settings we find varied assessments and approaches to change. A question we may ask concerns the sources of traditional knowledge understood to be operationalised in land management work among Indigenous rangers or other Aboriginal people. We suggest such an inquiry would engage with Indigenous peoples' use of land claim and native title documents and other anthropological research, published and archival historical work, photos, maps, and so on. These sources of traditional knowledge are hardly contrary to achieving continuity of customary environmentalism. However, our point is that such issues are characteristically unaddressed in accounts of Indigenous knowledge. In our field sites, these dynamics certainly underline how traditional knowledge arises from mixed and contested histories of documentation as well as oral communications, invariably also prompted by economic drivers associated with heritage surveys, mining and other development project negotiations, native title claims and the like.

Work with fire presents an instructive example. In the Gulf Country, customary Indigenous traditions regarding the use of fire as a land management tool have been profoundly impacted by pastoralism, to the extent that many Aboriginal people perceive the late dry season burning preferred by some pastoralists as a traditional practice (see Martin 2013b: 75–6). Through investment in regional fire management, such Indigenous perceptions are changing, as the early dry season mosaic burning patterns of precolonial times are revived. But it is clear that such practices are recovered traditions (Hobsbawn

& Ranger 1983) rather than straightforwardly reinstituted ones, and it is the conditions driving such revival and the extent to which it is sustainable across the continent that require clear analysis.

We agree with Altman, Kerins and others that land and sea management and environmental work more broadly is an important concern for Aboriginal people. Like many across the political spectrum in Australia, we are encouraged by Indigenous people's embrace of such work and commitment to its stated goals where this occurs. In our view, environmental work may well contribute to healthier lives on country for those who manage to secure such positions. However, our corrective to reified ideas of customary knowledge is that this process should be recognised as driven by the realpolitik of achieving funding and related resources, laudable aims of assisting young people to find meaningful work and a potential disposition inclined as much towards embracing new forms of knowledge as reviving traditions.

Conclusion

In this chapter we have asked a number of questions about what we term 'customary environmentalism' in Australian Indigenous communities. We return here to the question which we see underlying much of the recent work by Altman and some others at CAEPR as to whether assumptions about tradition and culture, howsoever understood, are a viable basis for achieving economic self-reliance. If so, where, and how? We should note that this is a separate question from the acknowledged value of successfully asserted pride and symbolic recognition of a continuing Aboriginal identity in Australian society.

We suggest it is not adequate to posit environmental work across the country being informed by tradition without a clear appreciation of how this tradition is itself an expression of intercultural relationships and the potential leverage achieved through strategic essentialism. While superficially attractive to many, including some Indigenous people, the reification of customary environmental knowledge may well risk forcing Aboriginal people into the corner of 'a state-resourced and mandated project of "traditionalism"' (Martin 2009: 108) of the kind that has been noted in native title cases. In the context of programs of environmental work among Aboriginal people, this may occur through assumptions or implicit requirements that they mobilise and implement traditional knowledge as a pathway into modernity and economic development. This may well be fine and productive in regard to some places and in respect of certain aspects of knowledge of the country. But analyses will also usefully encompass how environmental work has as much to do with people looking for job opportunities and learning from professional scientists and others as it does with drawing on traditional knowledge.

An interesting question in this regard is whether non-Indigenous people could or should be employed together with Aboriginal people in environmental management programs (other than supervisory roles)? Related to the above is the question of whether environmental work for Indigenous people is to continue only or mainly in the more remote locations. Can there be Indigenous rangers working with non-Indigenous rangers in mixed communities and towns as well as cities like Sydney or Melbourne? We suggest the adequate study of Indigenous environmental work requires engagement with the broader context in which such work is situated, including empathetic attention to the non-Indigenous people and institutions involved (cf. Fache 2014).

Indigenous development remains a central challenge, and promise, of Australian Government policy. We see this challenge as the central preoccupation of much of Jon Altman's work over many years. In engaging with a key aspect of CAEPR's research for this chapter we note the empirical rigour and strength of the writing we have focused on. However, in our view, there is an unmistakeable element of utopianism in the approach we have critiqued. While that idealism is in some respects attractive and symbolically satisfying for those of us who are committed to supporting aspirations among Aboriginal people, we argue for a thorough examination and discussion of fundamental concepts underlying the idea of customary environmental work.

References

Altman JC (2012). Preface. In Altman JC & Kerins S (eds), *People on country: vital landscapes, Indigenous futures*, The Federation Press, Sydney.

Altman JC & Kerins S (eds) (2012). *People on country: vital landscapes, Indigenous futures*, The Federation Press, Sydney.

de Rijke K (2013). Book review. People on country: vital landscapes, Indigenous futures. Altman JC & Kerins S (eds). *The Australian Journal of Anthropology* 24(3):259–61.

Ens E (2012). Conducting two-way ecological research. In Altman JC & Kerins S (eds), *People on country: vital landscapes, Indigenous futures*, The Federation Press, Sydney.

Fache E (2014). Caring for country, a form of bureaucratic participation. Conservation, development, and neoliberalism in Indigenous Australia. *Anthropological Forum: A Journal of Social Anthropology and Comparative Sociology* 24(3):267–86.

Gelder K (2005). Reading Stephen Muecke's ancient and modern: time, culture, and Indigenous philosophy. *Australian Humanities Review* 36, July.

Hobsbawn E & Ranger T (1983). *The invention of tradition*, Cambridge University Press, Cambridge.

Kowal E (2008). The politics of the gap: Indigenous Australians, liberal multiculturalism, and the end of the self-determination era. *American Anthropologist* 110(3):338–48.

Langton M (2013). *The quiet revolution: Indigenous people and the resources boom*, HarperCollins, Sydney.

Martin DF (2009). The governance of agreements between Aboriginal people and resource developers: principles for sustainability. In Altman JC & Martin DF (eds), *Power, culture, economy: Indigenous Australians and mining*, CAEPR Research Monograph No. 30, ANU E Press, Canberra.

Martin R (2013a). Book review. People on country: vital landscapes, Indigenous futures. Altman JC & Kerins S (eds). *Australian Book Review* 348:48–9.

Martin R (2013b). Sometime a fire: re-imagining elemental conflict in northern Australia's Gulf Country. *Australian Humanities Review* 55:67–91.

Merlan F (1998). *Caging the rainbow: places, politics, and Aborigines in a north Australian town*, University of Hawaii Press, Honolulu.

Merlan F (2013). Theorizing relationality: a response to the Morphys. *American Anthropologist* 115(4):637–8.

O'Dea K (1984). Marked improvement in carbohydrate and lipid metabolism in diabetic Australian Aborigines after temporary reversion to traditional lifestyle. *Diabetes* 33(6):596–603.

Scelza BA, Bird DG & Bliege Bird R (2014). Bush tucker, shop tucker: production, consumption, and diet at an Aboriginal outstation. *Ecology of Food and Nutrition* 53(1):98–117.

Sutton P (2003). *Native title in Australia: an ethnographic perspective*, Cambridge University Press, Cambridge.

Sutton P (2009). *The politics of suffering: Indigenous Australia and the end of the liberal consensus*, Melbourne University Publishing, Melbourne.

Trigger D (1986). Blackfellas and Whitefellas: the concepts of domain and social closure in the analysis of race relations. *Mankind* 16(2):99–117.

Trigger D (1997). Land rights and the reproduction of Aboriginal culture in Australia's Gulf Country. *Social Analysis* 41:84–106.

5

What is the policy significance of the hybrid economy?

Nicolas Peterson

Introduction

The future of Aboriginal people living on remote lands either in the large ex-mission and government communities or in small outstations is problematic both for government and ultimately for the people themselves. Not only are these people remote from mainstream economic activity in many, but by no means all cases, but, by and large, there is no regional demand for their labour. Were people much better educated, perhaps 15–25 per cent could be employed in administration and service delivery in their communities, if all jobs were Aboriginalised. Such a situation is at least a generation or two away even from the possibility of realisation. This situation parallels the situation in a number of countries such as South Africa and parts of Asia where there are also populations that are surplus to the labour requirements of the mainstream economy. The prospects of substantial proportions of the remote Aboriginal population ever being employed in the mainstream are remote.

This faces policymakers, and the people themselves, with the question as to whether there are desirable long-term forms of dependency that are not only satisfactory to Aboriginal people but which are not going to be a cause of concern to others, and to ask what resources Aboriginal people might have to draw on to structure such a life (cf. Ferguson 2013).

Since at least 2001 Jon Altman has been a strong advocate of one possible solution for some of those people living on Aboriginal lands in the tropical savannah and coastal areas of north Australia. His solution is for the government to recognise that these people are part of what he calls a hybrid economy and for the government to support a particular sub-group to build on this for an alternative development paradigm that is more accepting of cultural difference (Altman 2010: 270). The thinking behind this idea goes back to at least his experience and research for his PhD thesis in 1979–80 living at Mumeka (Momega) outstation south of Maningrida, with a small, fluctuating population averaging 19 people. In a fine study he documented the income and expenditure patterns and the time allocation of people living there, quickly coming to appreciate the value and significance of the customary economy (see Altman 1987).

On the basis of extended fieldwork at Mumeka outstation in western Arnhem Land, Altman estimated that the imputed value of subsistence income (i.e. hunted and gathered foods at the outstation) was 175 per cent of the people's cash income. Clearly this was a major contribution to people's livelihood and fundamental to understanding their circumstances at that time. The outstation life provided a much better protein diet and much less stress than living at Maningrida.

Jon developed the term 'hybrid economy' in 2001 during his collaboration with the members of the Key Centre for Tropical Wildlife Management at Charles Darwin University, emphasising that the notion of Aboriginal economy in remote Australia needed to be broadened and developed especially because both policymakers and politicians failed to understand the important contribution that remote area Aboriginal people make to their own support: they are not just welfare dependent but contribute to their own support through the production of bark paintings and artefacts for sale, and through hunting, foraging and fishing for food.

Since developing the framework he has been strongly promulgating it in both academic and applied forums. From 2007 he has elaborated his ideas under the project title People on Country: Healthy Landscapes and Indigenous Economic Futures. This refers to what Altman describes as a social and environmental movement based around the recognition of how much of the national environmental estate and biodiversity is on Aboriginal lands. Further, he argues that across this Indigenous estate are many hundreds of small communities that are in an ideal position, properly supported by government, to help look after it both in their own interests and those of the nation.

The Northern Territory Emergency Response in 2007 is a key turning point in Altman's work. This is marked by outspoken criticism of the government's approach in Indigenous affairs and 'a growing dis-enchantment with the ability of evidence based research to inform productive Indigenous policy and practice' (Thomassin & Butler 2014: 4). Altman saw Indigenous affairs as increasingly influenced by particular ideologies and interest groups. For 30 years Altman has devoted himself to the production of high quality evidenced-based research, both by himself and through the Centre for Aboriginal Economic Policy Research (CAEPR), directed to the betterment of Aboriginal lives by assisting government and others in the formulation of policy in Indigenous affairs.

There is no doubt that Altman's work has been enormously effective in developing understanding of the nature and significance of, and securing support for, outstations, the art and craft movement, Indigenous tourism projects and, more recently, ranger programs and other aspects of working on country. He has also been a strong advocate for the Community Development Employment Projects (CDEP) scheme, so mistakenly criticised and attacked by many.

Given that Altman is now in full advocacy mode for the significance of the hybrid economy, not just as a framework for describing the economies of remote Australia but as the basis for policy, I want to ask whether the thinking behind the hybrid economy holds out the promise of a desirable form of long-term dependency and if it is really coherent as a basis for policymaking for Aboriginal people in remote Australia.

The hybrid economy

The hybrid economy is usually presented in the form of a Venn diagram of three intersecting circles, one representing the economic aspects of the state, another representing the market and the third the customary economy. This gives rise to four intersections between these three sectors (4, 5, 6, 7 in Fig. 5.1) and it is the linkages indicated by these intersections that highlight the areas where Altman considers the most productive activity occurs (Russell 2011: 2).

State

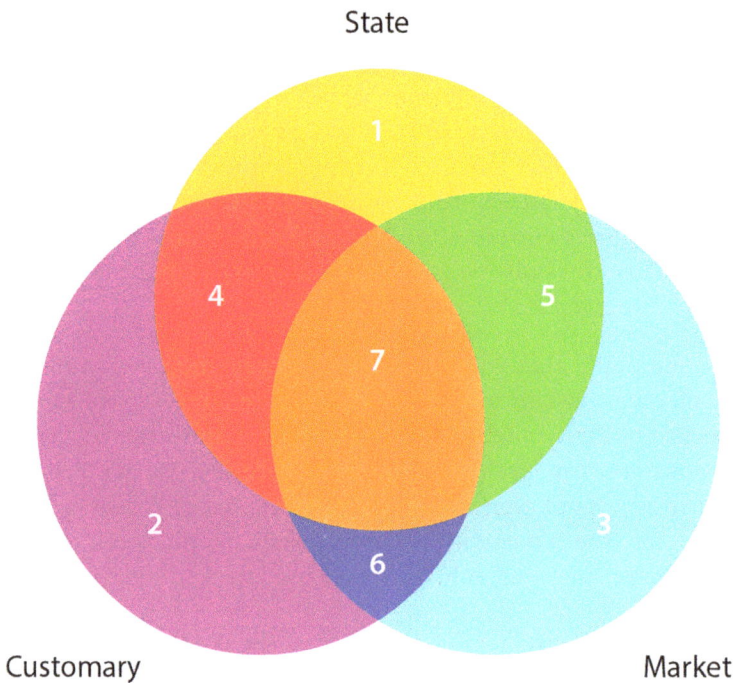

Customary   Market

Fig. 5.1 The hybrid economy
Source: Altman (2005)

Thus in respect of the intersection between the customary and the state (4), social security or the CDEP scheme underwrite some customary activities; in respect of the intersection between the state and the market (5) there are commercial enterprises that are underwritten by the state through CDEP or other enterprise support; in respect of the intersection between the customary and the market (6) there are joint ventures that are not predicated on any state support;

and in respect of the intersection between market, state and customary (7) the clearest example is the marketing of arts and crafts but also cultural tourism and some environmental services (Altman 2001: 4–5). The model could be further developed and is not always consistently presented (see Gregory, this volume). In many illustrations the three domains vary in size, as does the extent of the overlaps, and generally speaking there is a lack of quantification associated with the sectors and overlaps.

The hybrid economy: A desirable long-term form of dependency?

The hybrid economy model focuses on production and income sources. Thus the state (1) mainly supplies direct income in the form of social security payments and, in the outstation contexts, a limited number of jobs. The customary sector (2) mainly provides imputed income through import substitution as a result of hunting and fishing. The market sector (3) provides cash through the sale of artefacts. In the outstation contexts segments 4, 5, 6, and 7 are mainly related to the generation of income through the production and sale of artefacts subsidised through the CDEP scheme, occasional involvement in tourism, and more recently through wages earned in relation to the provision of environmental services.

A central issue is the robustness of the hybrid economy. Does the customary sector continue to play the same important role in import substitution today when there are greater constraints on hunting than in the past, and possibly depletion? The imputed contribution to income in Mumeka, at least, seems to have dropped.

This might not be an issue if jobs have become available in the environmental services area, but given the limited number of such jobs available in the Maningrida area (around 40) the possibilities for increased cash income from this source seem small. There are certainly opportunities for increased tourism ventures but only a limited number of these could possibly function in the range of one regional centre. As to the art and craft market this can be very valuable but is quite fragile, as Altman has documented, and highly dependent on government funding of the relevant infrastructure.

The principal source of cash income in the hybrid economy has always been social security, which depends substantially on the age structure and composition of the population. Given that outstation populations are groups of closely related kin, sharing practices are likely to ensure that everybody has some access to cash and in-kind resources. So while the actual mechanisms and tensions in distribution are not known it can be assumed that sharing practices will, generally speaking, ensure a level of access by all.

The most obvious challenge to long-term satisfaction with this existence is in respect of consumption. As long as people's consumer dependency remains low then the levels of income generated by the ever-changing nature of the hybrid economy are likely to remain satisfactory. However, there is evidence of an increased desire for a wider range of goods and services in outstations that require cash. This suggests that levels of consumer dependency are rising. Housing is one example. People's desire for better accommodation is faced with the costs of providing it in remote locations, with consequent declarations by government that no new houses will be built in such places. But there are other expensive and new dependencies, especially associated with the phone and other information and communication technology, the costs of which will, in all probability, rise. Any decline in food from the customary economy will ratchet up the need for cash. Further, people are now being asked to contribute to the cost of services being supplied to them. Together, these factors will diminish outstation residents' discretionary income.

There is good evidence that people in outstations flourish in a number of ways, including in terms of physical and mental health and socially in terms of greatly increased control over their lives (e.g. see Burgess et al. 2009). Outstations probably are a desirable long-term form of dependency for those people living on them. This leads to the question of how many people that involves and foreshadows another: why, if it is desirable, does only a small proportion of the remote population appear to think so?

How many people live on outstations?

The difficulties of estimating outstation populations are several. Not least is the high level of mobility between outstations in a region and the regional centre, an issue that has been present since Altman carried out his fieldwork (see also Taylor 2006: 49). Then there is the issue of the definition of outstation which, as far as the statistical and legal agreements between the Northern Territory and Commonwealth go, is highly confusing, as any residence group outside the core 70 or so designated townships is called an outstation. This leaves not only ample room for confusion but also considerable scope for ambiguity in claims made for the numbers of people covered by the hybrid economy.

In 2001 the number of discrete Aboriginal communities Australia-wide was 1,216. Of these, 577 had 19 or less people and 785 had less than 49 (Taylor 2006: 47). It is not clear from these figures how vacant outstations were or are dealt with in these calculations. Such outstations can range from a few tin sheds to very sophisticated housing which may be vacant for years at a time, as is the case in the 19 outstations around Yuendumu and some outstations in Arnhem Land.

The total population of these 'less than 49 people' outstations in 2006 was estimated at 11,343 out of a very remote region total population of 80,680 (Taylor 2006: 47). The high level of mobility between regional centres and outstations can be seen in two different lights. It can be used to argue that many more than simply the residents of the outstations benefit from them, as people whose permanent residence is in the regional centres can go out to an outstation from time to time for recreation and holidays, thus spreading their benefit. But it can also be seen as a potential sign of weakness in the permanency of the outstations in that the regional centres have the enduring resources, services and many other attractions. Orbiting from outstations can lead to people getting stuck in the regional centres.

Either way, outstations (and providing environmental services from them) are a Rolls-Royce option for a very small portion of the Aboriginal population in remote areas. But, as has been suggested, there is some reason to suppose that the viability of outstations is quite fragile, even if government policy remains unchanged.

A coherent basis for policy?

In 2005 Altman and Morrison argued that the proper foundation for Indigenous economic development will need to be on the basis of property rights in commercially valuable assets like water, fisheries and minerals (Altman & Morrison 2006: 52). Elsewhere Altman has emphasised the carbon economy: the payment of rent to traditional owners by government and others for use of land. As with the hybrid economy, the emphasis is on income which underwrites Aboriginal people's own unilateral definition of economic development objectives (Altman 2012: 16). Apparently this is a right that Indigenous Australians have. The basis for this right or the responsibilities that go with it is nowhere stated, nor are there any indications of substantively worked out economic development objectives for particular remote regions. Further, there is no indication of why increasing unearned income will not result in increased dependency. The implied image is of a rentier class. But what this leisured people would do with their income and time is never addressed, although what past experience suggests is not good.

A further cloud reducing the clarity of the policy implications of the hybrid economy is the emphasis placed on the significance of cultural difference. The specific nature of cultural differences relevant to Aboriginal life in the 21st century to be built on or accommodated are not spelt out. Further, the emphasis on culture is often in danger of being backward-looking and failing to acknowledge the huge changes that have taken place in the last 60 years. There is no reason to suppose that the rate of change will decrease, although its trajectory is hard to predict. By emphasising cultural issues, the much more complex sociological ones are avoided and discussion of the future becomes slogans that get in the way of clear, evidenced-based argument, analysis and thinking.

The positive intentions behind the promotion of the hybrid economy cannot be questioned, but at best it is only focusing on the easy stuff and avoiding dealing with any of the difficulties the majority of remote area populations are facing. One obvious reason for doing so is that Altman, like everybody else, Aboriginal or non-Aboriginal, has no clear ideas about what to do for the majority of the population. We all wish people in remote Australia a good life but what that might be and how to secure it is another question altogether. Some people, however, do not have the luxury of doing nothing about the future—they are the government and the policymakers. Altman is an influential commentator from among one important set of opinion makers who all want things done—church members, the medical profession, Aboriginal and other public intellectuals, and members of the United Nations are others. They mainly work in slogans or critiques of existing policy, offering palatable but implausible solutions such as suggesting that all that is required is to listen to Aboriginal people. Were it so easy. If we look at what Aboriginal people in remote Australia actually do, it is clear that working in the customary economy and living on an outstation is only desirable for a small proportion of the total population. Helping the majority to develop desirable long-term life projects under conditions of dependency is clearly going to be highly challenging.

Acknowledgements

I would like to thank Jon Altman, Maggie Brady, William Arthur, David Martin, Julie Finlayson, Paul Burke, Chris Gregory and Francesca Merlan for many stimulating conversations around topics related to this contribution.

References

Altman JC (1987). *Hunter-gatherers today: an Aboriginal economy in north Australia*, Australian Institute of Aboriginal Studies, Canberra.

Altman JC (2001). *Sustainable development options on Aboriginal land: the hybrid economy in the twenty-first century*, Discussion Paper 226, Centre for Aboriginal Economic Policy Research, The Australian National University, Canberra.

Altman JC (2005). Economic futures on Aboriginal land in remote and very remote Australia: hybrid economies and joint ventures. In Austin-Broos D & Macdonald G (eds), *Culture, economy and governance in Aboriginal Australia*, University of Sydney Press, Sydney.

Altman JC (2010). What future for remote Indigenous Australia? Economic hybridity and the neoliberal turn. In Altman JC & Hinkson M (eds), *Culture crisis: anthropology and politics in Aboriginal Australia*, UNSW Press, Sydney.

Altman JC (2012). People on country as alternate development. In Altman JC & Kerins S (eds), *People on country: vital landscapes, Indigenous futures*, The Federation Press, Sydney.

Altman JC & Kerins S (eds) (2012). *People on country: vital landscapes, Indigenous futures*, The Federation Press, Sydney.

Altman JC & Morrison J (2006). Enhancing economic independence. *Journal of Indigenous Policy* 5:48–53.

Burgess C, Johnston F, Berry H, McDonnell J, Yibarbuk D, Gunbarra C, Mileran A & Bailie R (2009). Healthy country, healthy people: the relationship between indigenous health status and 'caring for country'. *Medical Journal of Australia* 190(10):567–72.

Ferguson J (2013). Declarations of dependence: labour, personhood, and welfare in southern Africa. *Journal of the Royal Anthropological Institute* 19(2):223–42.

Russell S (2011). *The hybrid economy topic guide*, Centre for Aboriginal Economic Policy Research, The Australian National University, Canberra.

Thomassin A & Butler R (2014). *Engaging indigenous economy: a selected annotated bibliography of Jon Altman's writings 1979–2014*, Working Paper 96, Centre for Aboriginal Economic Policy Research, The Australian National University, Canberra.

Taylor J (2006). *Population and diversity: policy implication of emerging indigenous demographic trends*, Discussion Paper 283, Centre for Aboriginal Economic Policy Research, The Australian National University, Canberra.

6

If the market is the problem, is the hybrid economy the solution?

Katherine Curchin

Introduction

One of Jon Altman's preoccupations in recent years has been the impact of neoliberal ideology on Indigenous affairs policy. He has been a critic of the policy goal of incorporating more Indigenous Australians in remote regions into the mainstream economy, believing that Indigenous Australians joining the labour market are destined for the least desirable place within it. He has also argued that the values orientation promoted by market society is at odds with the kin-based societies in which many Indigenous people live today. Altman maintains that an ideological commitment to the market has blinded many policymakers to the viable alternatives to market-based development in Australia's north (Altman 2005: 122). His hybrid economy framework challenges the dominant way of thinking about economic development for Indigenous peoples by highlighting a range of productive activities currently performed by Indigenous groups in Australia's north. These innovative activities occur within the intersection of the customary, market and state sectors of local economies. Livelihood strategies based on these activities enable

Indigenous people who live in regions remote from urban centres to generate income while resisting the full commoditisation of their labour and their land.

Scholars from a range of disciplines have found Altman's hybrid economy model useful in analysing past and present regional economies (Smith 2003, Gill 2005, Kwan et al. 2006, Lloyd 2010, Holcombe et al. 2011, Sullivan 2011, White 2011). The distinctive approach to Indigenous development that Altman has derived from the hybrid economy model has also been embraced with enthusiasm by some scholars (Morphy 2008, Scambary 2009, Watson 2009, Howitt 2012, Buchanan 2014), but there remains a need for further scholarly interrogation of the strengths and weaknesses of this approach. This chapter responds to this need by asking whether the hybrid economy offers a convincing way of resolving the tension Altman identifies between Indigenous cultural dispositions on the one hand and the attitudes and priorities underpinning market society on the other. In particular it grapples with what might appear to be a paradox: that protecting non-market values associated with Indigenous lifeworlds can best be achieved by focusing on the articulations of the customary economy with the market.

This chapter begins by examining the ways in which 'the market'—or to be more precise, development approaches underpinned by an ideological fixation on markets—figures in Jon Altman's writings as a problem for Indigenous peoples. I then examine the key characteristics of the livelihood activities at the core of Altman's hybrid economy approach to Indigenous development. I argue that the concept of partial commodification is useful for understanding what is appealing about these activities. My articulation of the concept of partial commodification draws on the work of the political philosopher Elizabeth Anderson (1993). She uses the notion of partial commodification to defend hybrid institutions in which the norms of the market are co-present with non-market norms derived from spheres such as the arts, the academy, sport and medicine. The desire of artists, academics and other professionals to make a living while resisting the full commodification of their talents finds a parallel in the aspiration of Indigenous people to make a living while resisting the full commodification of their unique knowledges, skills, traditions and lands.

Emphasising that partial commodification is at the core of the hybrid economy model is important because it averts a possible misinterpretation of Altman's approach. Altman is not blindly endorsing all articulations of the customary with the market or state. Partial commodification of Indigenous practices opens up opportunities, but as Altman recognises, it also poses dangers. In light of this I make some brief remarks in the final section of this paper about the 'bliss point' of the hybrid economy, a concept surrounding which there seems to be some misunderstanding.

The problems with markets

Altman takes issue with policymakers' faith in the power of labour market engagement to lift Indigenous Australians out of poverty and improve their well-being. He insists there are 'structural and other impediments that will limit the overall growth of the market in the remote regions where Indigenous people live on Aboriginal land' (Altman 2001: 8). The contemporary effects of the historical barriers Indigenous Australians have faced in accessing education and employment opportunities reduce their prospects of securing well-rewarded work. In remote regions in which the great majority of the Indigenous estate is located, the conditions necessary for the efficient operation of markets (such as a sufficiently large pool of buyers and sellers) are not present. Moreover, he observes that the reason these areas remained unalienated by settlers, and were therefore available for claim by Indigenous groups within the processes of the settler legal system, was their lack of promise as sites of commercial development (Altman 2001: 2). Yet many Indigenous people still aspire to live on (or close to) their ancestral lands located beyond the reach of a functioning labour market. This prompts Altman to take seriously the need for alternative means of alleviating Indigenous poverty.

At the same time Altman exhibits a further concern about market-oriented solutions to Indigenous poverty. As other economic thinkers have recognised, markets promote a distinctive ethos (Bowles 1998). This ethos entails certain conceptions of personhood and sociality which conflict with the distinctive Indigenous forms of personhood and sociality Altman has observed during fieldwork in central Arnhem Land. The contrast between market societies and kin-based societies is vital to Altman's critique of market-based development. Before proceeding further it is worth making the nature of this distinction clear.

Within market societies many interactions are relatively short-lived and impersonal, consisting of mutually beneficial trade facilitated by money. People are encouraged to think of themselves as individuals and as competitors. They are expected to invest in human capital—in other words, the education and occupational skills of their children and themselves. Adults derive a sense of personal identity from their job role. They surrender some of their autonomy to the will of their employer or else run enterprises shaped by the demands of their customers. The accumulation of material wealth is treated as honourable. Economic dependence on others is stigmatised. Saving and budgeting are prioritised over meeting the immediate needs and wants of extended kin.

By contrast, in kin-based societies such as those Altman has documented, personal interactions are among networks of kin. The sense of self is larger than the individual.

Personal identity is derived from relationships with people. The accumulation of material wealth is treated as dishonourable. People are less willing to sacrifice autonomy by submitting to authority for the sake of material gain. Economic interdependence with others is viewed positively. Meeting the immediate needs of self and kin is prioritised over saving and budgeting.

Altman considers economic development policies predicated on the displacement of a customary ethos with a market ethos ill-advised. He views such policies as assimilationist and therefore unjust. Altman also appears sceptical that top-down attempts to shift Indigenous conceptions of personhood and sociality will actually work. In other words, these social forms might prove more resilient than governments anticipate. In Altman's judgement the shift in worldview that successful competition in the mainstream labour market demands cannot be made without great suffering. The unsatisfactory gains likely to come from full integration into the market economy make this painful process seem all the more unfair. The hybrid economy is designed to address at once both these problems with market-based approaches to Indigenous development.

The hybrid economy approach

The foundational premise of the hybrid economy approach is that the regional economies within which some Indigenous Australians today make a living are comprised not just of the market and state sectors but of a third, often overlooked sector: the customary sector. These three sectors do not merely coexist but interact to make possible a range of distinctive livelihood opportunities (see Curchin 2013: 18–9). Of the livelihood opportunities that groups of Indigenous people have chosen or might choose to pursue in the future, Altman has particularly sought to draw attention to those which:

1. Provide an income.
2. Give working-age people something productive to do.
3. Support the continuation of distinctively Indigenous forms of personhood and sociality.

Livelihood opportunities which meet these three criteria are at the core of Altman's distinctive approach to Indigenous development. The productive activities most associated with the hybrid economy approach to Indigenous development are:

- self-provisioning through hunting and gathering;
- wild harvesting for sale of bush foods, marine species, native wildlife and introduced species;
- production for sale of Indigenous art, crafts and artefacts;
- environmental management services including ecological monitoring and research, fire management, invasive weed control, feral animal management and marine debris collection;
- cultural heritage management; and
- cultural tourism, festivals, and performances such as dance, music and storytelling.

These activities share a number of important features. The most noteworthy is that they enable people to reside on or close to their ancestral land and to maintain a valued connection with a sentient landscape. They use resources from the local environment in ways which can be sustained.

All but the first are a source of cash: they involve using the comparative advantage derived from customary and local knowledge and identity to produce goods or services for sale or payment. At the same time these activities provide opportunities to pursue distinctly Indigenous purposes—such as fulfilling obligations as traditional custodians of particular areas of land. The motivations for engaging in these activities go beyond cash remuneration, for example, the opportunities they provide to visit hard-to-access places. All of these activities entail the use and development of ecological, cultural or linguistic knowledge and skills derived from the Indigenous domain. They create opportunities to transmit this knowledge and identity to younger generations, and to receive recognition from outsiders of their mastery and their cultural survival in the face of colonisation. In comparison with conventional forms of employment, there is more scope for self-direction and less emphasis on submission to the will of an employer. The timing and duration of work effort is less likely to be organised around clock-time and the Western calendar and more likely to reflect ecological and ceremonial cycles. Work practices depend upon cooperation rather than competition with other workers within the workplace. Work groups are likely to be comprised of people whose kin-relationships make them comfortable working together. In sum, these activities enable people to earn income—including cash income derived from market exchange—while resisting the full commoditisation of their labour, their cultural inheritance or the local environment.

Many of the activities at the core of the hybrid economy approach involve the state as well as the customary and market sectors. These activities are too small scale, too labour intensive, too seasonal or too geographically remote from markets to attract private capital investment or to be economically profitable without government or philanthropic subsidisation through funding of, for example, equipment or marketing expertise.

Other activities that share many of these characteristics but feature less prominently in the hybrid economy literature, if at all, include:

- monitoring Australia's borders on behalf of the Australian Government;
- running cattle stations;
- translating, interpreting and teaching Indigenous languages;

- media production including film, television, radio and digital media;
- social, cultural and linguistic research; and
- providing consulting services in fields such as bush survival, bush pharmacology and cultural awareness.

It is important to note that the productive activities at the core of the hybrid economy approach to development are only a subset of the activities through which Indigenous people residing in remote regions earn a cash income. Municipal services, road building and repair, construction and building maintenance, transport, food and alcohol retail, mining, health services, school education, childcare, disability care and aged care, as well as government and non-government administration are all industries providing some employment for Indigenous people in remote regions. Though technically all part of the hybrid economies of these regions, these avenues for making a living are not at the core of the hybrid economy development approach because they meet the first two criteria I outlined above but not the third. Whether Altman is wise to place such emphasis on the third criteria is a matter of debate (see Austin-Broos 2011: 122–3, 141–5), but I do not have the space to engage with this issue here.

Partial commodification

The concept of partial commodification—familiar to non-Indigenous people from fields of endeavour such as medicine, science and the arts—is useful for thinking about the livelihood activities which typify the hybrid economy. It also illuminates some of the current threats to these activities. Though goods such as artwork, artefacts and crocodile eggs, and services such as weed control, fire management and cultural tours are exchanged for money, this does not necessarily mean they become mere commodities, mere instruments of profit and use. Rather, as Elizabeth Anderson argues, 'what confers commodity status on a good is not that people pay for it, but that exclusively market norms govern its production, exchange, and enjoyment' (Anderson 1993: 156). Even when goods and services are produced for sale, criteria other than profitability may be used to make decisions. Commodification need not be all or nothing; it admits of degrees. This is important because the full commodification of certain types of goods degrades them.

This thought has been central to the development of professions in the West. Professions have traditionally been characterised by the honouring of non-market values. Even though money changes hands, market norms are not the only norms governing the interaction. Ethical judgements are also in play, and may at times trump considerations of profitability. Artists and scholars too derive their livelihoods from the partial commodification of their talents. They accept payment for their efforts yet still recognise aesthetic values and truth-seeking as guiding ideals. Honouring such ideals will sometimes entail forgoing opportunities to make money (Anderson 1993: 147). Partial commodification is not to be regretted according to Anderson: it is important that professionals, artists and scholars can be paid for their work, because this is what enables them to devote most of their productive hours to it without sliding into destitution. Though the engagement of market and non-market spheres creates potential for conflict, this does not rule out the possibility of arrangements that are mutually beneficial.

When thinking about the hybrid economy it is helpful to remember that Indigenous Australians are not alone in seeking engagement with the market without total colonisation by market norms. Just as there are Indigenous people who wish to make their livelihoods while honouring standards deriving from a local Indigenous value system, there are professionals who make their livelihoods by providing services for payment while pursuing the non-market ideals of their chosen fields (Anderson 1993: 156). Within societies Altman would characterise as market-based there are many people—scientists, artists, sportspeople, doctors and so on—whose livelihoods are enabled by institutions which mediate market and non-market norms.

One of the distinctive features of partial commodification is the recognition of standards of excellence that exist independently from 'instrumental criteria such as profitability' (Anderson 1993: 147). Partial commodification depends upon a willingness to acknowledge domains of human pursuit with intrinsic value regardless of their market value. It depends on recognition that deviation from market norms does not indicate deficiency or failure on the part of artists and scientists. Securing state funding—an important element of the hybrid economy approach—is a classic strategy for resisting full commoditisation. This requires respect by policymakers for the autonomy of separate spheres within civil society that operate according to their own frameworks of value (Anderson 1993: 149). It demands that the state refrain from 'regarding itself as a customer for the projects it funds' (Anderson 1993: 149), in other words, specifying what it will purchase and refusing to fund anything else. This is important for the integrity of these separate spheres.

There is always the risk that partial commodification will slide into full commodification. Greed or pressure to make a profit can compromise the pursuit of higher purposes (Anderson 1993: 147). As Michael Sandel (2012) has cogently argued, market values can displace other values when market principles are brought to bear. Vigilance is required to guard against the over-intrusion of norms from other spheres. There is a need to continually reaffirm that some goods should not be treated as mere commodities. The conditions which enable partial commodification are fragile and are threatened by market fundamentalism.

How then does this discussion of partial commodification enhance our understanding of the hybrid economy? The Venn diagram with which Altman represents the hybrid economy directs our attention to the question of whether or not an activity involves multiple overlapping spheres (Altman 2006: 2). But what really matters is the answer to a more nuanced question: How do the norms and expectations originating in the different spheres interact? In the activity under consideration, which are more powerful: market norms or customary norms? Are customary norms crowded out by market incentives? Has commodification changed the character of the activity in regrettable ways? Alternatively, do customary norms dominate in a way that makes the activity unprofitable and incompatible with making a decent living? The concept of partial commodification suggests a continuum between no commodification and full commodification. In a given activity there might be some influence of market norms though customary norms clearly dominate. In another, customary norms might prevail with a trace of market influence also evident. The point at which market intrusion becomes too great is a matter for contestation. Minds will differ as to how much compromise is worth making for the sake of generating greater income.

Altman (2010: 275) writes of the 'bliss point' of the hybrid economy. Our discussion of partial commodification clarifies that the bliss point is not simply any economic activity in which the customary, state and market sectors are overlapping. Indeed the three sectors can potentially overlap in regrettable ways—ways which ensure the displacement of customary norms but result in no compensating benefits. The point is that the hybrid economy potentially brings customary and market expectations into tension. Valorising the articulation of customary with market economies is too simple, and this is not what Altman intends. He insists that he does not 'seek to present this commodification of culture as unproblematic, be it in tourism, the arts or the provision of environmental services' (Altman 2010: 273). Rather he emphasises the importance of selectivity when thinking about opportunities for development. Altman is aware that the challenge is to 'nurture the hybrid economy in ways that mesh with Indigenous values' (Altman 2001: 10).

My discussion of partial commodification is also intended to draw attention to the threats to the income-generating activities that typify the hybrid economy. They depend not just on the ongoing recognition that there are autonomous spheres of such value, but that the contemporary Indigenous domain is one of these spheres. Indigenous people judge their performance of obligations to country and kin in accordance with the values internal to the Indigenous domain. It is to be expected that the standards thought most important by Indigenous producers may not fully overlap with the standards held by providers of external funds whether they are for-profit firms seeking carbon abatement services, philanthropists or the state. Outside funding creates difficulties when funders are reluctant to acknowledge the Indigenous domain as an autonomous source of value. To advocate for the hybrid economy is to struggle against the market fundamentalist mindset which refuses to honour the legitimacy of non-market norms.

Conclusion

This paper has highlighted the concerns about the market system explicit and implicit in Altman's work that have driven his search for alternative economic forms. One impetus for Altman's development of the hybrid economy approach to Indigenous development has been his scepticism that the market economy will ever deliver adequate opportunities for Indigenous people who are culturally or geographically remote from urban centres. But in this chapter I have argued that his concern about the social costs of moving from a kin-based to a market-based economy have also been vitally important to the development of this innovative approach. Altman fears that making the shift from a kin-based economy to a market-based economy demands a profound transformation of people's values, desires and relationships.

I have argued here that the hybrid economy can be understood as a project of alternative livelihood generation through partial commodification of goods and services deriving from the Indigenous customary domain. Assessing whether (and under what conditions) the partial commodification of particular Indigenous practices can resolve the tension Altman identifies between Indigenous cultural dispositions and the attitudes and priorities underpinning market society requires empirical research by economic anthropologists and others. Clearly political philosophy can only take us so far. Nonetheless, what I have tried to do in this chapter is show that the challenge inherent in deriving a livelihood from uniquely Indigenous practices while safeguarding the distinctive moral understandings which inform these practices has analogies in many other fields. Knowing that partial commodification does not always lead to corruption of non-market values provides grounds for optimism. At the same time we should avoid a blind celebration of hybridity. Economic hybridity threatens lose-lose scenarios just as much as it promises win-win ones. It would be a mistake to equate the bliss point of the hybrid economy with the overlapping of all three sectors. Rather what matters are 'the norms governing the production and circulation of goods' in particular contexts (Anderson 1993: 166). To know this we will need further careful empirical study of the details of local Indigenous economies.

References

Altman JC (2001). *Sustainable development options on Aboriginal land: the hybrid economy in the twenty-first century*, Discussion Paper 226, Centre for Aboriginal Economic Policy Research, The Australian National University, Canberra.

Altman JC (2005). Economic futures on Aboriginal land in remote and very remote Australia: hybrid economies and joint ventures. In Austin-Broos D & MacDonald G (eds), *Culture, economy and governance in Aboriginal Australia*, University of Sydney Press, Sydney.

Altman JC (2006). *The Indigenous hybrid economy: a realistic sustainable option for remote communities?* Topical Issue 2/2006, Centre for Aboriginal Economic Policy Research, The Australian National University, Canberra.

Altman JC (2010). What future for remote Indigenous Australia? Economic hybridity and the neoliberal turn. In Altman JC & Hinkson M (eds), *Culture crisis: anthropology and politics in Aboriginal Australia*, UNSW Press, Sydney.

Anderson E (1993). *Value in ethics and economics*, Harvard University Press, Cambridge MA.

Austin-Broos D (2011). *A different inequality: the politics of debate about remote Aboriginal Australia*, Allen & Unwin, Sydney.

Bowles S (1998). Endogenous preferences: the cultural consequences of markets and other economic institutions. *Journal of Economic Literature* 36(1):75–111.

Buchanan G (2014). Hybrid economy research in remote Indigenous Australia: seeing and supporting the customary in community food economies. *Local Environment* 19(1):10–32.

Curchin K (2013). Interrogating the hybrid economy approach to Indigenous development. *Australian Journal of Social Issues* 48(1):15–34.

Gill N (2005). Aboriginal pastoralism, social embeddedness, and cultural continuity. *Society & Natural Resources* 18(8):699–714.

Holcombe S, Yates P & Walsh F (2011). Reinforcing alternative economies: self-motivated work by central Anmatyerr people to sell Katyerr (Desert raisin, Bush tomato) in central Australia. *The Rangeland Journal* 33(3):255–65.

Howitt R (2012). Sustainable Indigenous futures in remote Indigenous areas. *GeoJournal* 77:817–28.

Kwan D, Marsh H & Delean S (2006). Factors influencing the sustainability of customary dugong hunting by a remote indigenous community. *Environmental Conservation* 33(2):164–71.

Lloyd C (2010). The emergence of Australian settler capitalism in the 19th century and the disintegration/integration of Aboriginal societies: hybridisation and local evolution within the world market. In Keen I (ed.), *Indigenous participation in Australian economies: historical and anthropological perspectives*, ANU E Press, Canberra.

Morphy F (2008). Redefining viability: Aboriginal homelands communities in north-east Arnhem Land. *Australian Journal of Social Issues* 43(3):381–96.

Sandel M (2012). *What money can't buy: the moral limits of markets*, Allen Lane, London.

Scambary B (2009). Mining Agreements, developments, aspirations, and livelihoods. In Altman JC & Martin DF (eds), *Power, culture, economy: Indigenous Australians and mining*, CAEPR Research Monograph No. 30, ANU E Press, Canberra.

Smith BR (2003). Pastoralism, local knowledge and Australian Aboriginal development in northern Queensland. *The Asia Pacific Journal of Anthropology* 4(1–2):88–104.

Sullivan P (2011). *Belonging together: dealing with the politics of disenchantment in Australian Indigenous policy*, Aboriginal Studies Press, Canberra.

Watson V (2009). From the 'Quiet Revolution' to the 'Crisis' in Australian Indigenous affairs. *Cultural Studies Review* 15(1):88–109.

White JM (2011). Histories of Indigenous-settler relations: reflections on internal colonialism and the hybrid economy, *Australian Aboriginal Studies* 1:81–96.

7

Valuing Aboriginal cultural activity: Beyond markets

Kaely Woods

Introduction

It was an honour to speak at the conference that celebrated the contribution of Jon Altman, the founding Director of the Centre for Aboriginal Economic Policy Research (CAEPR), and to hear others reflect on his work. My lifelong interest and involvement in Indigenous issues, particularly sustainable economic development on terms that meet the needs of Aboriginal and other Australians, has motivated me to undertake a PhD somewhat later in life.

While Altman was establishing his research career, I was at The Australian National University (ANU) studying undergraduate economics part-time, juggling study with full-time work. The welfare and public economics that stirred my interest was grounded in utility theory, premised on individualism and material objectives. This left me wondering how this framework could accommodate non-monetary utility including Aboriginal cultural values.

After completing an economics degree my career turned to challenging, sometimes rewarding, social and economic policy in the Australian Government departments of Finance, Prime Minister and Cabinet, and Health, and with Indigenous Business Australia.

In central agency policy roles from the early 1990s, I engaged with Altman and CAEPR across a range of issues, including reviews of the Community Development Employment Projects (CDEP) scheme and related economic development programs. Altman actively sought to engage with policymakers and bureaucrats to achieve two ends: to influence policymakers through imparting knowledge and contextual understanding; and to better inform his own understanding of emerging policy issues and positions.

Here I reflect on aspects of Altman's work that have been, and continue to be, of particular relevance and interest to me. I outline what led to my doctoral research and how this research will extend Altman's project of quantifying the value of Indigenous cultural activity.

Professor Altman's contribution

I am struck by the extraordinary efforts Altman made to observe, document and analyse economic activity in Arnhem Land, particularly his visits to Mumeka outstation where he embedded himself in the community for two years in order to undertake his doctoral research, and regularly visited in following years.

Altman's early work on hunter-gatherer economies in northern Australia was positioned in a production-focused framework. Reflecting his initial training as an economist, Altman conducted quantitative assessments of production as a participant observer over extended periods. Through these studies he was able to measure and analyse the dietary and market-equivalent values of production; the time and effort exerted in bush food gathering, fishing, and hunting activities; and the seasonality of these activities (Altman 1983, 1984, 1987, 2009). This research built on the foundation of post-World War II studies of the nutritional value of customary hunting and gathering practices in Arnhem Land (Specht et al. 2000) and paralleled work being done elsewhere in Arnhem Land (Meehan 1982).

Altman's observation and analysis of hunting and gathering in Kuninjku country over extended periods clearly demonstrated the substantial calorific and market-equivalent values of the goods produced or caught (Altman 1983, 1984). The extended immersion and continuing connection that Altman built with the people provided him with a greater depth of understanding than previous shorter studies in Arnhem Land. It arguably also ensured less distortion, given that aspects of experimentation in the earlier studies have been shown to impact directly on production and consumption choices (Bird-David et al. 1992).

As an active participant in hunting activity, Altman's observations were not limited to the economic efficiency of cooperative efforts. He also recognised the cultural and social aspects of the production activity. The participatory nature of Altman's research led him to note the significance of other aspects of the customary economy, including distributive arrangements, particularly for large game; trade between groups; tool production; and the production of ritual or religious items. The asymmetry of distribution of game and concepts around demand sharing, which are important aspects of the economic framework operating in these societies, were further explored by Altman, including in work with Peterson (Altman 2009, 2011; Altman & Peterson 1988).

Recently, Altman (2009) reflected on a 1980 fire drive for hunting macropods in which he participated, considering a number of different aspects of the hunting activity in the hybrid economy model. He identified many spin-off benefits of this activity, including an increased sense of well-being resulting from the demonstration of Kuninjku social norms (including demonstration of older men's authority, sharing and consumption practices, and increased camaraderie); the education of young initiates in both cultural and ecological skills; and ecological management. In economic terms, these activities built social and human capital as they equipped individuals and the society with the skills for ongoing survival and created utility beyond the net calorific benefit of the catch. The apparent value of these activities is more than a market value equivalent to the cost of obtaining a comparable food product from a shop or another provider. Distribution mechanisms for larger game, which Altman noted to be asymmetrical towards more senior hunters in acknowledgement of their standing, could be typified as a return on their social or cultural capital.

Altman's research into Aboriginal involvement in tourism (Altman 1988, 1989b; Altman & Finlayson 1992) and the Aboriginal arts sector (Altman 1989a) also broke new ground by demonstrating the limits of the market and intersections with the customary and government sectors (see also Altman 2001, 2003, 2005). Altman's hybrid economy model is essentially a descriptive tool that sets out to highlight the role of the customary, non-market economy for Aboriginal people in remote areas. In particular, Altman refers to the flexibility hybridity affords in increasing production possibilities in ways that accommodate social and cultural practice, thereby improving well-being above the level that could be achieved by any single sector. Altman has calculated market-equivalent values of productive activity in order to highlight the value of the customary, non-monetary economy.

Activity that builds social and cultural capital is recognised in much of Altman's work but is not given a market-equivalent value. Additional benefits and value are recognised in participation in social hunting, gathering and art creation events, including the way these enable the building and passing on of cultural skills and enhance the standing and recognition of elders (Altman 1983, 2001, 2009). Altman has also recognised the value from activities in the customary economy in quality of life (Altman 1980), building cultural and ecological knowledge or intellectual property (Altman 1983) and biodiversity and ecological management (Altman 2001). These examples demonstrate the role of non-monetised, culturally based activities in building cultural, social and human capital.

Altman recognised the importance of data and greatly strengthened the evidence base for policy development. Altman identified the opportunity for a national survey of Aboriginal and Torres Strait Islander people following a recommendation from the Royal Commission into Aboriginal Deaths in Custody. He convened a workshop of academics and select officials to discuss options and implications of such a survey (Altman 1992). This resulted in a national socioeconomic survey of Australia's Indigenous people, which has continued to develop with ongoing input from Altman and other academics. Sections of the survey reflect Altman's influence in consideration of productive cultural activities such as fishing, hunting, gathering, art production, and performance. Resulting quantitative studies of the relationship between cultural activity and employment using data from the 2002 and 2008 National Aboriginal and Torres Strait Islander Social Surveys are inconsistent (Hunter &

Gray 2001, Dockery 2010, Stephens 2010, Dockery 2011). This points to the challenges of interpretation of cultural attachment which may reflect localised sociocultural influences.

Culture and economic development in policy

Aboriginal perspectives on the relationship between culture and economics have not influenced policy development. Indeed, they have rarely been part of the framework used by policymakers working on Indigenous issues. Aboriginal voices were heard more strongly during the Aboriginal and Torres Strait Islander Commission (ATSIC) years, with the development of strategies and increased funding for programs aimed at the survival and revival of languages and supporting Indigenous art and tourism. In central government policy, programs and approaches that promoted the continuity of cultural practice were never given the same priority as land rights, health, housing, education, and economic development. However, across the country, Aboriginal people have demonstrated continuity in cultural activity and connection to country through native title processes and through land management and employment programs such as CDEP.

CDEP was so central to Indigenous policy for three decades that no consideration of Indigenous employment or economic activity is complete without it. I witnessed CDEP activities in several remote communities that were grounded in social and cultural norms, supporting cultural activity and maintenance. Programs such as women's centres, caring for older people, sharing stories, and arts and crafts development are examples. These activities were consistent with the intent of the Aboriginal Employment Development Policy (AEDP) which was to create appropriate jobs for Aboriginal people in the places they lived while recognising that there were limited market opportunities in remote areas. The AEDP specifically supported 'traditional Aboriginal economic activities as a legitimate form of employment' (Australian Government 1987).

Two common success factors for CDEP were, in my experience, active community engagement in planning and development and implementation that reflected the social and cultural settings of individual communities. The prerequisite of a community plan for entry into CDEP encouraged the strengthening of community governance. However, during the period of rapid growth of CDEP in the late 1980s and early 1990s, many community plans were developed by external consultants with little sense of community ownership, resulting in a reduced sense of ground up community development. As a result, some CDEP activities became programmatic work-for-welfare, rather than avenues for community development and employment. As policy debate shifted from self-determination towards the 'real economy' and 'real jobs', CDEP was increasingly viewed as welfare or 'sit down money'. CDEP was sometimes seen as an effective veil over underemployment and unemployment, without due recognition as an effective avenue for community-driven and controlled development.

The 2007 Northern Territory Emergency Response, or Intervention as it became known, confirmed Indigenous policy development as centralised and top down, without broad-based involvement of Aboriginal people. The evolution of economic development policy from the AEDP in an era of self-determination through mutual obligation, the Intervention, and the current promotion and consultation on the Forrest Review (Forrest 2014) has had little consideration of cultural activity, except where it is central, as in art and tourism.

Government documents frequently acknowledge the value of culture to Aboriginal people and society in general, but not in economic terms beyond market value (Macklin et al. 2010). This market value is not necessarily the same as the value to Aboriginal people. Research into well-being and health points to the contribution of culture in providing Aboriginal people with a sense of identity and purpose (McDermott et al. 1998, Eckersley et al. 2001, Dockery 2011).

Cultural policy, which is generally the domain of the federal government, is framed in the 2013 statement *Creative Australia* with a declared aim to 'ensure that the cultural sector—incorporating all aspects of arts, cultural heritage and the creative industries—has the skills, resources, and resilience to play an active role in Australia's future' (Australian Government 2013). Aboriginal and Torres Strait Islander cultures are prominent in *Creative Australia*, with the first of five goals being to 'Recognise, respect and celebrate the centrality of Aboriginal and Torres Strait Islander cultures to the uniqueness of

Australia's identity'. However, there are limited specific actions and recommendations dealing with Indigenous culture. The major focus of the policy relevant to Aboriginal and Torres Strait Islanders, beyond maintaining existing programs, is the preservation of languages and the updating of the National Indigenous Languages Policy. Perusal of the Register of Cultural Organisations (ROCO)[1] suggests only 30 (1.9 per cent) of the 1,573 organisations recognised and supported by the Australian Government are identifiable as Aboriginal-owned or -controlled. A large proportion of these are performance-based organisations operating in the mainstream market. It seems that there has not been substantive financial support and recognition of culture as determined by Aboriginal people themselves since the ATSIC Cultural Industry Policy of 1997.

Moving beyond market value

While Altman and others have documented the value of production in the customary economy by considering market price equivalents, I seek to go beyond this by quantifying the value of products and processes that are not commodified.

The question of what is the complete value of cultural activity has not been fully answered by research to date. How can we value the process of group hunting and gathering beyond the calorific and market price equivalent of the product? Can ceremony be valued only according to the tourist dollars it may generate? Does the market value of Aboriginal art reflect its value to artists or does the process of production bring other benefits? By quantifying value beyond markets, is it possible to influence policy consideration of employment and cultural activity?

To answer these questions, it is worth considering developments in environmental economics over the past 30 years. Valuation of environmental amenities, where no explicit market exists, has been a central area of research and development. Partial equilibrium models

---

1   Register of Cultural Organisations (ROCO) organisations and funds as of 11 September 2013, accessed most recently on 3 November 2014 at arts.gov.au/sites/default/files/collections/register-of-cultural-organisations-roco.pdf.

from neoclassical welfare economics have been used to calculate shadow prices as estimates of the social prices of public goods or social costs of environmental damage or pollution (Parks & Gowdy 2013).

The recognition of non-market values has also been achieved in cultural economics, led by Throsby. Research in this field has predominantly focused on the value of cultural goods consumed or cultural heritage assets as public goods using similar methods to those used in environmental economics (Throsby & Withers 1985; Throsby 1999, 2003; Snowball 2008). Throsby (2006) has also examined the creativity involved in the artistic productive process and its value in terms of innovation and contribution to the artist's human capital. Less attention has been directed to cultural activity as a process of producing cultural goods and services, particularly in Indigenous cultural contexts.

What has been shown in both environmental and cultural economics is that market values are incomplete measures of the value of goods. The demonstration of broader values can justify government support for activities that preserve, enhance and support environmental and cultural activities.

Indigenous cultural tourism and arts are predominantly discretionary goods. Market demand is limited and can fluctuate widely with currency movements and international events (Acker et al. 2013, Ruhanen et al. 2013). Despite this fragility, cultural tourism continues to attract Aboriginal people as a way of earning an income while remaining connected to country and kin. The perceived benefits of these hybrid economic activities extend beyond income generation to the continuity of cultural practices and management of country.

Building and sustaining cultural capital requires ongoing effort and investment. For Aboriginal people, cultural practices such as speaking languages, practicing rituals, and teaching the young are essential to ongoing, living culture and associated identity. This is a much broader understanding of the importance of culture compared to a narrow economic production framework that only counts the market value of food production, artefact sales or cultural tours.

The limitations of market values are also evident in government-funded natural resource management programs such as Caring for our Country. The public good nature of the ecological management, border protection and biosecurity functions undertaken mean that they are unlikely to underpin sustainable private businesses in the commercial world. They are dependent on government or philanthropic funding for survival. While cultural tourism and art markets are critical elements of economic development in northern Australia, fragility limits their sustainability. Despite this, Aboriginal people participating in these activities frequently report high levels of satisfaction with work of this nature. Using cultural knowledge in the market meets financial needs while also enabling continuing connection to culture and country. This reflects the flexibility and range of production possibilities in the hybrid economy.

For Aboriginal people the choice is sometimes stark: development or culture. In the Kimberley, where I am planning to do fieldwork, Aboriginal people have articulated a desire for economic development and jobs, while also stressing the importance of maintaining culture, expressed through language, traditions and ongoing relationships with country. People often move for work and communities often schedule major cultural business at times that minimise disruption to education and work. These tensions and trade-offs can be used to inform the question of the value of cultural activity.

My research

My research question is: What is the association between Aboriginal cultural activity and labour supply in remote Australia? I intend to test the tensions and trade-offs between paid employment and cultural activity, using choice modelling to reveal the (non-market) value of cultural activity relative to paid employment. My consideration of cultural activity includes customary production such as hunting, fishing, and gathering; the creation of functional utensils and goods; participation in ceremony and ritual; and associated social interaction.

While my research interests are much broader than employment, a useful lens is to measure the non-market value of cultural activity by testing the trade-offs between cultural activity and paid employment. We know that there is significant disparity in employment levels between Indigenous and other Australians, and there has been considerable research into the education and training differentials that contribute to the labour supply side of this inequity. There have been two notable programs in recent years focusing on the demand side with corporate entities setting targets for Indigenous employment: the Australian Employment Covenant (now Generation One); and Reconciliation Action Plans. Both appear to have fallen short of employment targets. The lack of transparency in the Australian Employment Covenant makes assessment difficult (Jordan 2010, Australian National Audit Office 2013, Reconciliation Australia 2013).

There is an identified gap in quantitative research about the relationship between cultural practice and labour supply (Gray et al. 2012). Anthropological studies have variously identified tensions between paid work and maintenance of cultural practices and family obligations (Musharbash 2001, Austin-Broos 2006, McRae-Williams & Gerritsen 2010, McRae-Williams 2011). Others have pointed to employment income supporting households and facilitating engagement in cultural activity through vehicle ownership and other financial capacity (Sercombe 2008, Scambary 2013). Official measures of employment do not include cultural and social production. Better understanding of the influence of cultural practice on Aboriginal choices to engage with employment is needed to ensure appropriate and effective policies and programs.

My initial qualitative phase of research will confirm the appropriate attributes and levels for the choice modelling. My research will contribute to understanding the association of cultural activity and labour supply in a number of ways:

- Develop an empirical means to compare cultural practice and paid employment that will provide new insights into the relationship between cultural practice and maintenance and the labour supply in remote areas.
- Develop methods to identify and quantify the value of cultural practices, which can in turn indicate employment conditions that maximise the recruitment and retention of Aboriginal employees on mutually acceptable terms with employers.
- Provide explicit valuation of cultural practice that could support a re-examination of national employment policies and targets, perhaps through a classification of remoteness.

The essence of my project is the recognition of the value of culture and how to ensure Aboriginal viewpoints and choices are integrated into policy. While the idea of capturing the non-market value of cultural activity may seem theoretical, its relevance to behavioural influences for Aboriginal people is stark in policy debates about Aboriginal employment, health, education, and training. Understanding the motivations and values in activities undertaken within and outside the workplace is at the heart of effective employment policies and practices. Understanding why people make the choices they do in employment, training, diet, and other lifestyle factors is the key to successful policy interventions. While economics today is often about Big Data, at its core are still questions about human behaviours and what drives them.

The valuation of cultural activity beyond markets does not equate to commoditisation of culture. Nor is it the solution to entrenched poverty and disadvantage that exists in communities with limited commercial or state-sponsored economies. As I see it, the role of valuation is the explicit recognition of the relative importance of cultural activity as a key to cultural maintenance when considering economic development opportunities and options.

Conclusion

To say that Altman has influenced my work and research is an understatement. His engagement with senior officials was notable when I worked in central government agencies. The hybrid economy model prompted explicit recognition of Aboriginal economies beyond the market and state sectors. Altman's efforts in quantifying particular aspects of the hybrid economy were relevant in considering arts and tourism opportunities. Going beyond a time study and product assessment approach to valuing Aboriginal cultural activity and its relationship with market employment is breaking new ground. I look forward to the robust engagements with Altman and others that may ensue.

Acknowledgements

I would like to thank Jon Altman, Katherine Curchin and Matthew Gray who commented on earlier drafts of this paper.

References

Acker T, Stefanoff L & Woodhead A (2013). *Aboriginal and Torres Strait Islander art economies project: literature review*, CRC-REP Working Paper CW010, Ninti One Limited, Alice Springs.

Altman JC (1980). The Aboriginal economy. In Jones R (ed.) *Northern Australia: options and implications*, Research School of Pacific Studies, The Australian National University, Canberra.

Altman JC (1983). Eastern Gunwinggu fish trapping at Gunbatgarri. *The Beagle, Occasional Papers of the Northern Territory Museum* 1:59–71.

Altman JC (1984). The dietary utilisation of flora and fauna by contemporary hunter-gatherers at Momega Outstation, north-central Arnhem Land. *Australian Aboriginal Studies* 1:35–46.

Altman JC (1987). *Hunter-gatherers today: an Aboriginal economy in north Australia,* Australian Institute of Aboriginal Studies, Canberra.

Altman JC (1988). *Aborigines, tourism, and development: the Northern Territory experience*, North Australia Research Unit Monograph, The Australian National University, Darwin.

Altman JC (1989a). *The Aboriginal arts and crafts industry: report of the Review Committee, July 1989,* Australian Government Publishing Service, Canberra.

Altman JC (1989b). Tourism dilemmas for Aboriginal Australians. *Annals of Tourism Research* 16:456–76.

Altman JC (ed.) (1992). *A national survey of Indigenous Australians: options and implications*, CAEPR Research Monograph No. 3, Centre for Aboriginal Economic Policy Research, The Australian National University, Canberra.

Altman JC (2001). *Sustainable development options on Aboriginal land: the hybrid economy in the twenty-first century*, Discussion Paper 226, Centre for Aboriginal Economic Policy Research, The Australian National University, Canberra.

Altman JC (2003). *Economic development and participation for remote Indigenous communities: best practice, evident barriers, and innovative solutions in the hybrid economy*, presentation to the Ministerial Council for Aboriginal and Torres Strait Islander Affairs, Sydney, 28 November.

Altman JC (2005). Development options on Aboriginal land: sustainable Indigenous hybrid economies in the twenty-first century. In Taylor L, Ward GK, Davis R, Henderson G & Wallis L (eds), *The power of knowledge, the resonance of tradition*, Aboriginal Studies Press, Canberra.

Altman JC (2009). Manwurrk (fire drive) at Namilewohwo: a land-management, hunting and ceremonial event in western Arnhem Land. In Russell-Smith J, Whitehead, P & Cooke P (eds), *Culture, ecology and economy of fire management in north Australian savannas: rekindling the Wurrk tradition*, CSIRO Publishing, Collingwood.

Altman JC (2011). A genealogy of 'demand sharing': from pure anthropology to public policy. In Musharbash Y & Barber M (eds), *Ethnography and the production of anthropological knowledge: essays in honour of Nicolas Peterson*, ANU E Press, Canberra.

Altman JC & Finlayson J (1992). *Aborigines, tourism and sustainable development*, Discussion Paper 26, Centre for Aboriginal Economic Policy Research, The Australian National University, Canberra.

Altman JC & Peterson N (1988). Rights to game and rights to cash among contemporary Australian hunter-gatherers. In Ingold T, Riches D & Woodburn J (eds), *Hunters and gatherers—property, power and ideology*, Berg Publishers, Oxford.

Austin-Broos D (2006). 'Working for' and 'Working' among Western Arrernte in Central Australia. *Oceania* 76(1):1–15.

Australian Government (1987). *Aboriginal Employment Development Policy statement*, Australian Government Publishing Service, Canberra.

Australian Government (2013). *Creative Australia. National cultural policy.* Commonwealth of Australia, Canberra.

Australian National Audit Office (2013). *Indigenous employment: the Australian Government's contribution to the Australian Employment Covenant*, ANAO Audit Report No. 55 2012–13, ANAO, Canberra.

Bird-David N, Abramson A, Altman J, Bicchieri M, Burch ES, Ember CR, Endicott KM, Grinker RR, Gudeman S & Ichikawa M (1992). Beyond 'The Original Affluent Society': a culturalist reformulation [and comments and reply]. *Current Anthropology* 33(1):25–47.

Dockery AM (2010). Culture and wellbeing: the case of Indigenous Australians. *Social Indicators Research,* 99:315–32.

Dockery AM (2011). *Traditional culture and the wellbeing of Indigenous Australians: an analysis of the 2008 NATSISS*, CLMR Discussion Paper Series 2011/01, Centre for Labour Market Research, Curtin University.

Eckersley R, Dixon J & Douglas RRM (2001). *The social origins of health and well-being*, Cambridge University Press, Cambridge.

Forrest A (2014). *The Forrest review: creating parity*, Commonwealth of Australia, Canberra.

Gray M, Hunter B & Lohoar S (2012). *Increasing Indigenous employment rates*, Issues Paper No. 3, Closing the Gap Clearinghouse, Australian Institute of Health and Welfare, Canberra & Australian Institute of Family Studies, Melbourne.

Hunter B & Gray M (2001). Indigenous labour force status re-visited: factors associated with the discouraged worker phenomenon. *Australian Journal of Labour Economics* 4(2):111–33.

Jordan K (2010). *The Australian Employment Covenant: is it taxpayers' money well spent?* Topical Issue 5, Centre for Aboriginal Economic Policy Research, The Australian National University, Canberra.

Macklin J, Evans C, Arbib M & Australian Government Department of Families, Housing, Community Services & Indigenous Affairs (2010). *Indigenous Economic Development Strategy 2011–2018*, Australian Government, Canberra.

McDermott R, O'Dea K, Rowley K, Knight S & Burgess P (1998). Beneficial impact of the homelands movement on health outcomes in central Australian Aborigines. *Australian and New Zealand Journal of Public Health,* 22(6):653–8.

McRae-Williams E (2011). Living with work in a remote Aboriginal community. In Gerritsen R (ed.), *North Australian political economy: issues and agendas,* Charles Darwin University Press, Darwin.

McRae-Williams E & Gerritsen R (2010). Mutual incomprehension: the cross cultural domain of work in a remote Australian Aboriginal community. *The International Indigenous Policy Journal* 1(2):1–27.

Meehan B (1982). *Shell bed to shell midden,* Australian Institute of Aboriginal Studies, Canberra.

Musharbash Y (2001). Yuendumu CDEP: the Warlpiri work ethic and Kardiya staff turnover. In Morphy F & Sanders WG (eds) *The Indigenous welfare economy and the CDEP scheme,* CAEPR Research Monograph No. 20, ANU E Press, Canberra.

Parks S & Gowdy J (2013). What have economists learned about valuing nature? A review essay. *Ecosystem Services* 3:e1–e10.

Reconciliation Australia (2013). *Reconciliation Action Plan impact measurement report 2012,* Reconciliation Australia, Canberra.

Ruhanen L, Whitford M & McLennan C (2013). *Demand and supply issues in Indigenous tourism: a gap analysis,* final report prepared for Indigenous Business Australia & Australian Government Department of Resources, Energy and Tourism's Indigenous Tourism Working Group, School of Tourism, University of Queensland & Griffith University, Brisbane.

Scambary B (2013). *My country, mine country: Indigenous people, mining and development contestation in remote Australia,* CAEPR Research Monograph No. 33, ANU E Press, Canberra.

Sercombe H (2008). Living in two camps: the strategies Goldfields Aboriginal people use to manage in the customary economy and the mainstream economy at the same time. *Australian Aboriginal Studies* 2:16–31.

Snowball JD (2008). *Measuring the value of culture: methods and examples in cultural economics*, Springer-Verlag, Berlin.

Specht RL, McArthur M & McCarthy FD (2000). Nutrition studies (1948) of nomadic Aborigines in Arnhem Land, northern Australia. *Asia Pacific Journal of Clinical Nutrition,* 9(3):215–23.

Stephens BJ (2010). The determinants of labour force status among Indigenous Australians. *Australian Journal of Labour Economics* 13(3):287–312.

Throsby D (1999). Cultural capital. *Journal of Cultural Economics* 23:3–12.

Throsby D (2003). Determining the value of cultural goods: how much (or how little) does contingent valuation tell us? *Journal of Cultural Economics* 27:275–85.

Throsby D (2006). An artistic production function: theory and an application to Australian visual artists. *Journal of Cultural Economics* 30:1–14.

Throsby D & Withers G (1985). What price culture? *Journal of Cultural Economics* 9:1–34.

8

Hybrid economies as life projects? An example from the Torres Strait

Annick Thomassin

Introduction

Over the last decade, a number of Indigenous and non-Indigenous scholars and activists worldwide have come to embrace the concept of life projects as a holistic, local and dynamic alternative to the dominant paradigm of development (see Blaser et al. 2004). Emerging in the late 1990s, notably through the work of Gow (1997) and Escobar (1998), the notion of life projects is described as 'being about the possibility [of Indigenous peoples] defining the direction they want to take in life, on the basis of their awareness and knowledge of their own place in the world' (Blaser 2004a: 30). These projects, Blaser suggests, are 'always in the making' (2004a: 38), and can be considered as 'a politics and epistemology of resilience that assume relations, flows and openendedness as their ontological ground' (2004b: 54).

Bound to local agendas, standpoints and aspirations, these life projects exist in 'relative autonomy' (Morphy & Morphy 2013) from timeframes, objectives, and associated constructions and measures of development. They are independent of attempts by government and non-government organisations to improve abstract and generic socioeconomic indicators and statistical gaps. As relatively autonomous

Indigenous articulations,[1] these life projects reveal the 'possibility of participating in economic or cultural activities that enable them to engage with aspects of the [wider society] without changing or compromising other aspects of their way of life or their beliefs' (Morphy & Morphy 2013: 176).

Since the early 2000s, and drawing from empirical research commencing in 1978, Jon Altman has developed the hybrid economy model to make sense of Indigenous Australians' diverse economies. Altman postulates that Indigenous economies consist of three sectors—the state and the market sectors to which he adds the customary sector, the latter often being overlooked in conventional models and official statistics (Altman 2001). Akin to life projects, hybrid economies are driven by and articulated through local ethos as well as sociocultural, ecological and economic circumstances.

A few authors have referred to the hybrid economy model in the context of today's Torres Strait, underlining the synergy between commercial and subsistence fishing, government transfer payments and paid work in the private or public sectors (Marsh et al. 2004, Arthur 2005, Grayson et al. 2006, Kwan et al. 2006, Busilacchi et al. 2013).

Busilacchi et al. (2013: 2) write that 'Even though Australia is a developed nation, indigenous people in Torres Strait *still* rely on what has been defined as a "hybrid economy"' (emphasis added). While it may not have been the authors' intention, the word *still* appears to position contemporary Islanders' economic strategies as an intermediate phase on a continuum progressing from purely 'traditional' to fully fledged capitalist economies.

I suggest, in line with Buchanan (2014: 12), that local hybrid economies are 'more than merely transitional to capitalist incorporation'. Local hybrid economies may be better understood, like Altman argues, as development alternatives (e.g. Altman 2011). They are the upshot of local Indigenous groups' positions, decisions and conditions

---

1   I am using the concept of articulation in the sense conveyed by James Clifford and not in reference to the Marxist theory of articulation of the modes of production. In Clifford's (2001: 473) words, 'Articulation ... evokes a deeper sense of the "political"—productive processes of consensus, exclusion, alliance, and antagonism that are inherent in the transformative life of all societies'.

about the nature and desired level of adherence to the capitalist system and mainstream norms. As such, Torres Strait Islanders' contemporary hybrid economies may be approached as enacted and emerging individual and collective life projects and as an expression of Islanders' self-determination, relational ontology, resistance, resilience, aspirations, and connections with lands and sea.

This chapter draws on 15 months of doctoral fieldwork conducted in the Torres Strait between 2008 and 2010. I approach Masig Islanders' original and fluid articulations of their participation in the state, market and customary sectors as manifestations of diverse life projects (as well as internal and external constraints and opportunities). In particular, the focus is on Masig's fishery system and its intricate connections with the island's broader economic system. I examine how Masig Islanders orchestrate their involvement with the three aforementioned economic sectors in a manner that reflects their way of life, relational ontology, values, knowledge systems, tenure regimes and circumstances. These life projects, like the community from which they stem, are heterogeneous and ever-changing. They also uphold far-reaching economic and political aspirations.

Amidst the political projects voiced by several Masig Islanders are the strong desire to regain control over their marine territory and resources and the ambition to see these resources used in ways that benefit their community rather than mainly profiting larger non-Islander operators.[2]

On Masig, as across the Torres Strait, there was a clear association made between the expansion of the Islander sector of the fishing industry and aspirations to achieve greater political and economic autonomy for the region. At the time this fieldwork was conducted, people expressed the desire to improve the efficiency of the local fisheries, partially to attain such goals. There were talks about ways to reduce fuel consumption and bring processing and freezing facilities closer to the fishers in order to reduce overall operating costs. Attempts were made to increase and diversify access to various markets. There were also stated objectives to strengthen their participation in and control

---

2   This does not necessarily imply the disappearance of non-Islander operators from the local water but a shift in power relations between Islander fisher groups, non-Islander operators and government managers.

over the various commercial fisheries in their marine domains. Such objectives were driven by Masig Islanders' rules and values relating to resource extraction, wealth accumulation and distribution. I return to this point later.

Setting the scene

Geopolitically, Torres Strait is Australia's northernmost frontier and closest international border. Covering approximately 35,000 km², it connects the Coral Sea to the Gulf of Carpentaria, and the tip of Cape York to the southern shores of Papua New Guinea. Torres Strait marine ecosystems are rich but vary greatly across the region—from the mangrove and seagrass meadows of the west to the reef-strewn channels of the east.

The Torres Strait Protected Zone Joint Authority (PZJA) is the institution responsible for the management of the region's commercial and 'traditional' fisheries. This institution is vested with three key mandates: to acknowledge and protect Islanders' traditional way of life and livelihood, to preserve and manage the marine environment within the Protected Zone and to facilitate the 'optimal sustainable utilisation' of the resources.

Masig is part of the Kulkalgal cluster and located in central Torres Strait (see Fig. 8.1 and Fig. 8.2). The teardrop-shaped coral cay measures approximately three kilometres long by 800 metres at its widest point and rises to a mere three metres above sea level. Between mid-2008 and early 2010 there were approximately 265 people living on the island of whom roughly 90 per cent self-identified as Indigenous, according to the 2006 Census (Australian Bureau of Statistics 2006).

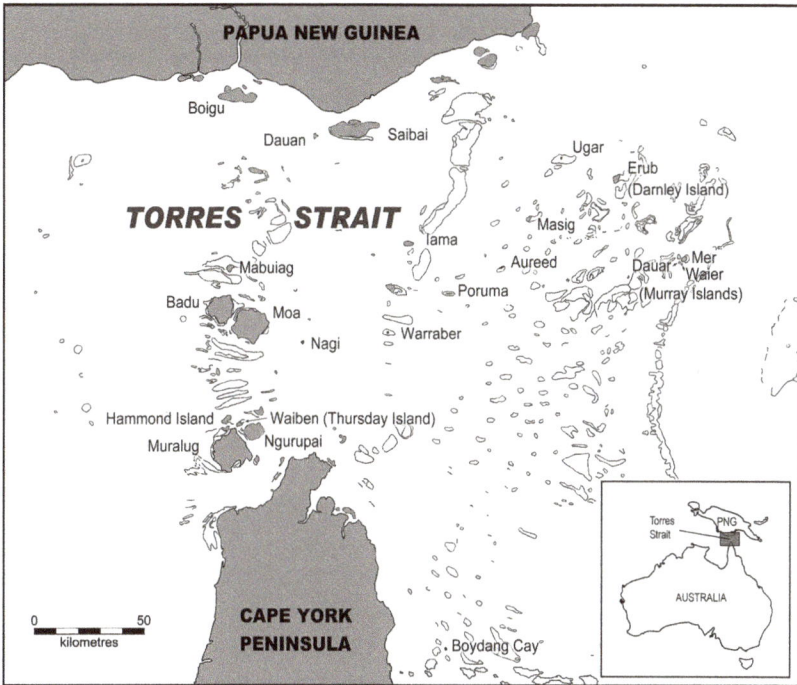

Fig. 8.1 Map of the Torres Strait
Source: Julie Lahn, 2003

Fig. 8.2 Aerial view of Masig and Koedal Islands
Photo: Annick Thomassin, 2009

Living from the land and sea

Masig Islanders describe themselves as seafarers. While anchored in an extensive web of ancestors who dwelled in, traded across, and defended the region for a few thousand years, this contemporary identity is also strongly associated with the lifeways and marine activities of their more recent forebears who were employed in the perilous pearling industry from the mid-1800s to the 1960s.

At least from the early 1900s Masig's fishers and broader community developed a dynamic mixed economy engaging in market, state and customary sector activities.[3] As Ganter (1994), Nakata (2004), Mullins (2012) and others have documented for the wider Torres Strait region, Islanders have creatively modulated their participation in the marine industry based on their needs and values and the booms and busts of the regional commercial fisheries. From 1904, schemes sponsored by missionaries, and later by the Australian government, allowed Islanders to buy pearl luggers and cutters and become owner-operators in the regional fisheries. Once owners, Nakata (2004: 161) writes, 'they preferred to use their boats as they wished, for travel and communication, for fishing and other community uses and, when they needed cash, for commercial purposes'. Their livelihood continuously overlapped the state, market and customary sectors of the regional economy.

In 2008–10, Masig Islanders were primarily employed in land-based activities as public servants, as workers for the few private employers, as participants in the Community Development Employment Projects (CDEP) scheme, or a combination of the above.[4]

---

3   Masig Islanders have developed a mixed economy since *bipotaim* (the precolonial era) engaging in trade, subsistence and ceremonial economic sectors. Their involvement with the market sector began around the mid-1860s while the state sector emerged in the early 1900s.

4   The Community Development Employment Projects (CDEP) scheme is a complex program through which members of participating Indigenous communities work part-time in community-led projects for slightly more than regular welfare entitlements. The participants have the possibility of supplementing their income through extra work for 'top up' pay or other sources of employment. CDEP projects are mostly land-based. Since 2013, CDEP has been gradually replaced by the Remote Jobs and Communities Program (RJCP) and is set to end on 30 June 2015.

Masig Islanders of working age tend to be occupationally mobile. Many hold multiple paid roles and positions—often simultaneously but also over time.[5] In addition, many earn regular or occasional extra income in commercial fisheries as independent, small owner-operators or fishing partners of Masig boat owners. Between 2008 and 2010, Masig had up to three men who derived their income solely from commercial fishing, despite the island freezer and processing plant not being in operation over this period.

On Masig, being a fisher is not so much a job or a profession. It is defined as a way of life, something that Masig people are socialised into, something they can turn to in times of need, that puts food on the table and can generate extra income. When CDEP was the principal source of government transfer payments in the Torres Strait, many Masig Islanders saw it as paying the bills, but regarded the real money as being in the sea. Land-based paid work (including CDEP), provided people with a certain economic stability which was complemented by a flexible level of engagement with the fishery system. While the community has only a few full-time fishers and a variable number of part-timers, the commercial and customary harvesting of marine resources are activities of economic significance for most, if not all, community members and contribute to the resilience of their whole socioeconomic system.[6]

The Masig fishery system

Masig's small-scale fishery system is characterised by a strong interplay between what are, somewhat artificially, characterised as commercial and customary fishing activities. Most fishing and hunting are conducted from small privately owned multipurpose dinghies (Fig. 8.3). During most, if not all, fishing trips, multiple species are caught simultaneously for commercial and non-commercial purposes using a combination of techniques and gear chosen by changing environmental circumstances and personal preferences. Wages earned

---

5   Arthur and David-Petero's survey on Torres Strait youth career aspirations has revealed similar patterns from 1999 to 2003 (Arthur & David-Petero 2000).
6   By customary I refer to any non-monetary harvesting for consumption, trading, ceremonial or sociocultural reproduction purposes.

through CDEP or land-based employment also help in supporting local marine activities, notably by providing some of the money needed to purchase the fuel consumed during these fishing excursions.

Fishers involved in commercial activities take seafood for their own sustenance over the course of fishing excursions and will also fish, hunt or collect a variety of species to share with their household.[7] Depending on the size of the catch, fishers may also share with members of their extended family and neighbours. In other words, market and customary sectors act in synergy with each other. Both are also embedded in a relational ontology which entails a logic of sharing.

Whether for cash, subsistence, or ceremonial purposes, fishing is an activity entangled in social relationships. Gifts of seafood help to create, maintain or strengthen relationships between community members and beyond (cf. Lahn 2006). These gifts are also used by fishers who may have borrowed boats or gear from relatives to reciprocate with their lenders.

Fig. 8.3 Masig Islanders' typical fishing boats
Photo: Annick Thomassin, 2009

---

7   This includes so-called 'commercial' species like tropical rock lobsters or trouts. A variety of fish, crustaceans, and molluscs are taken for subsistence. Masig Islanders' fishing methods do not usually produce by-catch. Thus, species taken for consumption are usually targeted as such.

Often invisible in reports or statistics about Torres Strait fisheries, the family unit and extended family members play a crucial supporting role. The time-consuming processing of trochus shell, for instance, brings family members together to clean and prepare the shells for shipping. The volunteers usually get their share of the prized trochus meat. This illustrates how the local fishery system blends the state, market, and customary sectors of the hybrid economy. It also highlights the social fabric that supports this model.

Masig Islanders' fishing activities do not happen in a sea that is simply 'out there', empty of relationships, open for anyone to access and exploit. Access to, and use of, sea territories and resources are regulated through a local customary marine tenure regime and a system of values which determines who holds rights over given territories and the extraction of marine resources from them.

The Masig marine estate covers an area of approximately 1,580 km^2— more than 950 times larger than the island itself (approximately 1.65 km^2). This estate includes 12 neighbouring islets and sand cays, the reefs, seagrass beds and the body of water connecting them. Every Masig Islander has the right to access this extensive marine domain and use the common pool of resources. Most fishing activities take place within this territory and the adjacent zones shared with the communities of Poruma, Warraber, Iama, Erub, Mer and Ugar (see Fig. 8.1).[8] Outsiders who wish to fish in these waters are expected to ask permission from Masig Islanders who will usually accompany the visitors on the fishing grounds.[9] In principle this rule applies to everybody (including non-Islander commercial operators). Yet, the presence of non-Islander fishing vessels in the area is legitimised through the PZJA's permit regime which ignores the Islanders' sea tenure system.

The quantity of seafood fished and hunted by Masig Islanders is governed by a principle many of them articulate as term 'take only what you need'. Being an appreciation of the shared and finite nature of the resources and a general disapproval of wastage, this principle is neither antithetical to, nor a perfect match with, the principle

---

8   For discussions about Torres Strait Islander customary marine tenure regimes see, for example, Sharp (1998), Mulrennan and Scott (1999), and Scott and Mulrennan (2010).
9   This rule can be better understood as an expression of mutual respect and respect of territorial boundaries. It is part of what Torres Strait Islanders call *gud pasin* (good ways).

of ecological sustainability as it draws on a different ontological standpoint. Taking more than considered sufficient in given situations, commercially or otherwise, or failing to share when one has more than enough for oneself and one's family, are behaviours associated with greediness. Such conduct may have negative social repercussions for the person or group considered at fault. This principle governs both commercial and customary use of the marine domain.

Masig small-boat fisheries in the hybrid economy

Contrasting with the non-Islander prawn, mackerel and finfish industries operating from larger vessels across Masig's waters, Masig Islanders' multispecies and multipurpose small-boat fisheries are greatly limited by weather conditions, seasonal migrations and market accessibility. Islander fishing efforts have a tendency to fluctuate with the seasons and the presence of buyers. For Masig Islanders the ability to combine or alternate between species or to shift to land-based activities constitutes a way of maximising returns from each excursion and securing a minimum income all year round. This flexible approach allows fishers to make the most of any circumstances—an aspect of their fisheries that is locally considered an advantage. Such an approach reduces reliance on a particular species or single source of income, results in periods of rest and rotation of target species, and increases the resilience of the whole system. This enables fishers to adapt to the vagaries of the markets, fuel prices and availability, family circumstances and obligations, and other socioeconomic factors. The combination of land-based and sea-based work allows fishers to stay close to their family, a desire seen as contrasting with more intensive fisheries models that require fishers to remain at sea for long periods of time.

Participation in the commercial and customary fisheries is also supported by small business grants from the Torres Strait Regional Authority (a statutory authority attached to the Australian Government). These enable Masig Islanders to buy boats and outboard engines.

From its introduction on Masig in 1985, CDEP has played a supporting role for the local fishery system (for discussions about the articulation between CDEP and Torres Strait fisheries see Arthur 2005, Altman et al. 1994, Kwan et al. 2006, Busilacchi et al. 2013). On Masig, a large number of regular commercial fishers combined work on the CDEP scheme and fishing activities.

I have been told on many occasions that 'CDEP is for the rent and the bills, fishing is for the rest'. For many years, to accommodate fishers, the CDEP schedule was based on two teams working in rotation (one week on, one week off) to allow fishers to go out. Arthur (2005) also suggests that, as a form of income support, CDEP helped relieve pressure on the fisheries. Indeed, the disappearance and reappearance of commercial options can destabilise the local economy. CDEP helped to minimise the impacts of such ebbs and flows and therefore constituted an important dimension of Masig's hybrid economy.

Debates about CDEP are too complex to detail here. However, it is important to note that perspectives on the scheme were are mixed. While there was a sentiment that CDEP had helped to support the local fishery system, there was also a view that the program might have impeded the local fishing effort. Arthur (2005: 11) notes that 'in part because of CDEP, the Islander fishery may not be (or need to be) as intensive as the non-Islander fishery'.

There was a shared view among Masig Islanders and across the Torres Strait that increasing returns from commercial fisheries was the main way by which they could achieve economic independence and political autonomy. Yet, in spite of the small size of the Masig community, people's aspirations for future development of the fisheries were diverse. Some Islander politicians and some of the more intensive fishers wished to see participation in commercial fishing increase significantly. Among them, a number hoped to see a small fleet of 8–9 metre boats developed, possibly in collaboration with the other three communities of the Central Strait. Along these lines, one of the island representatives stressed that a 'new breed of professional fishermen' was needed for the island's existing commercial freezer to be cost-effective and to get a better fuel price.

Others supported the existing dinghy model, which gives a lot of independence to each fisher, but wanted to see the island's most able-bodied men taking part in the fisheries in order keep the freezer going. As one of the full-time fishers interviewed mentioned, 'some people only use it when it's Christmas period', emphasising that if they shifted to full-time fishing, they would see the benefits from the freezer.

The schedule of having CDEP participants working alternate weeks was implemented to increase participation in fisheries and make the freezer profitable. Nevertheless, in most cases, aspirations to increase the fishing effort were circumscribed by fishers' positions on suitable levels of extraction and accumulation of capital. In other words, Masig Islanders' fishing behaviour was driven more by variable and finite needs and by the shared nature of the resource than by a desire to use the fisheries to their optimal yield.

Other community members were happy with a combination of part-time or occasional participation in various fisheries with land-based work, as opposed to larger-scale approaches. This model allowed them to be there for their families and participate in community life. It also meant that people could go fishing when money or seafood were needed for various celebrations, funerals and weddings, to send their teenagers to high school on the mainland, and so on.

Hence, the desire to increase individual levels of participation in fishing was not shared evenly among the community's fishers. Given the small size of the population, this diversity of views poses challenges for the development of the fisheries on a larger scale. Yet, as happened during the pearling era, arrangements between custodians of the broader Kulkalgal region may be a way to increase recruitment.

Other avenues for increasing participation are being envisaged. For example, Masig's hybrid economy was deployed to develop locally owned and based aquaculture projects, such as a pilot sponge farm; a project born of a collaboration between marine scientists, Masig project managers, and divers paid through CDEP. It is hoped that such initiatives will bear fruit in the near future in both jobs and profits.

Conclusion

I have necessarily simplified the socioeconomic, political and ontological standpoints of this dynamic island community. Whether the focus is on the local fishery or on the island's broader economic regime, Masig Islanders (as individuals, families or community) modulate the market, state, and customary sectors of their economy in ways that are informed by and foster their social relations and long-standing institutions.

Since the early 1900s, if not earlier, customised juxtapositions and superimpositions of these three economic sectors have allowed Masig Islanders to interact with their land and sea territories and resources on their own terms, that is, in accordance with their values, tenure regime, needs and aspirations. This strategy, to paraphrase a collaborator from another island, reveals their tendency to privilege lifestyle and families over a relentless pursuit of profit and accumulation of wealth. This strategy is also driven by objectives to regain control over their waters and resources, to continue living in and off their maritime domain, and to secure a future for those among their descendants who may wish to live on Masig.

Like several very remote localities in Australia, the island offers very few mainstream employment opportunities. In such circumstances, Masig Islanders' capacity to weave together the customary, state and market sectors of their local economy enables them to deal with the caprices of the weather, fish stocks and markets.

As a vessel for diverse life projects, a way to seize opportunities, and a means to respond to economic, demographic and political challenges, Masig Islanders' flexible hybrid economy can be described as an expression of their self-determination and relative autonomy. Accordingly, it seems wise to approach these economic strategies and underpinning institutions as the foundations and drivers of each island community's particular aspirations for development. External support could focus on recognising and supporting existing and emerging projects, economies and institutions. This would promote engagement with the marine environment that accords with Islanders' *pasin* (ways) and aspirations, rather than blanket solutions aimed either at closing statistical gaps or at the selective protection of Islanders' 'traditional' lifeways.

References

Altman JC (2001). *Sustainable development options on Aboriginal land: the hybrid economy in the twenty-first century*, Discussion Paper 226, Centre for Aboriginal Economic Policy Research, The Australian National University, Canberra.

Altman JC (2011). *Alternate development for Indigenous territories of difference*, Topical Issue 5/2011, Centre for Aboriginal Economic Policy Research, The Australian National University, Canberra.

Altman JC, Arthur, WS & Bek HJ (1994). *Indigenous participation in commercial fisheries in Torres Strait: a preliminary discussion*, Discussion Paper 73, Centre for Aboriginal Economic Policy Research, The Australian National University, Canberra.

Arthur WS (2005). *Torres Strait Islanders and fisheries: an analysis of economic development programs*, The National Oceans Office, Australian Government Department of Environment and Heritage, Hobart.

Arthur WS & David-Petero J (2000). *Education, training and careers: young Torres Strait Islanders, 1999*, Discussion Paper 207, Centre for Aboriginal Economic Policy Research, The Australian National University, Canberra.

Australian Bureau of Statistics (2006). *2006 Census community profile series: Masig Island (SSC 36655)*, ABS, Canberra.

Blaser M (2004a). Life projects: Indigenous peoples' agency and development. In Blaser M, Feit HA & McRae G (eds), *In the way of development: Indigenous peoples, life projects and globalization*, Zed Books/IDRC, London.

Blaser M (2004b). 'Way of life' or 'who decides': development, Paraguayan indigenism and the Yshiro people's life projects. In Blaser M, Feit HA & McRae G (eds), *In the way of development: Indigenous peoples, life projects and globalization*, Zed Books/IDRC, London.

Blaser M, Feit HA & McRae G (eds) (2004). *In the way of development: Indigenous peoples, life projects and globalization*, Zed Books/IDRC, London.

Buchanan G (2014). Hybrid economy research in remote Indigenous Australia: seeing and supporting the customary in community food economies. *Local Environment* 19(1):10–32.

Busilacchi S, Russ GR, Williams AJ, Sutton SG & Begg GA (2013). The role of subsistence fishing in the hybrid economy of an indigenous community. *Marine Policy* 37:183–91.

Clifford J (2001). Indigenous articulations. *The Contemporary Pacific* 13(2):467–90.

Escobar A (1998). Whose knowledge, whose nature? Biodiversity, conservation, and the political ecology of social movements. *Journal of Political Ecology* 5:53–82.

Ganter RJ (1994). *The pearl-shellers of Torres Strait: resource use, development and decline, 1860s–1960s*, Melbourne University Press, Melbourne.

Gow DD (1997). Can the subaltern plan? Ethnicity and development in Cauca, Colombia. *Urban Anthropology and Studies of Cultural Systems and World Economic Development* 26(3/4):243–92.

Grayson J, Marsh H & Hamann M (2006). *Information to assist Torres Strait Islanders manage their traditional fisheries for dugongs and green turtles*, final project report prepared for the Ocean Park Conservation Foundation, School of Tropical Environment Studies and Geography, James Cook University, Townsville.

Kwan D, Marsh H & Delean S (2006). Factors influencing the sustainability of customary dugong hunting by a remote indigenous community. *Environmental Conservation* 33(2):164–71.

Lahn J (2003). Past visions, present lives: sociality and locality in a Torres Strait community, PhD thesis, James Cook University, Townsville.

Lahn J (2006). Women's gift-fish and sociality in the Torres Strait, Australia. *Oceania* 76(3):297–309.

Marsh H, Lawler IR, Kwan D, Delean S, Pollock K & Alldredge M (2004). Aerial surveys and the potential biological removal technique indicate that the Torres Strait dugong fishery is unsustainable. *Animal Conservation* 7(4):435–43.

Morphy F & Morphy H (2013). Anthropological theory and government policy in Australia's Northern Territory: the hegemony of the 'mainstream'. *American Anthropologist* 115(2):174–87.

Mullins S (2012). Company boats, sailing dinghies and passenger fish: fathoming Torres Strait Islander participation in the maritime economy. *Labour History* 103:39–58.

Mulrennan M & Scott C (1999). Land and sea tenure at Erub, Torres Strait: property, sovereignty and the adjudication of cultural continuity. *Oceania* 70(2):146–76.

Nakata M (2004). Commonsense, colonialism and government. In Davis R (ed.), *Woven histories, dancing lives: Torres Strait Islander identity, culture and history*, Aboriginal Studies Press, Canberra.

Scott CH & Mulrennan ME (2010). Reconfiguring mare nullius: Torres Strait Islanders, indigenous sea rights and the divergence of domestic and international norms. In Blaser M, De Costa R, McGregor D & Coleman WD (eds), *Indigenous peoples and autonomy: insights for a global age*, UBC Press, Vancouver.

Sharp N (1998). Reimagining sea space: from Grotius to Mabo. In Peterson N & Rigsby B (eds), *Customary marine tenure in Australia*, Oceania Publications, University of Sydney, Sydney.

9

Indigenous country in the southwest Gulf of Carpentaria: Territories of difference or indifference?

Seán Kerins and Jacky Green

To remove the passive welfare trap, we need to break the nexus between indigenous development and geography. This means reorienting programs and incentives onto the development of individuals, rather than the development of geographical areas. It is a vital distinction (Tudge 2011: 22).

Introduction

The Abbott government is seeking to sever Indigenous peoples' cultural, spiritual and economic relationships with their land and other natural resources, while also breaking down Indigenous social relationships and kin structures. We are told this is being done 'to remove the passive welfare trap'. Facilitating the involuntary mobility of Indigenous Australians off their ancestral lands to areas where better education and job opportunities exist is not new. It was also one of the underlying principles of the 2008 Council of Australian Government's *National Indigenous Reform Agreement (Closing the Gap)* (COAG 2008: E-79).

It is also evident in the recent *Forrest review: creating parity* which, in Chapter 8, champions the break-up of Indigenous common property, along with the movement of Indigenous peoples off their country (Forrest 2014: 220). Forrest tells Indigenous peoples what success looks like for their remote communities. He says, 'remote communities are safe, vibrant and positive environments and local people and community members are able to orbit to larger town centres to take up work' (Forrest 2014: 191).

The idea, promoted by Australian governments and the economic elite, that Indigenous peoples should surrender their hard-won common property resources and abandon their ancestral lands to seek work elsewhere, is a view that Garawa, Gudanji, Marra, Waanyi and Yanyuwa peoples of the southwest Gulf of Carpentaria in the Northern Territory (Fig. 9.1) reject in their approach to development. Instead, they see development as a nexus between themselves, as Indigenous peoples, and their country, where their common property resources, networks, culture and ecological knowledge serve as reservoirs of creative alternatives to state development projects (Green et al. 2012).

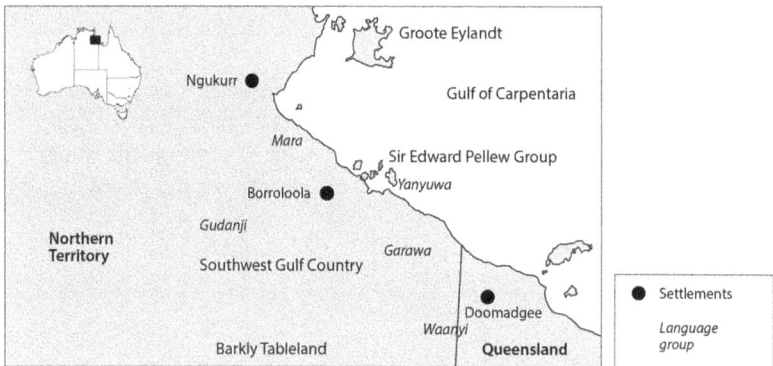

Fig. 9.1 Map showing Indigenous peoples of the southwest Gulf of Carpentaria

Source: Seán Kerins

The failure of top-down policy

Indigenous peoples in the Gulf region see the present structures and processes, which attempt to fit Indigenous interests to frameworks developed by the state, as not working and something that will not work for them. Many see current government policy, such as attenuating the communal attachment to land by individualising land ownership, as nothing more than government attempts to further alienate them from their country and kin and squash their long resistance to settler colonialism. They fear that if they are 'yarded up like cattle' and forced 'to live like white man in town with no culture' (Kerins 2013a) they will not be able to protect their country from the negative effects of large-scale development.

Over the past decade across the southwest Gulf region in the Northern Territory there has been a substantial increase in mining and energy resource extraction developments with few benefits flowing to Indigenous peoples, while it is they who bear the costs. Garawa, Gudanji, Marra, Waanyi and Yanyuwa peoples are alarmed at the increased environmental destruction and contamination of their country that they are witnessing (see Fig. 9.2 and Fig. 9.3). They are alarmed that species they once hunted, fished and gathered are quickly disappearing and that many of their important fishing and hunting places are now off limits because of access restrictions or pollution (Bardon 2014). They are increasingly alarmed that they cannot make their voice heard in the development debate. They are also alarmed that their long-term life project of living on and caring for country, which is 'embedded in local histories and encompassing visions of the world and the future that are distinct from those embodied by projects promoted by the state and markets' (Blaser 2004: 26), is being snuffed out.

It is important to remember that moving people off their country and usurping their land and other natural resources is not new to Indigenous peoples in the Gulf (see Fig. 9.4). 'The logic of elimination' (Wolfe 2006: 388) began in the 1870s when settler colonisers attempted to clear the land of Indigenous people with guns, poison and intimidation to make way for the first wave of European capital (Roberts 2005). It continued through to the 1960s when 133 Yanyuwa people were forcibly removed by the Welfare Branch from Borroloola to a reserve area (Dangana) 150 km east of Borroloola (Baker 1999: 99–100).

Fig. 9.2 Copper sulphide from Redbank mine flows directly into Hanrahan's Creek killing all aquatic life

Photo: Jessie Boylan

Fig. 9.3 Sulphur dioxide billowing from McArthur River Mine

Photo: David Morris

Fig. 9.4 Drawing of settler colonial violence in the Gulf Country, Dinny McDinny, (1927–2003)
Source: Private collection

As Wolfe (2006: 388) reminds us, the settler invasion is a structure rather than 'an event'. Jacky Green makes the same point in his artwork *Same story, settlers–miners* (Fig. 9.5), about which Green says:

It's not the first time we had people invade our country. It happened first time when whitefellas came with their packhorses, looking round to see what was there. Aboriginal people were watching from a distance, staying back, not wanting to be seen. Others were ready to spear them. The invasion is happening again. This time they come with their 'agreements' and their dozers.

Fig. 9.5 *Same story, settlers–miners*, Jacky Green, 2013
Source: Private collection

The success of Indigenous cultural and natural resource management

For the past decade, in this very remote and challenging region (Fig. 9.6), Indigenous peoples have been highly successful in building small-scale cultural and natural resource management enterprises, utilising their common property resources, cultural knowledge and kinship networks to provide social, economic and environmental benefits to themselves and wider Australia. It is important to note that these projects all have roots in the much maligned Community Development Employment Projects (CDEP) scheme (Kerins 2012a).

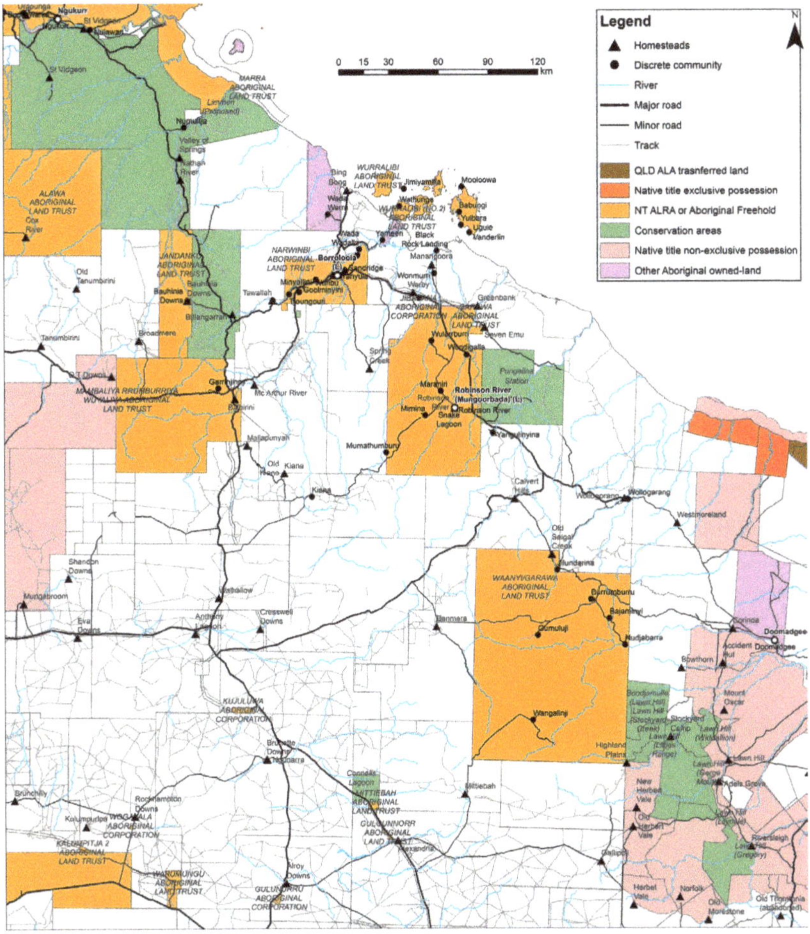

Fig. 9.6 Land tenure in the southwest Gulf of Carpentaria
Source: Francis Markham

Yanyuwa people operate a sea country ranger program employing 17 people through the Working on Country program. They recently declared their country an Indigenous Protected Area (IPA) where they focus, amongst other things, on creating meaningful employment opportunities for community members, managing important turtle and dugong breeding and feeding areas, fee for service work with fisheries, the removal of feral cats from the off-shore islands, and the transfer of cultural knowledge between generations (Yanyuwa Families et al. 2011). They are also engaging with market opportunities by developing an innovative cultural tourism enterprise based on wildlife in the region along with their cultural knowledge. If their property rights to fisheries resources were recognised by the Australian state, they would be able to pursue further opportunities, especially in the lucrative sports fisheries market.[1]

Garawa and Waanyi operate two ranger groups with seven full-time rangers and up to 40 casual workers. However, the flexibility of employing casual workers is fast disappearing under recent government employment policy (Green et al. 2012). Over the past decade Garawa and Waanyi rangers and landowners have taken control of fire, replacing the boom and bust cycle of wildfires with an early dry season mosaic burning regime which has seen a considerable reduction in greenhouse gas emissions (see Fig. 9.7). They have also reconnected many young people with their country, bringing them to camps to participate in burning activities, planning meetings and fauna surveys (Kerins 2012b). They have also developed a plan of management for an IPA over the Waanyi/Garawa Aboriginal Land Trust—the Ganalanga Mindibirrina Indigenous Protected Area—to help expand their work activities, engage young people, create more employment, and develop enterprises such as cultural tourism and carbon farming (Gambold & Kerins 2013).

To date, Gudanji and Marra have not been able to organise to develop formalised cultural and natural resource management activities on their country.

---

1   It is estimated that each year over 10,000 people fish in the saltwater country of the Yanyuwa people in the delta region of McArthur River and the coastal waters surrounding the Sir Edward Pellew Island Group. With little recognition of their property rights to fisheries, other than a non-commercial right recognised in the *Native Title Act 1993* (Cwlth), Yanyuwa people are excluded from market opportunities.

Fig. 9.7 Garawa ranger Donald Shadforth undertaking aerial controlled burning of his country at Robinson River
Source: Michael Lawrence-Taylor

Building social enterprise

For the past two years Garawa, Gudanji, Marra, Waanyi and Yanyuwa peoples have also been collaborating to develop a regional governance institution to operate across the southwest Gulf region in the Northern Territory as a social enterprise (Kerins 2013b). Social enterprises are 'not based on utilitarian-economic models but rather an economic model in which resources provide for broader goals, economic, social, cultural and political' (Berkes & Davidson-Hunt 2007: 211). This can include the creation of jobs and the strengthening of social capital by supporting people who have been inactive back into the wider activities of the community (Borzaga & Defourny 2001). While social enterprises can have a profit motive, their primary aim is to provide social and/or environmental dividends to community members, and in some cases to the wider public. They rarely distribute financial profit to individuals, with any surplus being reinvested for the long-term benefit of the community (Pearce 2003).

Garawa, Gudanji, Marra, Waanyi and Yanyuwa peoples aim, through establishing a regional governance institution, to break from the practice of relying entirely on government funding rounds for operational funds and move toward financial self-determination. They also intend to formalise their relationships with, and draw on the skills, expertise and financial contacts of, conservation and philanthropic organisations operating both nationally and internationally so that they can achieve their long-term development goal of sustainable land- and sea-based livelihoods throughout the region.

Government policy

Government support for these successful Indigenous cultural and natural resource management initiatives remains risk averse. Within the wider Indigenous policy framework they have been consigned, until recently, to the Australian Government's environment portfolio, where they were reliant predominantly on the IPA and Working on Country programs, as well as myriad other competitive short-term grant schemes (Kerins 2012b). The social, cultural, economic and environmental benefits they provide Indigenous groups and wider Australia were largely overlooked within the COAG Indigenous policy framework. The *National Indigenous Reform Agreement (Closing the Gap)* focused on 'the mainstream economy—real jobs, business opportunities, economic independence and wealth creation' (COAG 2008: 7).

There is also little evidence in the Northern Territory Government's Indigenous policy framework of its support for community-based enterprises operating across the Northern Territory. For example, the Northern Territory Government's *Draft Indigenous Economic Development Strategy*, in replicating the Australian Government's *Indigenous Economic Development Strategy* (Altman 2011), narrowly equates Indigenous economic development solely with increasing monetary wealth.

It states:

> While the definition of wealth in an Indigenous context encompasses financial wealth, connection to land, family and holistic health (physical, spiritual and emotional), the draft Indigenous Economic Development Strategy 2013–2020 refers to financial wealth (Northern Territory Government 2013: 1).

The Australian and Northern Territory governments are using the project of 'Northern Development' and their Indigenous economic development strategies as policy tools, not so much to assist

Indigenous peoples to achieve their own development aspirations, but as a legitimising strategy for their 'open for business' developmental agendas (Bevage 2013).

What we are witnessing across northern Australia is neoliberalism, which 'is the intensification of the influence and dominance of capital; it is the elevation of capitalism, as a mode of production, into an ethic, a set of political imperatives, and a cultural logic. It is also a project: a project to strengthen, restore, or in some cases, constitute anew the power of economic elites' (Thompson 2005: 23).

Jacky Green's provocative painting *FIFO—Fly In Fuck Off* (Fig. 9.8) captures something that many of us never see, the Aboriginal experience of dealing with state officials and mining company representatives in remote regions of the continent. It gives us a rare glimpse of the power relationship from an Aboriginal viewpoint. Green's artwork details how these meetings unfold after the planes arrive.

Fig. 9.8 *FIFO—Fly In Fuck Off*, Jacky Green, 2013
Source: Private collection

He says of his artwork:

> Aboriginal people sitting on the ground all focused on government and mining people standing with their whiteboard using complicated words. But we not really understanding, not getting our heads around what it really means. That's why some of them just sittin' there, on the ground, scratchin' their heads, and others got their hands up wantin' to ask questions. They just put something in front of us and when they think they got it right, they outta here. They just fly in and fuck off and we don't know what they really meant.

In *Whitefellas work like white ants* (Fig. 9.9), Green visualises the state's obsession with the individual as the death knell for Indigenous peoples.

Fig. 9.9 *Whitefellas work like white ants*, Jacky Green, 2014
Source: Private collection

He says:

> I call this painting 'Whitefellas work like white ants' because it tells the story of how whitefellas force their development projects on us and our country.

> On the left of the painting is the whitefella bulldozer pushing over what he thinks is just a tree. But it's not just a tree. It's a sacred site tied in with the songlines that run through our country. Above the bulldozer is a white ant. White ants destroy things.

On the right of the painting I show how white ants attack and kill healthy trees. The white ants find the weak spot, like a decaying root, they get in there and slowly start eating the tree from the inside out until they kill it.

This is what whitefellas do to us Aboriginal people, when they want to get us to agree to one of their development projects. They find the weak ones in our cultural groups. They look after them. They use them to sell their plans, and to tell us there will be jobs and good things from the development project, but there never is. There're only problems that we Aboriginal people are left with.

This way of working always causes conflict amongst our people. It starts to eat away at us and our communities from the inside out, just like white ants do.

When they pick us Aboriginal people off and separate the weak ones from our cultural groups they killing us and our culture. I symbolise this in my painting by the body hung by the neck in the tree.

Future opportunities

What is needed in the southwest Gulf region, and other regions of Australia, to assist Indigenous peoples further develop their cultural and natural resource management activities and social enterprises, is greater recognition of their property rights. Not only to land, but property rights to their fisheries, water and mineral resources.

To ensure that development projects benefit Indigenous peoples, policy frameworks need to link access to federal, state and territory support for major development projects to real steps to secure direct and substantial Indigenous benefits.

There is an urgent need to invest in Indigenous governance so that Indigenous peoples can build confidence, skills and institutions for positive and productive engagement with other industry and NGO sectors.

There is an urgent need for Federal and Territory governments to develop long-term investment frameworks for Indigenous cultural and natural resource management initiatives to create employment, new partnerships and market opportunities for Indigenous peoples.

There is also an urgent need for the completion of carbon farming methodologies for regions with rainfall under 600 mm per year, so that Garawa and Waanyi land owners can participate in new market opportunities which may assist them to further grow social enterprises across the region.

Finally, federal, state and territory governments should obtain Indigenous peoples' free, prior and informed consent before adopting and implementing legislative or administrative measures that may affect them.

Conclusion

We conclude with Jacky Green reflecting on Indigenous peoples' experiences in dealing with governments and their top-down policies.

> Once the government cleared us off our lands by shooting us and putting chains around our necks and dragging us off. Then, long time later, they said 'Here's your land back, we don't need it'. That tall man he poured the sand through that old man's hands. That made us real happy and we began to move back home. Government gave us a bit of help to get back and set ourselves up. But you know what? They never really took those chains off from round our necks, 'cos now they slowly pullin' on them. They pullin' us off our lands again and yardin' us up like cattle in town. They pullin' us off our land by not giving us schooling, health and housing services on our homelands. They not helpin' us. They sayin' to the parents if you don't send your kids to school we gonna stop your money and send you to prison. But there aren't no schools, so the parents have to move off their country to live like white man in town with no culture (Jacky Green, Borroloola, 17 April 2012).

Fig. 9.10 *Wundigala*, Myra Rory, 2008
Source: Private collection

References

Altman JC (2011). *The draft Indigenous Economic Development Strategy: a critical response*, Topical Issue 3/2011, Centre for Aboriginal Economic Policy Research, The Australian National University, Canberra.

Baker R (1999). *Land is life: from bush to town: the story of the Yanyuwa people,* Allen & Unwin, Sydney.

Bardon J (2014). *McArthur River Mine's burning waste rock pile sparks health, environmental concerns among Gulf of Carpentaria Aboriginal groups.* Australian Broadcasting Corporation, 27 July.

Berkes F & Davidson-Hunt IJ (2007). Communities and social enterprises in the age of globalization. *Journal of Enterprising Communities: People and Places in the Global Economy* 1(3):209–21.

Bevage A (2013). Giles warns 'Lefty' stirrers. *NT News*, 24 June.

Blaser M (2004). Life projects: Indigenous peoples' agency and development. In Blaser M, Feit HA & McRae G (eds), *In the way of development, Indigenous peoples, life projects and globalization*, Zed Books, London, New York.

Borzaga C & Defourny J (2001). *The emergence of social enterprise*, Routledge, London.

COAG (Council of Australian Governments) (2008). *National Indigenous Reform Agreement (Closing the Gap)*, Australian Government, Canberra.

Forrest A (2014). *The Forrest review: creating parity*, Australian Government Department of the Prime Minister and Cabinet, Canberra.

Gambold N & Kerins S (2013). *Ganalanga Mindibirrina Indigenous Protected Area, Plan of Management, 2013–2018,* Darwin.

Green J, Morrison J & Kerins S (2012). 'No more yardin' us up like cattle'. In Altman JC & Kerins S (eds), *People on country: vital landscapes, Indigenous futures*, The Federation Press, Sydney.

Kerins S (2012a). Building from the bottom-up: Indigenous development initiatives in the south-west Gulf of Carpentaria, Australia. In *Proceedings of Nga Pae o te Maramatanga Conference*, Auckland University, Auckland, New Zealand.

Kerins S (2012b). Caring for country to Working on Country. In Altman JC & Kerins S (eds), *People on country: vital landscapes, Indigenous futures*, The Federation Press, Sydney.

Kerins S (2013a). A key role for Indigenous peoples in Australia's sustainable future. In Craven R, Dillon A & Parbury N (eds), *Black and White: Australians all at the crossroads*, Connor Court Publishing, Melbourne.

Kerins S (2013b). Governing a Black commons. *Indigenous Law Bulletin* 8(8):30–4.

Northern Territory Government (2013). *Indigenous Economic Development Strategy 2013–2020: frequently asked questions*, Northern Territory Government, Darwin.

Pearce J (2003). *Social enterprise in Anytown*, Calouste Gulbenkian Foundation, London.

Roberts T (2005). *Frontier justice: a history of the Gulf Country to 1900*, University of Queensland Press, St. Lucia, Queensland.

Thompson MJ (2005). Review of A Brief History of Neoliberalism. *Democratiya* 3(Winter):22–7.

Tudge A (2011). A new deal for Indigenous Australians. *Institute of Public Affairs Review: A Quarterly Review of Politics and Public Affairs* 63(4):20–3.

Wolfe P (2006). Settler colonialism and the elimination of the native. *Journal of Genocide Research* 8(4):387–409.

Yanyuwa Families and li-Anthawirriyarra Sea Rangers with Stephen Johnson (2011). *Barni-Wardimantha Awara Yanyuwa Indigenous Protected Area Plan of Management and MERI Plan*, Mabunji Aboriginal Resource Association, Borroloola, Northern Territory.

10

Indigenous-owned art centres, tourism and economic benefits: The case of Maruku Arts

Marianne Riphagen

Art centres and public patronage

Jon Altman has written extensively about the Indigenous visual arts industry, including the roles played by community-owned Indigenous art centres and the importance of government support for artists and enterprises operating at considerable distance from key markets (Altman 2005, 2007a). He has repeatedly pointed to the economic, social and cultural benefits of government investment in art centres which accrue not just to Indigenous artists and to those who market their work but also to individuals and institutions in sectors like hospitality and tourism (Altman 2007b). Observing that Indigenous art centres constitute hybrid institutions which combine myriad commercial, cultural and social functions, Altman has consistently cautioned against pressuring such centres to operate independent of government funding. However, policymakers have often been reluctant to recognise art centres' mixed functions. As argued by Altman (2005), the ongoing failure to appreciate such hybridity lies at the core of Indigenous art centres' vulnerability and fragility.

Whilst concerned about policy pressures on Indigenous art centres to reduce their dependency on government subsidy, Altman (2000) has explored opportunities for commercialisation of the industry. Conscious of the popularity of certain forms of Indigenous cultural production amongst tourists, he has suggested that opportunities exist for Indigenous artists and art enterprises to expand into the market for tourist art (Altman 2007b). Altman has also observed that a number of art centres already engage with tourism as they attempt to attract inbound tourists to realise local sales and thus higher returns to their art practitioners. In this paper, I extend Altman's analysis of art centres by examining what happens when an Indigenous art centre does not just venture into the tourist art market but develops a commercial tourism arm. Such a move accords perfectly with the current Indigenous policy climate of mainstreaming (Altman 2010). Nonetheless, as I will demonstrate, it has yielded mixed cultural and economic results. These results illustrate concealed effects of mainstreaming and substantiate Altman's recurrent warnings against the forced commercialisation of Indigenous art centres.

Maruku Arts and tourism development

Maruku Arts is an Anangu-owned art centre located in Uluru-Kata Tjuta National Park. Established in 1984, Maruku represents a regional arts enterprise that services hundreds of artists across the Anangu Pitjantjatjara Yankunytjatjara (APY) and Ngaanyatjarra (NG) Lands. Its mandate is to buy wooden artefacts, known as punu, from artists based in remote Western Desert communities. These artefacts are subsequently sold wholesale or through Maruku's gallery inside the National Park. During the mid-1980s, Altman researched the economic impact of tourism on the Mutitjulu community, home to Maruku's warehouse and administration. He demonstrated that Maruku provided local and regional artists with important discretionary non-government income and the chance to profit economically from tourism without being forced to engage directly with tourists. Between April 1985 and May 1986 approximately 81 per cent of Maruku's payments to producers went to regionally based Anangu. During this 58-week period, $26,522 was paid to local artists from the Mutitjulu Community who could be identified in purchase books (Altman 1991a: 83; 1991b: 114). Altman suggested that with the expected growth in the tourism industry and expansion of the art centre, economic benefits for regional producers would only increase. In addition, he concluded that as long as no radical changes occurred in the regional economies of the APY and NG Lands, the supply of puṉu available for sale should be plentiful.

Thirty years later, as I commenced fieldwork in Muṯitjulu, Maṟuku's future no longer looked as bright as it did when Altman conducted his study. Like other Indigenous art centres, Maṟuku had been negatively affected by the downturn of the Aboriginal art market following the onset of the global financial crisis (GFC) (Wilson-Anastasios 2013). As private art galleries in the cities strained to make ends meet, several of the selling exhibitions planned by Maṟuku were cancelled (Scollay C, pers. comm., 24 March 2014). More importantly, this art centre suffered from the decline in visitors to Uluṟu—Maṟuku's principal market. The strong Australian dollar saw many domestic travellers forgo a trip to the Red Centre and journey overseas instead. International tourists who experienced reduced income security due to the GFC decided not to travel to Australia (Tourism Australia 2011). According to the Director of National Parks (2010: 54; 2011: 51; 2012: 51), the number of entry tickets sold to visitors to Uluṟu-Kata Tjuṯa National Park aged 16 years and above declined from 334,240 in 2009–10 and 269,242 in 2010–11 to 264,144 in 2011–12.

It is important to note that Maṟuku's applications for funding from the Australian Government's Indigenous Visual Arts Industry Support (IVAIS) program had been rejected for several years. As suggested by General Manager Clive Scollay (pers. comm., 15 September 2014), Maṟuku's inability to obtain support from IVAIS had been the result of an impression harboured by public servants that the art centre, regardless of the difficulties faced, is performing comparatively well. It is not entirely surprising that such an impression exists, since Maṟuku has long been promoted as an Indigenous entrepreneurial success story (e.g. Wright 2000: 115). Yet, while the art centre's performance has changed, its access to arts funding has not.[1] Recurrent operating losses combined with the absence of structural

---

1   Maṟuku Arts recently applied for funding under the Australian Government's Indigenous Advancement Strategy (IAS), which began on 1 July 2014. The art centre's proposal was not funded.

government support forced Maruku to identify new revenue options.[2] In 2012, its executive committee and management decided to diversify and develop arts-based tourism activities, most notably dot painting workshops. Several months earlier, in October 2011, Maruku had already established an art market in Yulara, the town outside of the National Park where tourists usually eat, sleep and shop. Unlike other art centres that dabble in tourism, Maruku Arts has since become an accredited tourism business. It has even enrolled in the Indigenous Champions Program run by Tourism Australia and Indigenous Business Australia.

Consequences of commercialisation

The decision to create a new sales outlet and arts-based activities for visitors to Uluru was aimed at improving Maruku's solvency for the benefit of the art centre's Anangu directors and artists. Nonetheless, the establishment of the art market and dot painting workshops has had unforeseen cultural and economic effects. Here, I will outline these effects by differentiating between Anangu producers in the Mutitjulu Community adjacent to Uluru and Anangu artists who reside regionally, at a distance from Maruku Arts.

Mutitjulu and the increase in income

For Mutitjulu-based artists, the art centre's new direction has resulted in an important income increase. To run the art market in Yulara, Maruku casually employs two local producers. Initially, the market operated on working days only. However, since the beginning of 2013 tourists have been able to shop at the market on a daily basis. Each day, Anangu from Mutitjulu are driven to and from Yulara where they demonstrate the art of painting to visitors.[3] Besides receiving a demonstration fee of $80 a day, these artists also earn money by

---

2   The audited financial statements for the 2009–10, 2010–11, 2011–12 and 2012–13 financial years respectively recorded an operating loss of $340,573, an operating loss of $231,289, an operating surplus of $85,185 and an operating loss of $96,841 (ORIC 2014).
3   Because Mutitjulu is located inside the National Park, its residents are not allowed to fell trees to make woodcraft. Therefore, Maruku has always made an exception from its focus on woodcraft by buying paintings from local producers.

selling paintings made at the market to tourists.[4] Until April 2013, Maruku fully paid artists for each painting produced at the market on the day. Since then, a consignment system has been introduced for all artworks except small items such as bookmarks and canvases sized 15 by 20 centimetres. Once paintings are sold, producers receive 40 per cent of the sale price.

I have analysed production and sales data for Maruku's art market from its launch in October 2011 until April 2014, focusing on four sample months each year. The sample months have been chosen to reflect the seasonal nature of tourism at Uluru, with February representing the low season, July representing the high season and April and October corresponding to the shoulder seasons. As demonstrated by Table 10.1, Maruku typically puts over $10,000 a month of market money into the Mutitjulu community.[5] Because artists attend the market on a casual basis, the income they derive from their work is not sufficient to realise economic autonomy. Yet, certain Mutitjulu residents are able to carve out a substantial salary. In July 2013, the three highest earning artists respectively received $1,968 for nine days' work; $1,260 for five days' work; and $1,021 for four days' work. In October 2013, the three highest earning artists respectively received $2,012 for seven days' work; $1,371 for five days' work; and $881 for four days' work. This amounts to well over $200 for an approximately six-hour work day, excluding travel.

---

4   Until the beginning of 2015 artists received a demonstration fee of $100 each day. Maruku reduced this payment to $80 because the art market at Yulara was operating at a loss.

5   My analysis of art market data after the introduction of Maruku's consignment system is based on market sheets. These sheets do not list payments to artists in cash for non-consignment items like bookmarks and small paintings. As a result, the income earned by Mutitjulu-based artists for April 2013, July 2013, October 2013, February 2014 and April 2014 is slightly higher in reality than reported here. The majority of producers earned an estimated $40 on top of their recorded income from the creation of non-consignment articles each day they worked at the market.

Table 10.1 Maṟuku Arts' art market in Yulara (payments in Australian dollars)

	Oct. 2011	Feb. 2012	Apr. 2012	July 2012	Oct. 2012	Feb. 2013	Apr. 2013	July 2013	Oct. 2013	Feb. 2014	Apr. 2014
No. days market open	9	8	19	21	24	20	30	30	29	4	24
No. different artists	12	14	18	21	22	22	32	29	28	7	22
Total income earned by all artists	3,830	2,940	11,262	11,000	12,805	8,235	13,110	13,020	12,870	1,455	11,256
Average income earned per artist	319	210	626	524	582	374	410	449	460	208	512

Source: Author's research

Table 10.2 Maṟuku Arts' dot painting workshops (payments in Australian dollars)

	Oct. 2012	Feb. 2013	Apr. 2013	July 2013	Oct. 2013	Feb. 2014	Apr. 2014
No. artists to have done workshops	17	4	16	19	14	5	15
Total income earned by all artists	1,200	200	1,840	3,490	1,570	1,490	2,690
Average income earned per artist	71	50	115	184	112	298	179

Source: Author's research

The 90-minute dot painting workshops, which also rely on local labour, are held twice daily provided that sufficient tourists have signed up. Until August 2014 the morning workshop would be staged in Yulara whilst the afternoon workshop took place inside Uluru-Kata Tjuta National Park. In the morning, one Anangu artist already at work for Maruku at the market would be asked to conduct the workshop alongside a non-Indigenous host. This artist would then receive $50 on top of his or her market earnings for the day as compensation. Afternoon workshops operated independent from the art market due to their occurrence inside the National Park, away from Yulara. To conduct these workshops, a Maruku employee would normally pick up a new artist from Mutitjulu and pay this producer $120 for demonstrating acrylic painting and the symbolism associated with Western Desert art to tourists. Table 10.2 demonstrates the income earned by Anangu from Mutitjulu from the dot painting workshops. As before, I focus on the four sample months which represent different tourism seasons at Uluru. While the total income earned by all artists through the workshops varies considerably and is by no means high, an estimated 78 per cent of all casual payments accrued to producers already at work at the art market. The money thus earned by artists from the dot painting workshops principally constitutes a top up on their existing Maruku income.

It is important to note that payments to Mutitjulu-based producers for their involvement in Maruku's new tourism activities represent an addition to the income already earned by local Anangu from selling their art, especially acrylic paintings, directly to Maruku's warehouse.

The regional economy

While Anangu residents of Mutitjulu have benefited from the introduction of Maruku's tourism activities, their regionally based relatives have been less fortunate. Due to their residence in remote communities at a distance from the National Park, Anangu who comprise Maruku's regional constituency have not been in the position to regularly work at the art market or present the dot painting workshops. During research trips to Mutitjulu in July and September 2014, I encountered an almost empty warehouse. The shelves normally stocked with wooden artefacts, predominantly purchased from regional Anangu communities, were largely unfilled. The lack of punu can be explained through an analysis of Maruku's community buying data. During the financial year 2013–14, Maruku spent almost $64,000 on puṉu in remote communities on the APY and NG Lands.[6] This is down considerably from the more than $175,000 spent on woodcraft during the previous financial year. Indeed, the amount spent by Maruku on buying puṉu from regional producers during the 2013–14 financial year was the lowest on record for the period between July 2006 and June 2014 (see Table 10.3).[7] Between July 2013 and June 2014, 12 out of 17 regional communities serviced by the art centre saw a drop in income earned by puṉu makers compared with the previous year.

Table 10.3 Maruku Arts' total annual expenditure on puṉu in 17 regional Aṉangu communities (expenditure in Australian dollars per financial year)

Year	Expenditure
2006–07	107,880
2007–08	305,118
2008–09	152,697
2009–10	113,256
2010–11	68,445
2011–12	150,378
2012–13	175,535
2013–14	63,953

Source: Author's research

In the 2011–12 financial year, Maruku received funding from the Aboriginals Benefit Account to upgrade infrastructure and encourage Aṉangu puṉu making regionally. This funding enabled the so-called puṉu man—the employee responsible for purchasing woodcraft on a regular basis—to spend more time with artists in communities serviced by Maruku, to provide art practitioners with the transport and tools needed to source wood for puṉu making and to focus on skills development. The staff member assigned to this role at the beginning

6   The regional communities serviced by Maruku and analysed here include Amata, Blackstone, Docker River, Ernabella, Finke, Fregon, Indulkana, Jameson, Kalka, Mimili, Nyapari, Pipalyatjara, Tjukurla, Wanarn, Warakurna, Warburton and Wingellina.

7   Maruku's total expenditure on puṉu during the 2010–11 financial year was also low. An overstocked warehouse combined with declining sales to tourists compelled the art centre to temporarily reduce its community buying trips (Scollay C, pers. comm., 17 March 2014).

of 2012 dedicated himself to these development tasks. However, in December 2013, this puṉu man left Maṟuku Arts disillusioned. As he explained to me, the new tourism activities had impacted his ability to spend time and money on facilitating puṉu making (Ellemunter E, pers. comm., 17 November 2013). In an attempt to get its commercial tourism business off the ground, Maṟuku had to reallocate scarce resources—money and labour—to the dot painting workshops and market stall. In 2013, the puṉu man found that on the rare trips he was able to undertake, Aṉangu no longer had a good supply of puṉu available. Indeed, people told him they thought the puṉu man would no longer be coming. Eventually, this puṉu man left as his efforts to stimulate puṉu production appeared unsuccessful.

The data for the 2012–13 and 2013–14 financial years tell a story of an almost $112,000 loss of income for regional Aṉangu communities, a decline in the production of an art form that has made Maṟuku stand out amongst Australia's Indigenous art centres and an apparent challenge to cultural maintenance. However, there is also a bigger narrative. Clive Scollay (pers. comm., 18 June 2013) argues that the decrease in Aṉangu woodcraft production and the diminishing expenditure on puṉu by the art centre are structural issues which can principally be attributed to the competition presented by painting. Scollay contends that since the establishment and flourishing of several art centres on the APY and NG Lands, Aṉangu who previously made puṉu have now turned their attention to painting. Painting usually costs less time and effort and the income derived from making such artworks tends to be higher than that realised through making woodcraft. The general manager thus explains Maṟuku's reduced expenditure on puṉu by highlighting problems with the supply side.

Fig. 10.1 demonstrates that between July 2006 and June 2014 Maṟuku's spending on puṉu in regional Aṉangu communities indeed represented a downward trend [$F(1,134)=4.3$, $P<0.05$, $r^2=0.03$]. Additional regression analysis conducted for communities individually revealed a downward trend of Maṟuku's expenditure on puṉu for 12 out of 17 communities. For Amata, Fregon and Indulkana, this downward trend was significant [$P<0.05$, $r^2=0.6$ for all three communities].

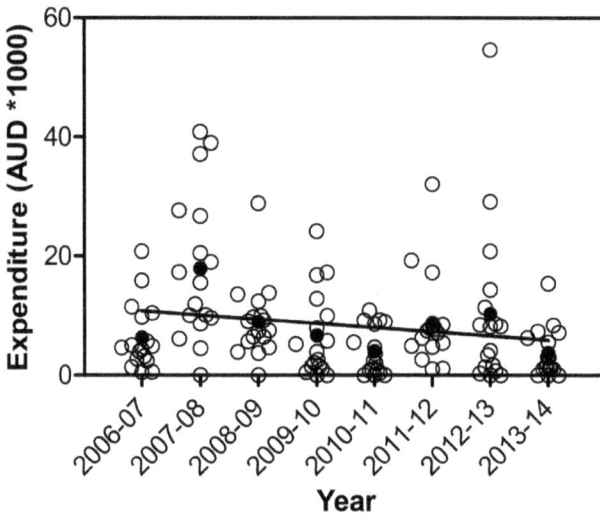

Fig. 10.1 Maṟuku Arts' expenditure on puṉu in 17 regional Aṉangu communities per financial year (data per community (open circles), yearly average (closed circles) and linear regression line shown)
Source: Author's research

Interestingly, 75 per cent of communities that manifested a trend toward declining puṉu expenditure were home to a community-owned Indigenous art centre. Among those communities that did not evince a downward trend, only 40 per cent had an art centre. Fig. 10.2 and Fig. 10.3 respectively show Maṟuku's annual expenditure on puṉu in 11 Aṉangu communities with an art centre and six communities without.[8] Whilst the downward trend observed in communities with an art centre is statistically significant [$F(1,86)=10.2$, $P<0.01$, $r^2=0.11$], no statistical significance has been established for communities without an art centre [$F(1,46)=0.1$, $P=0.8$, $r^2=0.002$].

---

8   Amata, Blackstone, Ernabella, Fregon, Indulkana, Kalka, Mimili, Nyapari, Pipalyatjara, Tjukurla and Warakurna all had independent, fully functional art centres for the entire period surveyed.

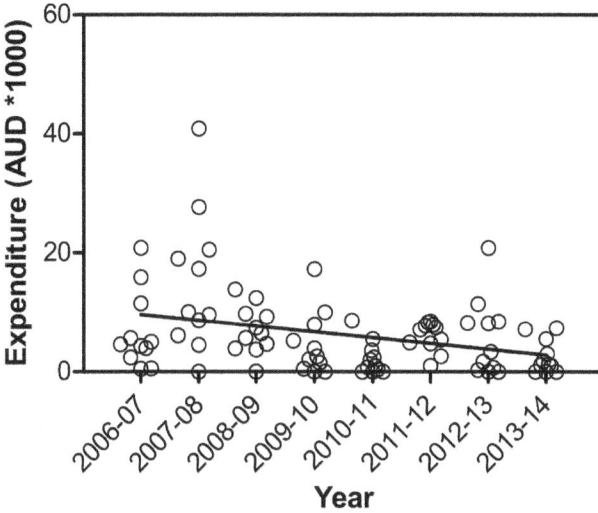

Fig. 10.2 Maruku Arts' expenditure on puṇu in 11 regional Aṇangu communities with an art centre per financial year (data per community (open circles) and linear regression line shown)

Source: Author's research

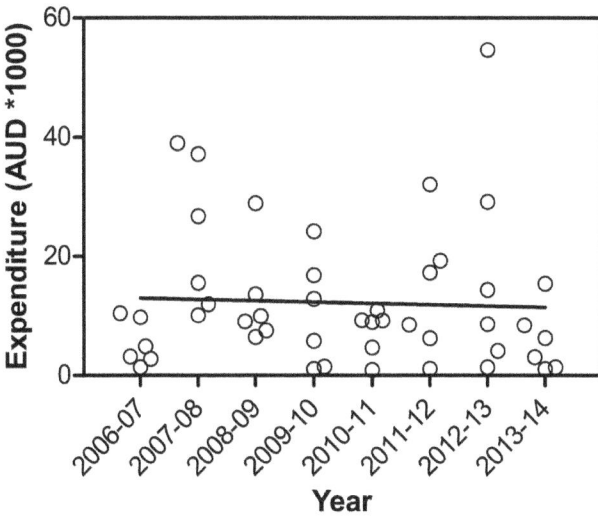

Fig. 10.3 Maruku Arts' expenditure on puṇu in six regional Aṇangu communities without an art centre per financial year (data per community (open circles) and linear regression line shown)

Source: Author's research

These preliminary findings provide support for Scollay's argument that the decrease in income realised by Aṉangu through puṉu production precedes Maṟuku's development of tourism activities and relates to the prospering of painting. They do not, however, detract from the impact of the new activities on Maṟuku's capacity to invest in the practice of puṉu making.

Concluding remarks

The case study of Maṟuku Arts illustrates what can happen when an Indigenous art centre is forced to commercialise. Whilst the art centre has readily received support from Indigenous Business Australia, Tourism Australia and Tourism NT to establish itself within the tourism arena, it continues to lack the resources to properly facilitate puṉu making regionally. Today, the balance between Maṟuku's payments to local and regional producers differs substantially from the strong emphasis on regional expenditure encountered by Jon Altman during his research in Muṯitjulu three decades ago. Those who have primarily benefited from Maṟuku's new direction have been locally based Aṉangu artists who already enjoyed access to more economic opportunities than their relatives living regionally.

Yet, it is not just about economics, as Altman has emphasised in his writings about Indigenous art. The decline in income earned by puṉu makers regionally has further impacted on a cultural tradition already in jeopardy because of structural changes to the regional economy since Altman's study during the mid-1980s. The production of high quality wooden artefacts is currently at risk. Maṟuku's recent investments in tourism products principally based on the art of dot painting have drawn attention and resources away from Aṉangu woodcraft. While policymakers may applaud the art centre's new profit-oriented direction, the advanced commercialisation and mainstreaming seen in the case of Maṟuku Arts evidently poses inadvertent risks to Indigenous economic and cultural sustainability.

Acknowledgements

The author would like to thank directors, staff and artists of Maṟuku Arts for permitting and supporting this research; Howard Morphy and David Throsby for initiating and leading this research project, Jon Altman for his advice and assistance; Katya Petetskaya for her useful comments on this paper; and H. Christiaan Stronks for his help with the regression analysis. This work was supported by the Australian Research Council under Grant DP120101387.

References

Altman JC (1988). The economic basis for cultural reproduction. In West W (ed.), *The inspired dream: life as art in Aboriginal Australia*, Queensland Art Gallery, Brisbane.

Altman JC (1991a). The economic impact of tourism on the Mutitjulu community. In Central Land Council, Pitjantjatjara Council & Mutitjulu Community, *Sharing the park: Aṉangu initiatives in Ayers Rock tourism*, Institute for Aboriginal Development, Alice Springs.

Altman JC (1991b). The economic impact of tourism at Uluṟu National Park on other Aboriginal communities in Central Australia. In Central Land Council, Pitjantjatjara Council & Mutitjulu Community, *Sharing the park: Aṉangu initiatives in Ayers Rock tourism*, Institute for Aboriginal Development, Alice Springs.

Altman JC (2000). The Indigenous visual arts industry: issues and prospects for the next decade. *Artlink* 20(1):86–92.

Altman JC (2005). *Brokering Aboriginal art: a critical perspective on marketing, institutions, and the state*, Centre for Leisure Management Research, Deakin University, Melbourne.

Altman JC (2007a). Art business: the Indigenous visual arts infrastructure. In Perkins H & West M (eds), *One sun, one moon: Indigenous art in Australia*, Art Gallery of NSW, Sydney.

Altman JC (2007b). *Inquiry into Australia's Indigenous visual arts and craft sector, submission to the Senate Environment, Communications, Information Technology and the Arts Committee*, Topical Issue 04/2007, Centre for Aboriginal Economic Policy Research, The Australian National University, Canberra.

Altman JC (2010). What future for remote Indigenous Australia? Economic hybridity and the neoliberal turn. In Altman JC & Hinkson M (eds), *Culture crisis: anthropology and politics in Aboriginal Australia*, UNSW Press, Sydney.

Director of National Parks (2010). *State of the parks report 2009–10*, Parks Australia, Canberra.

Director of National Parks (2011). *State of the parks report 2010–11*, Parks Australia, Canberra.

Director of National Parks (2012). *State of the parks report 2011–12*, Parks Australia, Canberra.

ORIC (Office of the Registrar of Indigenous Corporations) (2014). *Anangu Uwankaraku Punu Aboriginal Corporation Compliance Notice—s439–20(1)*, ORIC, Canberra.

Tourism Australia (2011). *Exchange rates: challenges and opportunities for Australian tourism*, Tourism Australia, Canberra.

Wilson-Anastasios M (2013). Desert artists draw a line in the sand. *Sydney Morning Herald* 4 May.

Wright F (2000). *The art & craft centre story volume three: good stories from out bush*, ATSIC, Canberra.

11

Five theses for reinstituting economics: Anthropological lessons from Broome

Stephen Muecke and Ben Dibley

Sometimes a visit to a country town can give you a feel for larger issues facing the nation. Broome is remote, strongly Indigenous, multicultural and its population swings seasonally from between 15,000 in the steamy wet to 40,000 in the dry, when people migrate north from the southern winter. As we research an ethnography for the Goolarabooloo people, who in 2013 successfully opposed the building of a gas plant on James Price Point, the need to think about competing economic claims arises.

On the one hand, the Western Australian Government, keen to industrialise the Kimberley, worked closely with the Woodside consortium and the Kimberley Land Council to make the gas plant happen, and so further develop a resources sector which on current estimates contributes about $1.1 billion annually to the region's economy (Department of Planning 2014). They argued that such industrialisation would bring infrastructure and jobs to the western Kimberley by plugging into 'its largely untapped wealth', which, in terms of offshore resources and energy assets, have a speculative value approaching $250 billion (Broome Chamber of Commerce & Industry 2014). On the other hand, the Goolarabooloo and an alliance of environmental groups argued that Indigenous law and culture, along with the environment, was worth protecting, in their own terms, but also as economic resources for an alternative 'cultural and conservation economy' (Australian Conservation Foundation 2011). The tourism industry, worth about $300 million to the region annually, kept pretty quiet as the battle raged from 2009–13, even though an oil spill on the famous Cable Beach would close down the industry in Broome, deterring the 210,000 or so tourists who presently visit the town each year (Department of Planning 2014).

These competing stories are of national interest, not least because of the economic boom Australia has experienced with commodity exports, even without a mining tax. But this boom is complicated by other factors: a 'two-speed' economy, the social damage done by fly-in/fly-out (FIFO) worker mobility, battles over native title, divisions in Indigenous communities, and environmental damage. Such factors are strong indicators that 'the economy' is not just about economics, which is where environmental humanists like us come in.[1] We ask questions about human factors as well as non-human ones, on the assumed need to monitor for human well-being, as well as a healthy environment to sustain life.

French philosopher and anthropologist Bruno Latour (2013) has recently written an 'anthropology of the Moderns' (referring to Western Europeans) and he claims that the Economy has become their most cherished institution, wielding a metalanguage of value. It has usurped Nature as it becomes 'second nature' to use this language to make the Economy the 'bottom line'. While he is overstating the case, and the capital E of Economy signals his bold generality, the tendency for economic language to allow 'all peoples to benefit from the same measuring instrument made explicit everywhere in the same idiom' (Latour 2013: 383–4) may well be a significant trend whose unifying, globalising power is the identifiable target of various—equally global—modes of resistance.

He further criticises the Economy's claims to science-driven accuracy or the way it is described as 'the ice-cold, rational, coherent, and continuous manifestation of the calculation of interests alone'

---

1   In this we share an affinity with the postcapitalist politics exemplified by Gibson-Graham et al. (2013).

(Latour 2013: 386). But where is this cold hard gaze exactly? Commerce is, in practice, full of heat: surprising new products, marketing tricks, testosterone and stimulant-fuelled traders, fictional goods, cooked books, and outright lies. For the sake of comparison, anthropologists might read Marcel Mauss on the gift and look at 'primitive' economies in the Pacific and 'recoil in panic before the imbroglios that they find described there. "But then," they sigh, "those poor wretches will never get out of it, they'll always be bound, attached, indebted, hooked, enmeshed, entangled"' (Latour 2013: 448–9). Whereas, Latour goes on, in our modern economies 'prolonged hardening exercises have accustomed them to being "quits" with respect to those with whom they enter into transactions … we've found the way to get ourselves out of such imbroglios by adding to them their exact opposite: "And now we're quits; I owe you nothing; we have exchanged equivalents; goodbye!"' (2013: 449).

What a strange ideal on which to found an economy! You turn someone close into a stranger; you want to close deals as if *getting away* from one another were the aim. But in fact nobody lives according to the principles of this idealised Economy, where equivalent values are precisely and coldly calculated. Our actual economic behaviour is just as mixed up and intimate as any Pacific bartering system. In economics as in everything, it turns out, we are *attached* to each other and to what we value. In Broome you might call it a lifestyle, on the trading floor in the city it might be a stock correction.

This somewhat loose characterisation of the Economy (with a capital E) is undertaken nonetheless with an anthropological attitude, where the anthropologist takes with a grain of salt the extravagant claims his informants are making about this 'system': its ubiquity, its providence for all, its objectivity, and its freedom. It is in this anthropological spirit that we turn to Broome where this same economy was invoked as embodying all the good reasons for putting a heavy LNG (liquefied natural gas) industrial precinct on Goolarabooloo ancestral land. Here we could be forgiven (with some hindsight given the project is now abandoned) for invoking the figure of Darryl Kerrigan from the film *The Castle* shouting 'Tell 'em they're dreaming!' as we search for a technical term to describe an economic model that is so out of touch with the local country's needs that it is … what? … fantastical?

The \$45 billion gas plant was to be built by the Joint Venture Partners led by Woodside without any economic modelling, as described by Matt Grudnoff (2012):

> The state government decided not to undertake an economic modelling process because it argued that 'no model was determined sufficiently appropriate to accurately quantify the economic impacts of the Precinct.'
>
> …
>
> Having stated that no economic modelling was done, the government's report then says it:
>
> 'seeks to broadly examine and qualitatively analyse the macroeconomic impacts of the expenditure and investment associated with the LNG Precinct, including the impacts on GDP, income, prices and fiscal variables'.
>
> Achieving this goal is extremely difficult without a robust economic modelling exercise.

Without going into all the details, Grudnoff's analysis demonstrates that the good reason for not doing the modelling would have been to hide the fact that the only significant beneficiaries would be the major shareholders of the companies involved.

The project was shelved after four years of massive expenditure of resources and energy, on the part of activists on both sides. Those seeking to protect Indigenous sites in the Kimberley see the next big threat coming from companies like Buru Energy seeking to frack the Canning Basin, but that too now looks highly doubtful. What is going on with these massive plans for industrialisation that the Government of Western Australia tries to push through without any viable planning? Naturally, they meet with resistance, which our ethnography will describe, but we also want to go another step, which anti-capitalist discourses generally do not take. We want to take the risk of sounding naïve by suggesting that the Economy, as deployed in these instances, needs to be reinstituted, reformed, or completely reset in the light of the actual interests of the significant (and indeed 'insignificant') stakeholders.

To this end we'd like to offer five theses—though perhaps it ought to be 11!—for resetting or reinstituting the Economy.

Thesis No. 1: Economies should recognise that their variables are contingent rather than necessary

Broome makes visible the possibility that there are whole communities of people relatively indifferent to the Economy, because they have another more 'traditional' economy to which to turn. Such communities might be somewhat immune to a narrative that tries to carry the imperative that 'it is only a matter of time' before Broome is 'developed'. If it is finally recognised that the Western template of economic modernity is but one among many, that even non-Western peoples can sustain different modernities, then it should be agnostic, finally, and begin more serious negotiations about its limits, what values it touches, and its limited mission in a place. Economic contingencies, then, are the 'sticky' localised factors to which economic endeavours inevitably find themselves attached. They are the additional expenses, the delays, the demands for a 'social licence', the roundabout negotiations and even corrupt deals, none of which are part of the template of a universalising modernist economics, but which are put down to 'skill', 'experience' or even 'business in confidence' secrets. Making these contingencies explicit in regards to local demands would have the effect of *renaturalising* in each new case, or meaningfully adapting to local circumstances.

Thesis No. 2: The Economy should be deflated so that it is not the only game in town, so that it does not (aspire to) determine all values, so that incommensurate values can continue to be sustained in parallel by religion, the law, politics, science and education

The redemptive promise of the economic script endlessly heralded in government reports and corporate prospectuses is one in which the horizon of universal prosperity is to be reached without friction. Through cool heads and hard work economic salvation awaits all.

Yet the calculative script belies the volatility of the people and the things that it sets in motion and whose passions and energies generate much friction and heat. The promise of prosperity to be piped from the beneath the ocean's floor and distributed from the James Price Point LNG precinct proved not to be the conduits through which commerce would indifferently flow, a flow to which nothing would stick, but rather the trenches from which a cosmopolitical war came to be waged. The sages of the Economy found themselves confronted by others with cosmologies in which the presence of 'the invisible hand' was nowhere to be found, and in which the 'second nature' of the Economy was anything but common sense. As other worlds, other logics, other values pressed in on those of the Economy, Premier Colin Barnett's ambition for an industrialised Broome was—for now at least—reduced to a pipe dream.

Yet, even in defeat, the sphere of the Economy remained inflated. True to the calculative script and apparently unmoved by its cosmopolitical skirmishes, Woodside coolly withdrew from the James Price Point project. With the risks outweighing the opportunities for shareholders, the project was considered no longer economically viable. Calling it quits—the company left town. Where did that leave the microcosmic 'Broome economy'? Some blamed a few retail closures on this pull-out, hopeful that there was evidence that heavy industry was always going to be the town's saviour. Others, like the Goolarabooloo, remained exhausted but unmoved since their relation to the mainstream economy was one that always saw it 'deflated', not as their main concern, not their main business. Their expression of sovereign indifference was a brave mask over the danger that this economic intrusion would have the capacity to reinforce their precarious economic marginality. Our third thesis, riffing on Jon Altman's hybrid economy, disrupts such a narrative that would have the mainstream inevitably swallowing up margins.

Thesis No. 3: Economies are—especially in Aboriginal Australia—hybrid

If the successful campaign which saw Woodside's retreat from James Price Point challenged the ruling elite's conviction that the Kimberley's industrialisation was inexorable, it also troubled Premier Barnett's assertion (there was no economic modelling after all) of a direct correlation between this development and Indigenous economic gain. Without gas development in the Kimberley, an embattled Barnett retorted, 'there will be no gas-related economic development in the Kimberley and there will be no economic benefit for the Aboriginal people of the Kimberley' (cited in Australian Conservation Foundation 2011). Repeating the received wisdom of dominant policy discourse in Australia, which assumes that Indigenous poverty can only be alleviated with modernisation and its development programs, the rationale behind Barnett's veiled threat was as familiar as it was unconvincing. Certainly the Goolarabooloo were unpersuaded. A gas plant was equivocally not an entity to which they saw their well-being as attached, financial or otherwise.

Altman's hybrid economy offers a way out of this impasse on Indigenous economic well-being. Taking an ethnographic turn within the discipline of economics, Altman's work contributes, we contend, to a certain deflation of the Economy, expelling the (hot) air of those who would elevate it as the only redress to Indigenous disadvantage. Altman's conceptual-cum-political innovation is in expanding and diversifying what counts as economic activity in remote Australia and considering how such activity cuts across the sectors of the market, the state and the customary (for a pertinent example see Altman 2009). Altman advances the hybrid economy as a critical analysis and alternative model of economic development to those rolled out by a neoliberal administration. His is a powerful heuristic for emphasising Indigenous engagement in a diversity of economic activities and livelihood sources which evidence creative postcolonial adaptation (e.g. Altman 2010). We continue and widen Altman's emphasis on Indigenous agency, and the issues of 'difference but relatedness' that he stresses, by insisting that the economies of remote Australia are not only institutionally hybrid, they are also ontological hybrids. This is in recognition that economic agents are organised, disorganised and reorganised not only in relation to different forms of institutional practice, but also in the relations between human and non-human actors. This is the contention of our fourth thesis.

Thesis No. 4: Economies are 'more than human' and as such they should recognise their non-human stakeholders

The Woodside fiasco makes clear that there are many more actors than those included in the calculative script of the Economy. From geological forces and cosmological entities to cyclones and bilbies, each performed a political agency in whose presence, as it turned out, economic decisions needed to be made. Such recalcitrant non-humans could not be ignored or abandoned as 'externalities' beyond the sphere of the idealised Economy. They were not grit in an otherwise frictionless flow. Rather, they demonstrated that the agency of an economic assemblage is always distributed across an overflow of human and non-human entities. Economies, we contend then, must be considered as 'confederations' in which the non-humans have a stake and a political claim for representation; that is, if the economic is to be brought down to earth (Bennett 2010).

Thesis No. 5: Economies must be earthbound

Economic activity based on country where people live has to recognise that it is earthbound; henceforth it will not be a case of 'closing deals' to 'get away' with extracted value. So for this to happen a few other concepts need to be reinstituted or reset, notably Nature. Now that the Anthropocene has moved front stage, Nature as the stable backdrop to human activity is an idea as dangerous to human existence as the notion of the Economy as second nature. Earthbound economies cannot be as the Economy was for the Moderns—one of detachment and freedom seemingly unconstrained by material limits, as if we have multiple planet Earths at our disposal. Rather, facing a 'ticklish' Gaia—an Earth whose systems respond to our actions—such economies must become ones of attachment, of responsibility. Earthbound economies, then, must be immunological by design, integral to the sociotechnical and organic envelope that sustains 'a breathable atmosphere' for humans, for their existence (see Sloterdijk 2013).

Was it really a kind of certainty derived from huge wealth that hardened the hearts of the oligarchs, leading them to think that 'we owe nobody anything'? The trouble is, the biggest creditor of all is coming back to bite them: the Earth. And it is telling them 'you owe me everything, your immense personal wealth does not make you unassailable. Your wealth is in "bonds drawn against the treasure of the Earth"' (Latour 2013: 449); dollars and euros mean nothing now, they give you a false freedom from debt. Your Earth bonds have always tied you to the values that really mattered to you: the good life. What you value most is actually in danger: a high-quality meal as opposed to an unhealthy one; really enjoyable associations with other beings as opposed to fake ones.

Could such a simple lesson really be learned from visiting a remote country town where rival economies are playing out their dramas? We hope to have shown that the evidence is there that assemblages of human and non-human values (what the Environmental Humanities takes seriously as a field) are so strongly held by local stakeholders that they have been able to deflect the might of a powerful consortium of multinational companies with the forceful backing of the state and sympathetic media campaigns. These were values that the universalising narrative of the Economy did not engage; this is why we have argued that economies need to be more realistic about what they do. They cannot arrive in new places with an old European idea of what Nature is and couple it to an overconfident machinery of the Economy as the predominant 'second nature' of human society. If organisations are not prepared to reinstitute economies under local conditions, negotiations will break down as they did every step of the way for Woodside's adventure in Broome.

References

Altman JC (2009). Indigenous communities, miners and the state. In Altman JC & Martin DF (eds), *Power, culture, economy: Indigenous Australians and mining*, CAEPR Research Monograph No. 30, ANU E Press, Canberra.

Altman JC (2010). What future for remote Indigenous Australia? Economic hybridity and the neoliberal turn. In Altman JC & Hinkson M (eds), *Culture crisis: anthropology and politics in Aboriginal Australia*, UNSW Press, Sydney.

Australian Conservation Foundation (2011). *Briefing paper: economic futures for northern Australia*, Australian Conservation Foundation, Carlton VIC.

Bennett, J (2010). *Vibrant matter: a political ecology of things*, Duke University Press, Durham, NC & London.

Broome Chamber Of Commerce & Industry (2014). *Submission No. 125 to the Inquiry into the development of northern Australia*, House of Representatives Joint Select Committee on Northern Australia, Parliament of Australia, Canberra, 28 March.

Department of Planning (2014). *Kimberley planning and infrastructure framework*, Department of Planning, Government of Western Australia, Perth.

Gibson-Graham JK, Cameron J & Healy S (2013). *Take back the economy: an ethical guide for transforming our communities*, University of Minnesota Press, Minneapolis.

Grudnoff M (2012). *James Price Point: an economic analysis of the Browse LNG project*, Policy Brief No. 40, The Australia Institute, Canberra.

Latour B (2013). *An inquiry into modes of existence: an anthropology of the moderns,* translated by Catherine Porter, Harvard University Press, Cambridge MA.

Sloterdijk P (2013). *In the world interior of capital: towards a philosophical theory of globalization*, Polity, Cambridge UK.

Part 2: Critiquing Neoliberalism and the Guardian State

12

Neoliberalism and the return of the guardian state: Micromanaging Indigenous peoples in a new chapter of colonial governance

Shelley Bielefeld

Introduction

Income management is a controversial and highly politicised policy initiative. Originally introduced as part of the 2007 Northern Territory Intervention, income management was applied only to Indigenous welfare recipients in prescribed areas.[1] In 2010 the government developed new income management,[2] which they claimed was non-discriminatory (Commonwealth of Australia 2009: 12787). New income management has several compulsory categories and can also be entered into voluntarily (for fuller discussion of problems with these specific types of income management see Bielefeld 2012: 539–56). However, Indigenous peoples continue to be heavily over-

---

1   *Social Security and Other Legislation Amendment (Welfare Payment Reform) Act 2007* (Cwlth).
2   *Social Security and Other Legislation Amendment (Welfare Reform and Reinstatement of Racial Discrimination Act) Act 2010* (Cwlth).

represented amongst those subject to income management (Senate Estimates 2014: 1), which gives rise to concerns about ongoing racial discrimination.

This chapter maintains that there is a nexus between colonialism, neoliberalism, and new paternalism in the income management context. Colonialism maintains that civilisation will only be attained when the norms of the coloniser displace the cultural norms of the colonised—the justifying discourse is that of a 'civilizing mission' (Said 1994: 131). Neoliberalism has varying manifestations; here it refers to the discursive narratives and policies adopted by the Australian Government that promote 'market-oriented "governance"' of Indigenous peoples (Altman 2012: xvi; Peck 2012: xiii, 20). Neoliberalism operates across relational, ideological and institutional spheres (Cahill 2014: ix). New paternalism claims that the poor suffer from deficiencies of reason and/or character, and require intense supervision because they are less inclined to adhere to mainstream behavioural norms. It therefore imposes 'mutual obligations' to emphasise the responsibilities of welfare recipients (Mead 1997: 4, 33–4).

At an ideological level, these governing frameworks share certain similarities in the disparaging characteristics they attribute to Indigenous welfare recipients. At an institutional level, they play a significant role in how the guardian state is experienced by Indigenous welfare recipients. Neoliberalism and new paternalism both claim to be post-racial policies. However, neoliberalism and new paternalism are useful tools for the colonial state because they reinforce the same hierarchical patterns of oppression and domination that have plagued Indigenous peoples since the commencement of colonisation.

Ongoing colonialism

Australia's colonial project remains unfinished. As Aileen Moreton-Robinson (2009b: 11) explains, colonialism 'continues to operate discursively and materially within cultural formations, institutions and public culture'. This is apparent in the development of contemporary forms of income management. The presence of the Indigenous poor serves as an unsettling reminder of the fact that despite repeated efforts by authorities, numerous Indigenous people have not been successfully disciplined into adopting the norms of colonial society. The response of the state has been to utilise a familiar discourse of financial irresponsibility and ineptitude on the part of Indigenous peoples, drawing upon many generations of colonial 'stock stories' (Anthony 2013: 90, 139). This is part of an inherently racialised dynamic. As a strongly interventionist style of governance, contemporary income management ascribes 'defective willpower' to the Indigenous welfare recipients 'it seeks to reform' (Nicoll 2012: 172–3) and benevolent intentions to the state.

The narrative of benevolent intentions serves the state well in reproducing relations of domination and subordination. This narrative underpinned the 'protection' legislation of Australia's earlier assimilation era, and was a key aspect of the Northern Territory Intervention. Through the Intervention, Indigenous welfare recipients living in prescribed communities were attributed with the characteristics of addiction. In introducing the income management scheme in 2007 it was said that '[w]elfare is not for alcohol, drugs, pornography or gambling' (Commonwealth of Australia 2007: 2). The suggestion made in the Parliamentary Debates was that cash given to Indigenous welfare recipients in prescribed areas was squandered on these items. Minister Mal Brough referred to 'Indigenous communities where normal community standards and parenting behaviours have broken down' and where 'ready access to drugs and alcohol has created appalling conditions for community members, particularly children' (Commonwealth of Australia 2007: 2).

Written into the Parliamentary record, this narrative has become part of the racialised knowledge constructed about Indigenous welfare recipients. It is a narrative which resonates with negative stereotypes of Indigenous peoples throughout Australia's colonial history (Bielefeld 2012: 528–35; Anthony 2013: 139, 141; Bielefeld 2014: 16). Consequently, income-managed Indigenous welfare recipients can still be presumed to suffer from deficiencies of character because 'racial group reputations can guide assumptions about target characteristics at either the collective or individual level' (Soss et al. 2011: 78). It is therefore unsurprising that income management disproportionately applies to Indigenous welfare recipients, especially forms of compulsory income management (Senate Estimates 2014: 1). Yet there is ongoing colonialism in the claim that so many Indigenous welfare recipients do not know how to manage money and require state-imposed restrictions to facilitate responsible spending patterns.

Neoliberalism and new paternalism

Neoliberalism promotes policies that continue to reproduce structural inequality for Indigenous peoples (Morris 2013: 6), whilst simultaneously being presented as 'ubiquitous, inevitable, [and] natural' (Peck 2012: xi). Neoliberalism lauds self-reliance as the only rational and moral way of life (Martin 2011: 209). Those relying upon welfare payments are therefore deemed defective by reason of their financial dependence. Unemployment is harshly represented as individual failure (Morris 2013: 6). The solution proposed by neoliberal governance is to restructure the delivery of welfare to push those who are dependent on state support in the direction of individual self-reliance (Neale 2013: 180). Yet as far as Indigenous welfare recipients are concerned, this decontextualised adverse judgement ignores the legacy of colonisation (Moreton-Robinson 2009a: 70). The 'historical, structural and institutional forms of violence' (Morris 2013: 9) which have contributed to Indigenous disadvantage are notably absent in neoliberal representations of poverty. However, it appears that 'the tight knots of entrenched economic power' (Peck 2012: 259) put in place by colonialism will not be easily untangled. Neoliberal ideology is a key aspect of this embedded power dynamic. As Paul Farmer (2004: 313) makes clear, '[n]eoliberalism is the ideology promoted by the victors [and] … is indebted to and helps to replicate inequalities of power'. In this sense, neoliberalism imposes 'economic violence' (Peck 2012: 110) which works in tandem with the violence inherent in the colonial project (Watson 2009: 48; Fanon 2008: 7, 10).

Early colonists represented Indigenous peoples as 'lazy, irresponsible and incompetent' for not adapting to European work habits (Moreton-Robinson 2007: 91); and under neoliberal discourse the same negative stereotype still holds. Neoliberalism aims to convert Indigenous welfare recipients into 'economically productive … Indigenous citizens' (Howard-Wagner & Kelly 2011: 115). However, this requires neoliberalism to be combined with new paternalism. Jamie Peck (2012: 7) explains that '[n]eoliberalism … has only ever existed in "impure" form, indeed *can* only exist in messy hybrids. Its utopian vision of a free society and free economy is ultimately unrealizable'. It is for this reason that neoliberalism must graft itself parasitically to other forms of governance (Peck 2012: 30), such as new paternalism. This amounts to neoliberal hybridity. The integration of neoliberalism with new paternalism facilitates the intervention required to transform the behaviour of those who exhibit reluctance to abide by the rules of the market, such as the Indigenous poor.

Although neoliberalism endorses the ideal of a minimal state (Wacquant 2009: 248; Morris 2013: 46–7), at least in terms of regulating the market, it is also committed to the ideal of self-reliant individuals functioning as part of capitalism. Indigenous welfare recipients who do not conform to this neoliberal ideal have been portrayed as deviants who fail to take responsibility for their behaviour (Moreton-Robinson 2009a: 70). Thus the stigmatising and intrusive tools of new paternalism are now being employed to remake these deviant subjects into good neoliberal citizens. New paternalism requires an amply resourced guardian state in order to bring this moralistic crusade to fruition. This is 'a *violation* of neoliberal principles of small government and reduced public expenditures' (Wacquant 2009: 262). However, the government's dream remains of a more minimalist state in the future, one in which all the idealised neoliberal citizens go to work each day, eventually reducing welfare expenditure. Consequently, the state directs resources towards bending 'so-called problem populations and territories to the common norm' (Wacquant 2009: 1). Unsurprisingly therefore, the vast majority of locations selected thus far for income management are Aboriginal communities (Department of Social Services 2014: 117).

There is an ideological imperative at stake in this ambitious political project. The use of neoliberalism and new paternalism 'allows state elites to reaffirm the ideological primacy of meritocratic individualism' (Wacquant 2009: 108–9). This is essential to maintain the myth that Australia is an egalitarian society, the land of the fair go, where anyone can succeed so long as they put in a sufficient effort. It is difficult to sustain the myth when the Indigenous poor are present to remind Australia of the 'long shadow' cast by the 'legacy of colonialism', a shadow which indicates that 'racism has not disappeared' (Morris 2013: 1, 4). Efforts are therefore increased to bring about what Jon Altman (2013: 92) refers to as 'neoliberal assimilation'. Income management is a key part of this process. It replicates the 'concept of tutelage' (Said 1994: 209) for welfare recipients, who are presumed by the government to be experiencing poverty due to a lack of financial discipline rather than systematically entrenched inequality.

Dominant colonial narratives about 'undisciplined', 'passive and dependent' Indigenous peoples (Morris 2013: 172; Ergas 2014) are consistent with the denigrating picture of welfare recipients painted by new paternalism. Like neoliberalism, new paternalism ignores structural factors contributing to poverty. Instead, new paternalists such as Lawrence Mead (in Standing 2014: 100) urge welfare recipients 'to "blame themselves"' for their poverty, which is ideologically convenient for governments. New paternalists claim to implement their coercive supervisory policies for the good of those subject to them, which is familiar rhetoric to Indigenous peoples. New paternalism therefore provides colonial governments with a convenient cover, a new label for their old racially discriminatory dynamics. It allows them to claim that they are simply seeking to correct the behavioural deficiencies of welfare recipients—despite the fact that those who are deemed deficient and dysfunctional are disproportionately Indigenous (Bray et al. 2012: 192; Senate Estimates 2014: 1).

The heavy influence of new paternalism is seen in discourse which has portrayed Indigenous welfare recipients as drug-addled irresponsible parents, and Indigenous communities as places where abnormal behaviours flourish due to Indigenous cultural deficiencies (Commonwealth of Australia 2007: 2; Ergas 2014). This makes Indigenous welfare recipients a prime catchment pool for income management as a form of disciplinary regulation. Under this framework the poverty of Indigenous welfare recipients has been attributed to a crack in their cultural values that needs to be plugged with paternalistic policy in order to promote neoliberal hegemony.

Nevertheless, the rhetoric of neoliberalism and new paternalism allows the Australian Government to persist in maintaining that they are being helpful when they impose infantilising and degrading measures upon Indigenous peoples—even when there is scant evidence of beneficial outcomes as a result of such intervention and considerable evidence of harmful effects (Altman & Russell 2012: 11; Altman 2013: 138, 150–1). On harm, the government-commissioned report undertaken by Bray and others quoted an Indigenous woman from Darwin who stated that:

> One thing I find is your depression and other added stresses from it (income management). It is making it harder and [people are] stressed when not … able to get to funerals [which is] causing depression from not having closure (Bray et al. 2012: 94).

They quote another Indigenous woman from Darwin: 'It's really embarrassing people … They got to remember not everyone is dysfunctional.' (Bray et al. 2012: 95) The stress from income management has also led to 'medical problems' in the form of 'heart palpitations' (Equality Rights Alliance 2011: 19).

Whilst the government has been castigating Indigenous welfare recipients for financial irresponsibility, they have simultaneously committed vast resources to micromanaging finances via income management.[3] This is despite a lack of evidence as to its efficacy. Is this not financial irresponsibility on a grand scale? There is a paradox present in this scenario. In government-commissioned, independent, university-based research, Bray et al. (2012: 267) found that 'there is little indication that income management is itself effective in changing parenting behaviour, reducing addiction or improving capacity to manage finances'. Evidence that income management is largely ineffective has been brought to the government's attention on numerous occasions (see Equality Rights Alliance 2011: 40; Bray et al. 2012: 267; Department of Families, Housing, Community Services and Indigenous Affairs 2012: 207). Yet the government does not appear to be interested in any evidence opposed to its ideological position. This is reaffirmed in two recent government reports dealing with welfare reform which suggest that forms of income management be further expanded. The first, the *McClure report*, erroneously claimed that:

> Overall … the evidence to date suggests income management has assisted individuals and families to stabilise their financial circumstances, helped them meet priority needs, particularly the needs of children, and can protect vulnerable people from financial harassment and exploitation (Department of Social Services 2014: 84).

This wording echoes the government's stated purpose for introducing income management contained in the Parliamentary Debates and the Explanatory Memorandum accompanying the income management legislation (see Commonwealth of Australia 2007: 2, 4, 6; 2009: 12786; 2011, 13540; Explanatory Memorandum 2011: 2). However, repeating the government's rhetorical assertions does not amount to evidence.

---

3   The Australian National Audit Office estimates that income management for each welfare recipient living in remote areas costs approximately '$6600 to $7900 per annum' (Australian National Audit Office 2013: 17).

The second report is the *Forrest review*, overseen by mining magnate Andrew Forrest, which ironically claims that the time for paternalism is over (Forrest 2014: 3). Ongoing income management rebadged as a 'Healthy Welfare Card' is the substance of Recommendation 5, which would affect approximately 2.5 million welfare recipients (Forrest 2014: 28, 102, 107). This would lead to a cashless system for the vast majority of welfare recipients, all in the name of supporting the 'vulnerable' (Forrest 2014: 103). In this model the cause of socioeconomic vulnerability experienced by welfare recipients repeats the rhetoric of new paternalism—welfare recipients are (mis)represented as impoverished because they engage in irresponsible spending patterns. That new paternalism coincides neatly with the neoliberal project is clearly seen in the *Forrest review*. Those in receipt of welfare payments are portrayed as costly citizens who 'generate no tax and incur substantial costs to the nation' and who must be transformed into productive workers (Forrest 2014: 37, 68).

Indigenous peoples are over-represented in the welfare system, which means they would continue to be disproportionately affected by the 'Healthy Welfare Card' (Forrest 2014: 27), just as they are currently over-represented under the income management system. Like the *McClure report*, the *Forrest review* fails to engage with numerous pertinent reports which have pointed to limited evidence of benefits from income management and some significant shortcomings of the scheme (see Australian Indigenous Doctors' Association & Centre for Health Equity Training, Research and Evaluation 2010: 23–5; Australian Law Reform Commission 2011: 260, 267–8, 271, 279; Equality Rights Alliance 2011: 40; Bray et al. 2012: 94–5; Commonwealth Ombudsman 2012: 6, 9–10, 12–6, 30; Commonwealth Ombudsman 2013: 43–6; Parliamentary Joint Committee on Human Rights 2013: 61–2). This testifies to the power of ideology over evidence and a return of the guardian state as the oppressive frameworks of neoliberalism, new paternalism and colonialism converge. As Peck (2012: 30) states, in reality neoliberalism 'must always cohabit with others'.

Conclusion

Income management represents a new chapter of colonial governance in its intensive, stigmatising, paternalistic control over the lives of Australia's First Peoples, which is once again proclaimed to be for their own good. Yet as a technology of governance, income management cannot eradicate the poverty encountered by Indigenous welfare recipients, because micromanaging the paltry sums they receive will never redress the structural disadvantage Indigenous people experience. Nor can income management effectively address generations of impoverishing government policies. However, it will ensure that the colonial status quo remains, and if the goals of neoliberalism and new paternalism are attained, this may well lead to the completion of the colonial project.

Postscript

Since September 2014 there have been four more reports released on income management which are worth mentioning due to their resonance with the issues discussed in this chapter. However, the first three reports do not deal with income management in the Northern Territory, where 90.2 per cent of those who are income managed are Indigenous (Bray et al. 2014: 54).

The first report was government-commissioned, independent, university-based research and concerns the voluntary income management scheme operating in the Anangu Pitjantjatjara Yankunytjatjara (APY) Lands. Communities in the APY Lands had requested voluntary income management as a means of addressing a range of concerns, including financial harassment or 'humbugging' (Katz & Bates 2014: 1). Their consent to the measure is a crucial distinction between this form of income management and the compulsory income management to which most Indigenous welfare recipients are subject in the Northern Territory. Although the data in this report is presented as tentative, with further research required, it noted that 'people on income management appear to be more likely to run out of money than those not on income management' (Katz & Bates 2014: 22).

The second and third recently released income management reports were undertaken by Deloitte Access Economics for the Department of Social Services and concern place-based income management operating in Playford in South Australia, Greater Shepparton in Victoria, Bankstown in New South Wales, and Rockhampton and Logan in Queensland (Deloitte Access Economics 2014a, 2014b). The problem of income managed welfare recipients being more likely to 'run out of money' than their non-income managed counterparts was also mentioned in the Deloitte May report (Deloitte Access Economics 2014a: 68). Over two thirds of surveyed participants subject to compulsory income management as vulnerable welfare payment recipients considered that income management 'was not an appropriate measure for them given their current circumstances' (Deloitte Access Economics 2014a: 4). Social stigma arising from income management and use of the BasicsCard was a problem for some welfare recipients, especially for those who were Indigenous (Deloitte Access Economics 2014a: 4, 8, 95–6, 101, 135, 137, 151; 2014b: 120).

Although there is much useful information contained in these government-commissioned income management reports, they do have their limitations (Deloitte Access Economics 2014a: 39). For example, the aim of the Deloitte Access Economics evaluations was to determine whether place-based income management was implemented effectively (2014a: 16; 2014b: 8), not whether the ideological assumptions underpinning the expansion of income management were sound.

The fourth recently released report was government-commissioned, independent, university-based research on the operation of income management in the Northern Territory. Released in December 2014, some of the main findings were that:

- The evaluation could not find any substantive evidence of the program having significant changes relative to its key policy objectives, including changing people's behaviours.
- There was no evidence of changes in spending patterns, including food and alcohol sales, other than a slight possible improvement in the incidence of running out of money for food by those on Voluntary Income Management, but no change for those on compulsory income management ...

- There was no evidence of any overall improvement in financial well-being, including reductions in financial harassment or improved financial management skills …
- More general measures of wellbeing at the community level show no evidence of improvement, including for children …
- The evaluation found that, rather than building capacity and independence, for many the program has acted to make people more dependent on welfare (Bray et al. 2014: xxi–xxii).

Significantly, Bray et al. (2014: xxi) also noted that '[a] substantial group of people subject to income management felt that income management is unfair, embarrassing and discriminatory'. This is hardly surprising given the ideology underpinning income management critiqued in this chapter, and that Indigenous peoples are still grossly over-represented in income management categories. In December 2013, 18,300 people in the Northern Territory were income managed, with '16,514 Indigenous and 1,786 non-Indigenous people subject to the measures' (Bray et al. 2014: 54). Only 20.1 per cent of these were voluntary income management.

The response to this December 2014 report by then Minister for Social Services, Kevin Andrews, was to claim that income management had not worked in the Northern Territory because 'income management at 50% is too low to achieve the positive social outcomes that income management can bring' (Kevin Andrews, quoted in Davidson 2014). Instead, Andrews asserted that a higher percentage of income subject to income management would lead to better outcomes—a view with no evidence to substantiate it. Given the ideological commitment both major political parties have demonstrated, income management seems likely to continue for the foreseeable future.

Acknowledgements

The author wishes to thank Professor Jon Altman for his feedback on an earlier draft of this chapter.

References

Altman JC (2012). Foreword. In Fijn N, Keen I, Lloyd C & Pickering M (eds), *Indigenous participation in Australian economies II: historical engagements and current enterprises*, ANU E Press, Canberra.

Altman JC (2013). Arguing the Intervention. *Journal of Indigenous Policy* 14:1–151.

Altman JC & Russell S (2012). Too much 'Dreaming': evaluations of the Northern Territory National Emergency Response Intervention 2007–2012. *Evidence Base* 3:1–28.

Anthony T (2013). *Indigenous People, Crime and Punishment*, Routledge, London and New York.

Australian Indigenous Doctors' Association & Centre for Health Equity Training, Research and Evaluation (2010). *Health impact assessment of the Northern Territory Emergency Response*, University of New South Wales, Sydney.

Australian Law Reform Commission (2011). *Family violence and Commonwealth laws: improving legal frameworks*, Report No. 117, Commonwealth of Australia, Sydney.

Australian National Audit Office (2013). *Administration of new income management in the Northern Territory*, Audit Report No. 19, Commonwealth of Australia, Canberra.

Bielefeld S (2012). Compulsory income management and Indigenous Australians: delivering social justice or furthering colonial domination? *University of New South Wales Law Journal* 35(2):522–62.

Bielefeld S (2014). History wars and Stronger Futures laws: a stronger future or perpetuating past paternalism? *Alternative Law Journal* 39(1):15–8.

Bray J, Gray M, Hand K, Bradbury B, Eastman C & Katz I (2012). *Evaluating new income management in the Northern Territory: first evaluation report*, Social Policy Research Centre UNSW, Sydney.

Bray J, Gray M, Hand K & Katz I (2014). *Evaluating new income management in the Northern Territory: the final report*, Social Policy Research Centre UNSW, Sydney.

Cahill D (2014). *The end of laissez-faire? On the durability of embedded neoliberalism*, Edward Elgar Publishing, Gloucestershire & Massachusetts.

Commonwealth of Australia (2007). *Parliamentary Debates*, House of Representatives, 7 August 2007 (Malcolm Brough, Minister for Families, Community Services and Indigenous Affairs and Minister Assisting the Prime Minister for Indigenous Affairs).

Commonwealth of Australia (2009). *Parliamentary Debates*, House of Representatives, 25 November 2009 (Jennifer Macklin, Minister for Families, Housing, Community Services and Indigenous Affairs).

Commonwealth of Australia (2011). *Parliamentary Debates,* House of Representatives, 23 November 2011 (Jennifer Macklin, Minister for Families, Housing, Community Services and Indigenous Affairs).

Commonwealth Ombudsman (2012). *Review of Centrelink income management decisions in the Northern Territory: financial vulnerability exemption and vulnerable welfare payment recipient decisions*, Commonwealth Ombudsman, Canberra.

Commonwealth Ombudsman (2013). *Ombudsman 2012–2013 Annual Report*, Commonwealth Ombudsman, Canberra.

Davidson H (2014). Kevin Andrews defies report to argue for more control of welfare recipients' cash. *The Guardian* 18 December.

Deloitte Access Economics (2014a). *Place based income management— baseline evaluation report*, Department of Social Services, Canberra.

Deloitte Access Economics (2014b). *Place based income management— process and short term outcomes evaluation*, Department of Social Services, Canberra.

Department of Families, Housing, Community Services & Indigenous Affairs (2012). *Cape York welfare reform evaluation*, Commonwealth of Australia, Canberra.

Department of Social Services (2014). *A new system for better employment and social outcomes—interim report of the Reference Group on Welfare Reform to the Minister for Social Services*, Commonwealth of Australia, Canberra.

Equality Rights Alliance (2011). *Women's experience of income management in the Northern Territory*, Equality Rights Alliance, Canberra.

Ergas H (2014). Unweaving the web of Aboriginal welfare dependency won't be easy. *The Australian* 1 September.

Explanatory Memorandum, *Social Security Legislation Amendment Bill 2011* (Cwlth).

Fanon F (2008). *Concerning violence*. Penguin Books, London.

Farmer P (2004). An anthropology of structural violence. *Current Anthropology* 45(3):305–17.

Forrest A (2014). *The Forrest review: creating parity*, Commonwealth of Australia, Canberra.

Howard-Wagner D & Kelly B (2011). Containing Aboriginal mobility in the Northern Territory: from 'Protectionism' to 'Interventionism'. *Law Text Culture* 15:102–34.

Katz I & Bates S (2014). *Voluntary income management in the Anangu Pitjantjatjara Yankunytjatjara (APY) lands*, Social Policy Research Centre UNSW, Sydney.

Martin D (2011). Policy alchemy and the magical transformation of Aboriginal society. In Musharbash Y & Barber M (eds), *Ethnography & the production of anthropological knowledge*, ANU E Press, Canberra.

Mead L (1997). The rise of paternalism. In Mead L (ed.), *The new paternalism: supervisory approaches to poverty*, Brookings Institution Press, Washington.

Moreton-Robinson A (2007). Witnessing the workings of White possession in the workplace: Leesa's testimony. *Australian Feminist Law Journal* 26:81–93.

Moreton-Robinson A (2009a). Imagining the good Indigenous citizen: race war and the pathology of patriarchal White sovereignty. *Cultural Studies Review* 15(2):61–79.

Moreton-Robinson A (2009b). Introduction: critical Indigenous theory special issue. *Cultural Studies Review* 15(2):11–2.

Morris B (2013). *Protests, land rights and riots: postcolonial struggles in Australia in the 1980s*, Aboriginal Studies Press, Canberra.

Neale T (2013). Staircases, pyramids and poisons: the immunity paradigm in the works of Noel Pearson and Peter Sutton. *Continuum: Journal of Media & Cultural Studies* 27(2):177–92.

Nicoll F (2012). Bad habits—discourses of addiction and the racial politics of intervention. *Griffith Law Review* 21(1):164–89.

Parliamentary Joint Committee on Human Rights (2013). *Examination of legislation in accordance with the Human Rights (Parliamentary Scrutiny) Act 2011: Stronger Futures in the Northern Territory Act 2012 and related legislation*. Commonwealth Parliament, Canberra.

Peck J (2012). *Constructions of neoliberal reason*, Oxford University Press, Oxford.

Said E (1994). *Culture and imperialism*, Vintage Books, New York.

Senate Estimates (2014). Parliament of Australia, House of Representatives, *Income management summary—27 December 2013*.

Soss J, Fording R & Schram S (2011). *Disciplining the poor: neoliberal paternalism and the persistent power of race*. University of Chicago Press, Chicago and London.

Standing S (2014). *A precariat charter: from denizens to citizens*, Bloomsbury, London and New York.

Wacquant L (2009). *Punishing the poor: the neoliberal government of social insecurity*, Duke University Press, Durham and London.

Watson I (2009). In the Northern Territory Intervention what is saved or rescued and at what cost? *Cultural Studies Review* 15(2):45–60.

13

Media stars and neoliberal news agendas in Indigenous policymaking

Kerry McCallum and Lisa Waller

Introduction

Our essay uses a media studies lens to examine the ascendancy of neoliberal policy agendas in Indigenous affairs. The Media and Indigenous Policy project[1] has been investigating the dynamic interplay between news media and the complex, politically sensitive and uneven bureaucratic field of Indigenous affairs. A particular focus has been to investigate the news media's power to construct problems and suggest solutions in the Indigenous policy field. This essay draws on that research to argue that conservative news outlets have sponsored a narrow range of Indigenous voices to articulate and promote neoliberal policy agendas to government. We examine how *The Australian* newspaper, as the keystone media on Indigenous affairs, was integral to the rise of Noel Pearson as the singular influence on Indigenous affairs. In doing so, we acknowledge and pay tribute to the thinking of Jon Altman in the development of our ideas, and for his support throughout this project. Altman's public discussion

---

1   Australian News Media and Indigenous Policymaking 1988–2008 (DP0987457).

of the 2007 Northern Territory Emergency Response made him one of the few Australian public intellectuals to think and act outside the dominant neoliberal discourse on Indigenous policy.

Neoliberal agendas in Indigenous affairs policy

The constructivist approach to policymaking (Colebatch 2002, Bacchi 2009) foregrounds the discursive battles that frame some issues as problems to be solved and enable some solutions to be heard more clearly than others. This approach problematises the dominant assumption that Indigenous affairs is 'intractable', 'wicked' or an area of 'policy failure', and helps explain sharp swings and occasional dramatic announcements such as the 2007 Northern Territory Emergency Response (NTER or Intervention). It reminds us that the policies that govern Indigenous peoples are rooted in the history of Australian colonisation and the complex processes of federalism. It tells us not to assume a direct effect of media content on policy, but rather see news media are part of the discursive environment in which problems are constructed and policy solutions are developed to address those problems.

Altman (2010) has documented the shift to a neoliberal agenda in Indigenous affairs policy by Labor and Coalition governments since the mid-1990s. We use the term neoliberalism, drawing on Altman, to mean the adoption of 'market-based technical solutions to complex, deeply entrenched and diverse development problems' (Altman 2010: 268). Despite the range of possible policy responses, and Aboriginal and Torres Strait Islander peoples' resilience and determination to represent the diversity of their opinion, a neoliberal perspective has come to dominate the Indigenous policy field. Federal governments have increasingly implemented social policy that has intervened in Indigenous Australians' lives with the explicit aim of exposure to the market. Interventionist policies such as welfare quarantining may appear to contradict neoliberalism's promise of free market individualism, but as Peters (2011) observes, neoliberalism emphasises the dominance of the individual over the state while simultaneously and selectively raising the social above the individual. In this way, neoliberalism can be offered as a rationale for coercive and interventionist policies, as well as for policies that promote free market activity.

Indigenous affairs reporting in Australia

There is a widespread belief that the news media wield great influence in the Indigenous policy sphere (Manne 2011). Our project builds on a long line of research that finds that the content of news is, indeed, an important influence on policy. But we would argue that media influence is frequently subtle and deeply embedded in the relationships between influential players in the media and policy fields.

The Media and Indigenous Policy project mapped the reporting of Indigenous health in three Australian newspapers from 1988–2008. While not a comprehensive content analysis of all media coverage of all Indigenous news, our findings paint a stark picture of the content and quality of reporting, and provide a basis for our wider analysis. We conclude that Indigenous health was of limited and uneven interest to mainstream news media (see Fig. 13.1). Reporting followed a 'shallows and rapids' pattern, whereby Indigenous issues were most often ignored, but when they were reported, coverage was intense, sensationalist, and short-lived (Fleras & Kunz 2001).

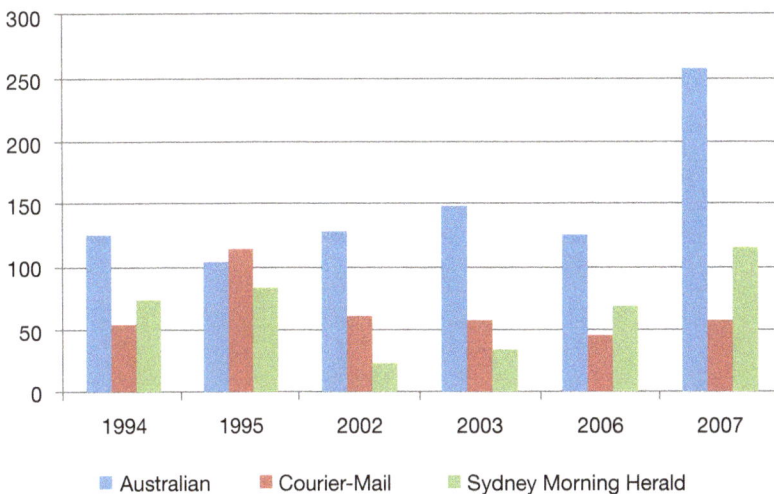

Fig. 13.1 Indigenous health reporting: Number of stories in *The Australian*, *Sydney Morning Herald* and *Courier Mail*, 1994–95, 2002–03, 2006–07

Source: Authors' research

Social policy domains such as Indigenous health were represented as political issues, with federal parliamentary leaders given the overwhelmingly loudest voice in news coverage. Qualitative analysis identified that news stories about Indigenous issues are typically told through frames of crisis, failure of government policy and individual responsibility, whereby Indigenous people are blamed for their own plight (McCallum 2011, 2013).

The Australian, Noel Pearson and Indigenous affairs

Our research has shown that between 1988 and 2008 *The Australian* was the only newspaper to report substantially on Indigenous health. Our finding that *The Australian* set the news agenda on Indigenous affairs is not surprising. As the flagship of Rupert Murdoch's NewsCorp and Australia's only national daily broadsheet newspaper, *The Australian* is an influential organ of news; it is a 'campaigning', loss-making but politically significant newspaper (Cryle 2008, McCallum & Reid 2012, McKnight 2012). We argue that *The Australian* is the keystone media source in the Australian Indigenous reporting landscape. Keystone media, according to Nielsen (2015), are defined not by their reach or ubiquity, but in terms of their systemic importance, their significance not for the majority of media users, but for the wider information environment they inhabit. The public servants, journalists and Indigenous policy advocates interviewed for our study contended that *The Australian* occupied the strongest position in the field of Indigenous reporting. *The Australian* had the biggest and most specialised reporting staff, the highest number of exclusives, devoted the most editorial space, committed resources both in Canberra and in remote Australia, and, most importantly, was the most closely listened to by opinion leaders, senior bureaucrats and political leaders. Its award-winning journalists bring substantial symbolic capital to the field (McCallum & Waller 2013). *The Australian*'s editors have deliberately and self-consciously made national discussion of Indigenous affairs a focal point (Brook 2012). Former editor Paul Kelly laid out *The Australian*'s contribution to Indigenous affairs in a keynote address at a 2014 conference to mark its 50th anniversary:

On Indigenous issues in recent decades the paper, I think, has taken some landmark positions. We have been very committed to moving away from what we feel was the commitment to progressive and unsuccessful policies in Indigenous affairs. We have worked with a number of Indigenous leaders in particular, Noel Pearson, to try to change the agenda and put a much greater emphasis on individual responsibility (Kelly 2014).

Participants in our study commented on the rise of conservative commentators during the Howard era as key players in policy debates, acknowledging in particular Noel Pearson's 'stunning success in engaging the eye of the mainstream'. Maddison (2009: xxxvi) however noted the contested ascendance of Noel Pearson among 'other Indigenous leaders'. Pearson is an Aboriginal Queenslander with deep cultural, political and economic capital (Curchin 2013). A senior Indigenous affairs bureaucrat told us:

And you know, he's incredibly well connected in government so every government wants a Pearson tick of approval. Every government actively seeks it out. They just can't help themselves because there isn't any other Indigenous leader with the same credit rating.

The Australian's political reporter Patricia Karvelas (2007) even went so far as to credit Pearson with convincing John Howard that 'his desire to activate the biggest social reform of his decade in power [the NTER] was right'. A policy insider noted his impact on government policy when he said:

So [Pearson's] notion about individual responsibility, that it's not all up to governments, is a really, really important one … [then Prime Minister] Tony Abbott is one of his biggest fans. And Tony, to his credit, has done things very much as a result of Noel … He has a very strong ideology.

We are interested in how certain individuals, like Pearson, come to occupy the intersection between news media and Indigenous policymaking by appearing to define the terms of public discourse and suggesting policy solutions. Waller (2010b) developed the concept of 'singular influence' to understand the power of the state and the media to consecrate a certain individual, such as Pearson, to promote their hegemonic, neoliberal rationalities, which are presented as so much common sense (Couldry 2010). We argue that *The Australian* newspaper aligned its reporting with the state's neoliberal policy agendas through its deployment of Noel Pearson as a regular commentator, anointed Indigenous leader and a singular influence on Indigenous affairs.

Pearson became an influential news source for *The Australian* during the Howard years. Our content analysis found that he was reported as a spokesperson on Indigenous health in *The Australian* twice as often as any other Indigenous person. More significantly, for a decade and a half, its editors gave Pearson a platform to present his views unmodified, through a series of invited columns. An analysis of 137 of these columns, published most often in the influential *Weekend Australian* between 2004 and 2011, revealed that Pearson used this platform to articulate his neoliberal policy agenda of individual responsibility, welfare reform, engagement with the mainstream economy, mobility, and home ownership.

In an invited column on 27 July 2004 for the 40th anniversary of *The Australian*, Pearson established the argument against what he and others, such as Peter Sutton (2009), have referred to as the 'liberal consensus':

> The liberal consensus during *The Australian's* lifetime was that Aboriginal disadvantage was caused by the denial of self-determination and denial of rights and services, and by discrimination ...
>
> *The Australian*, for all its faults, is the main national forum for this painful reassessment (Pearson 2004b).

Through his columns, Pearson set about systematically dismantling the liberal consensus. He idealised life prior to the 1967 referendum, criticised the move to legally enforce equal wages for Aboriginal workers, and blamed welfare rights for the current dependence among many Indigenous people on 'passive welfare'. While supporting land rights, Pearson strongly advocated private home ownership. He also promoted mobility—one of the currents of neoliberalism (Torres & Carte 2014)—arguing that Indigenous people move away from community to attend school or to find work (Pearson 2004a). In a 2005 piece he asserted:

> Indigenous social, educational and economic progress depends at least as much on increased geographic mobility and economic interaction with the national and global economies (Pearson 2005).

He extolled the importance of engagement with the 'real economy', noting that 'Work for the dole is always better than sit-down money, but it should never become a permanent alternative to work in the real economy' (Pearson 2006b). As Altman (2013) points out, Pearson is often vague about the 'real economy', but suggests that people should move away from programs such as CDEP, (which he refers to as passive welfare despite its requirement to work), to engagement with market capitalism through employment in mining or tourism. Pearson has been consistent in his insistence on personal responsibility to cure the ills that keep many Indigenous Australians in the margins of society, advocating that: 'For most people, the road to self-reliance ascends the "staircase of opportunity"' (Pearson 2006c). In the tradition of key neoliberal thinkers such as Hayek and Friedman, he advocates private choice as the answer to economic and social problems:

> The analogous sclerosis afflicting indigenous society is the pervasive absence of responsibility at the individual, family and community levels (Pearson 2006c).

In what might at first appear a contradictory stance, but in line with neoliberal thinking, Pearson has supported coercive, interventionist measures as necessary first steps toward breaking the dependency of Indigenous communities on government (Pearson 2006a). Despite his argument that their relationship with government was one of the biggest problems faced by Indigenous people, Pearson insisted the first step on the road to responsibility was 'the immediate need for government to intervene in those communities where the safety and protection of children and community members is an urgent priority' (Pearson 2006a). This view was reiterated in 2007 following the announcement of the NTER. In a series of articles where Pearson appeared to distance himself from this dramatic suite of policies, he nevertheless gave tacit support to measures such as welfare quarantining on the basis that at least the Howard government was acting on child sexual abuse (e.g. Pearson 2007a). Shortly after, Pearson commented as follows:

> … I believe liberal and conservative insights and policies currently have more to contribute to indigenous uplift than some outdated conventional progressive thinking (Pearson 2007b).

Conclusion

On 15 July 2014, at a dinner to celebrate the 50th anniversary of *The Australian* newspaper, Pearson came together with Rupert Murdoch and then Prime Minister Tony Abbott. In his speech to that dinner, Pearson (2014: 53) said: 'For those like me whose reform policies have been steadfastly supported by the paper's editorials, we have not been spared contrary views and criticism in news reporting and commentary. The dialectic of the national conversation plays out in the pages of *The Australian*'. We agree with Pearson's assessment that *The Australian* has committed significant resources to the reporting of Indigenous affairs, and its journalists have done much to raise awareness of the range of issues facing Indigenous Australians (Waller 2010a, 2013). We also agree that *The Australian*'s framing of Indigenous affairs news was not identical to Pearson's, and Pearson's views were not always in accord with those of the governments he influenced, or *The Australian*'s editorial line.

We do not, however, agree with Pearson's suggestion that *The Australian* fairly represented the diversity of views on Indigenous affairs. Our analysis leads us to conclude that Pearson, *The Australian* and federal government decision-makers were discursively aligned— 'a singular influence'. *The Australian*'s sponsorship of Noel Pearson gave him an unprecedented univocalism and effectively blocked from view other ways of imagining Indigenous policy issues. We contend that *The Australian*'s sponsorship of Pearson effectively narrowed the scope of debate on Indigenous affairs. This chapter has briefly outlined theoretical and empirical insights into the role of keystone news outlets like *The Australian* in promoting neoliberalism as the point of view of the dominant, which presents and imposes itself as a universal. In other words, neoliberalism has emerged as the hegemonic way of understanding the social world and the news media plays a key role in promoting neoliberal 'realities'.

References

Altman JC (2010). What future for remote Indigenous Australia? Economic hybridity and the neoliberal turn. In Altman JC & Hinkson M (eds), *Culture crisis: anthropology and politics in Aboriginal Australia*, UNSW Press, Sydney.

Altman JC (2013). Evidently: seeing through the smoke and mirrors of a black job hunt. *Tracker* 12 November.

Bacchi C (2009). *Analysing policy: what's the problem represented to be?* Pearson, Frenchs Forest.

Brook S (2012). Intellect and work ethic keep Mitchell in chair for 20 years. *The Australian* 4 June.

Colebatch HK (2002). *Policy*, 2nd edn, Open University Press, Maidenhead.

Couldry N (2010). *Why voice matters: culture and politics after neoliberalism*, Sage, London.

Cryle D (2008). *Murdoch's flagship: twenty-five years of* The Australian *newspaper*, Melbourne University Press, Melbourne.

Curchin K (2013). Discursive representation and Pearson's quest for a radical centre. *Australian Journal of Political Science* 48(3):256–68.

Fleras A & Kunz JL (2001). *Media and minorities: representing diversity in a multicultural Canada*, Thompson, Toronto.

Karvelas P (2007). Moved by Pearson's passion, *Weekend Australian* 23–24 June:1.

Kelly P (2014). Paul Kelly, keynote address to symposium marking 50 years of The Australian, video recording, Macquarie University, 7–8 July, Sydney. Retrieved from www.youtube.com/watch?v=g9EeVUSk7CU.

Maddison S (2009). *Black politics: inside the complexity of Aboriginal political culture*, Allen & Unwin, Sydney.

Manne R (2011). Bad news: Murdoch's *Australian* and the shaping of the nation. *Quarterly Essay* 43:1–119.

McCallum K (2011). Journalism and Indigenous health policy. *Australian Aboriginal Studies* 2011(2):21–31.

McCallum K (2013). Distant and intimate conversations: media and Indigenous health policy in Australia. *Critical Arts* 27(3):324–44.

McCallum K & Reid H (2012). Little children and big men: campaigning journalism and Indigenous policy. *Australian Journalism Review* 34(2):71–84.

McCallum K & Waller L (2013). Media interventions in Indigenous policymaking. *Media International Australia* 149:139–49.

McKnight D (2012). *Rupert Murdoch: an investigation of political power*, Allen & Unwin, Sydney.

Nielsen RK (2015). Introduction: the uncertain future of local journalism. In Nielsen R (ed.), *Local journalism: the decline of newspapers and the rise of digital media*, IB Taurus, London.

Pearson N (2004a). No danger of another stolen generation. *The Australian* 5 November.

Pearson N (2004b). Two stories of Indigenous affairs. *The Australian* 27 July.

Pearson N (2005). Reconciliation a building block. *The Australian* 19 April.

Pearson N (2006a). Big government hurts Aboriginal population. *The Australian* 26 June.

Pearson N (2006b). Join the real world. *Weekend Australian* 16–17 December.

Pearson N (2006c). Road to responsibility. *Weekend Australian* 30 September – 1 October.

Pearson N (2007a). Politics aside, an end to the tears is our priority. *The Australian* 23 June.

Pearson N (2007b). Leftist policies pave kids' road to hell. *The Australian* 21–22 July.

Pearson N (2014). A rightful place: race, recognition and a more complete Commonwealth. *Quarterly Essay* 55:53–4.

Peters M (2011). *Neoliberalism and after? Education, social policy and crisis of Western capitalism*, 2nd edn, Peter Lang, New York.

Sutton P (2009). *The politics of suffering: Indigenous Australia and the end of the liberal consensus*, Melbourne University Press, Melbourne.

Torres R & Carte L (2014). Community participatory appraisal in migration research: connecting neoliberalism, rural restructuring and mobility. *Transactions of the Institute of British Geographers* 39(1):140–54.

Waller L (2010a). Indigenous research ethics: new modes of information gathering and storytelling in journalism. *Australian Journalism Review* 32(2):19–31.

Waller L (2010b). Singular influence: mapping the ascent of Daisy M. Bates in popular understanding and Indigenous policy. *Australian Journal of Communication* 37(2):1–14.

Waller L (2013). It comes with the territory: 'Remote' Indigenous reporting for mainstream Australia. *Australian Journalism Monographs* 14:5–38.

14

Trapped in the gap

Emma Kowal

All my life gaps have drawn me in.

The gap between my privileged, middle-class upbringing and the oppressed people of the world drove me to write Amnesty letters on flimsy blue air mail paper in high school and sent me into activist groups as a medical student at the University of Melbourne in the early 1990s. In 1996 at the Canberra protests against the Howard government's first budget, it dawned on me that, as an Australian, the gap of Aboriginal disadvantage was the one that should trouble me most.

Along with some smart, politically aware friends, I helped to start an Indigenous solidarity group back on campus, working with Kooris to raise awareness of Indigenous issues and address White racism. As soon as I finished my combined medicine and arts degree, at the age of 25, I drove a second-hand Toyota 4 across the country to begin a new life as an intern at the Royal Darwin Hospital.

It was not long after starting work in the hospital that I became interested in the Indigenous health research institute close by, the (pseudonymous) Darwin Institute of Indigenous Health.[1] In my personal journey of methodically applying myself to what I thought to be the most urgent gap in the most effective way, the Darwin Institute

---

1   Parts of the following few paragraphs draw on the Preface to Kowal (2015).

seemed the next logical step. Having trained as a doctor, Indigenous health was the most important area to work in; within Indigenous health, public health was the most effective way to improve health; and to ensure that public health methods worked as well as they could, we needed good public health research. I knew the legacy of exploitative, disempowering research practices, and I believed the only way to close the gap was for researchers to truly commit to Indigenous control, a belief that seemed to align with the goals of the institute. I began infiltrating the institute, introducing myself to people after lunchtime meetings, having coffee with researchers after ward rounds, even studying Yolngu Matha at the Northern Territory University in anticipation of remote community work. I had soon lined up my first job at the institute as a public health researcher.

I spent a few years engaged in intermittent remote community work, combined with long stretches in front of a computer in town, translating the work into quantifiable outcomes, academic publications and community reports. I was finally working to close gaps through culturally appropriate, community-led health interventions.

Having reached the pinnacle of my own instrumentalism, the place where the rhetoric and level of resources meant there was the most potential to close the gap, I found myself disillusioned. My enthusiasm was dissipated at the power plays that went on between staff that overshadowed the cooperation that was needed; at the way that some projects which were widely promoted by the institute and governments as 'the answer' seemed full of dysfunction on the inside; and at the ease with which staff would criticise other projects as disempowering or even racist, but would not offer any useful assistance. Above all, I came to question the arguments circulating within the institute explaining why research had not worked in the past and why Indigenous control would fix the problem. The tendency to demonise White researchers in particular seemed an inadequate way to explain the situation, once I had got to know many of them and of course become one myself.

I became sensitive to the prominent role played by the moral politics of race and identity in public and private exchanges at the institute. In a seminar, for example, a question from an audience member about the method of payment of Indigenous research staff could imply that the White researcher was not paying their Indigenous staff sufficiently and was therefore exploitative or racist. A detailed explanation and justification would always follow such a question to deflect the implication, whether or not the implication was intended. Where projects were presented to the public, White researchers would take great pains to present an 'Indigenous face', editing themselves out of videos, preparing presentations for Indigenous colleagues to deliver but remaining silent themselves, and perhaps exaggerating the role of community members in a project. Whites were reluctant to question anything an Indigenous person said, even if it was clearly wrong. My interest in the source and effects of these racialised behaviours intensified, and the institute became the ethnographic field site for my PhD research. As I cynically wrote in my journal in the first months of my research: 'In the political world of Indigenous health we don't have arguments, we have positions. And the position of the "authentic Aboriginal voice" trumps even the most eloquent argument, and has no need for it.'

Over the course of my research, I recognised that much effort expended in the name of closing the gap was channelled into creating and maintaining racialised identities. In an *Indigenous* health institute, those who walk through the front doors every day are not just *people*, they are Indigenous people or non-Indigenous people. The institute is an always already racialised space. When the racial identities circulating in people's minds are examined more closely, they immediately multiply: the Indigenous people could be 'community people', or 'urban people'; the non-Indigenous people could be 'White people' or both non-White and non-Indigenous; the Whites could be 'rednecks' or 'anti-racists'; those not yet known to the viewer would best be classified as 'possibly Indigenous' until their Indigenous status has subtly been ascertained. Much work went into maintaining one's racial identity. For non-Indigenous people, this meant maintaining a specific racial identity as a 'good' White person and not an ignorant, exploitative, 'racist' White person: part of the solution and not part of the problem.

Having recognised the intense identity work that consumes so much energy in Indigenous affairs, I tried to understand what drove it. My explanation forms the heart of my book, *Trapped in the gap: doing good in Indigenous Australia* (Kowal 2015).

The racialised performances that characterise efforts to close the gap are far more than the 'moral vanity' Noel Pearson once diagnosed in the 'liberal left' (Pearson 2007); they are driven by the politics of the gap that continues to trap many of us.

Those who seek to close the gap experience two equal and opposing fears. First, they understand that improving Indigenous health requires systemic change, and they question their ability to overcome the institutional racism of post-settler society. While 'the gap' remains as an organic barometer of continued colonial oppression, they fear they are doing too little. At the same time, they fear they are doing too much. Encounters with radically different Indigenous ways of life leave White anti-racists concerned that their efforts to improve the health and social status of Indigenous people might be furthering the neo-colonial expansion of biopolitical norms. If the gap is due to the ways of life requisite to cultural survival, it follows that erasing the gap erodes Indigenous cultural distinctiveness. Despite the postcolonial mantra of community control, White anti-racists worry that their labours will be judged as indistinguishable from those of racist bureaucrats and missionaries of the past.

In the book I explain these fears as the product of tension between the two poles of equality and difference. White anti-racists manage the tension between attaining statistical equality (explored as 'remedialism') and maintaining essential Indigenous difference (explored as 'orientalism') by constructing a particular mode of Indigenous difference I call 'remediable difference'. Remediable difference is a difference that can be improved. This construction of difference works to manage the tension between 'remedialism' and 'orientalism' by promising that Indigenous people are different from non-Indigenous people, but not *so* different that interventions to close the gap will be ineffective, or will make them less Indigenous. In the book I recount how remediable difference was commonly unravelled by contact between White anti-racists and *radically* different Indigenous people, threatening the perceived moral integrity of both parties. The intense identity work I observed were attempts to manage or prevent this unravelling, and preserve the possibility of ethical White anti-racist intervention on deserving, authentic Indigenous subjects.

Illustrations of these arguments and their implications can be found in the book. But in this brief piece I want to sketch out how Jon's work has been crucial to my understanding of the gap and its traps.

In a sense, my work has sought to illustrate the affective and psychic costs to White anti-racists who inhabit the gap's contradictions on a daily basis.

For me, it was his 2007 Topical Issue paper, written as a rapid response to Howard's Northern Territory Intervention, that most succinctly expressed the dilemma of *all* attempts to address Indigenous disadvantage:

> Does the externally defined aim of normalization accord with Indigenous aspirations across the 73 prescribed communities, or put another way, do non-mainstream, culturally-different Australians want to be like 'the rest of us'? … The big picture is that equality of socio-economic status will not occur if people continue to live on their land in remote Australia, if they retain distinct cultural practices and priorities and if they resist or do not desire to move up the settlement hierarchy to towns and cities (Altman 2007: 9–10).

This is what haunts White anti-racists and threatens to unravel remediable difference. The possibility of radical difference makes closing the gap both impossible and immoral. As I put it in the book,

> If Indigenous people really have radically different priorities, then the project of improving their health, of making the lines on the graph converge, becomes a burden imposed upon them. As one colleague mused about a project he was involved in, 'The thing that bothers me is if it hasn't been taken up well and the community don't own it, well do they really want it?' There is a dual threat contained here: the fear that Indigenous people are not the innocent moral victims of structural causes but are actively determining their own radically different fates, and the fear that White anti-racist efforts to help them are merely the most recent colonial imposition (Kowal 2015: 48).

Jon has repeatedly and eloquently described the traps of the gap. What my work adds is an understanding of the high moral stakes involved in recognising or ignoring those traps. White anti-racists, many Indigenous people and the liberal state in general, have much invested in the logic of closing gaps, perhaps explaining why it has been so hard to take any alternative seriously.

In my first email correspondence with Jon in 2008 I naively asked him if his view in that 2007 paper was new, or at least expressed in a new way. He promptly provided a list of other places where he had previously made similar arguments. And more recently he sent me back to his very first book published in 1979 where he already flags the assumptions of economic equality.

> In discussing the possibility of effecting economic improvements in Aboriginal living conditions, it is not presumed that all people concerned would necessarily opt for economic changes, however beneficial materially, if the price for these was to be high in terms of social dismemberment or ecological disfiguration (Altman & Nieuwenhuysen 1979: 175).

He made this point again in the very first Centre for Aboriginal Economic Policy Research (CAEPR) publications. Discussion Paper No. 1 by Jon and Will Sanders, published in 1991, says that remote-living Aboriginal people seek 'to maintain important cultural and economic components of their traditional lifestyles, and consequently reject total economic assimilation' (Altman & Sanders 1991: 16–7).

The same year CAEPR's 2nd Research Monograph was published, analysing the form and progress of the 1987 Aboriginal Employment Development Strategy. In Jon's conclusion he explicitly argues that better definitions of 'equity' beyond statistical equality need to be developed that take into account 'cultural issues', recognising that 'many Aboriginal people in rural and remote locations … do not seek full incorporation into mainstream labour markets' (Altman 1991: 161).

In 2005 Altman and Rowse made the tension between difference and equality clear in an important chapter:

> to change people's forms of economic activity is to change people culturally. Some anthropological studies of regional economic activity argue that certain economic adaptations made by Indigenous Australians embody complex trade-offs between peoples' desires for cultural continuity and for material prosperity (Altman & Rowse 2005: 176).

Jon's critique of closing the gap is perhaps most forcefully expressed in his 2009 Working Paper:

> Cultural plurality suggests that there might be multiple interpretations of life worlds—where the state might see failure, mendicancy, dysfunctionality, and poor outcomes measured by social indicators, many Aboriginal people identify certain features that lie at the heart of their worldview (Altman 2009: 13).

The traps of the gap have perhaps never been more clearly expressed.

But despite his annihilating critiques of the gap, I think Jon understands its attraction. In an email to me he admitted that he too was once drawn into the gap:

> I started my career 'shocked' by the gap in 1976 in the economics department of Unimelb and now I see talk of the gap as unhelpful and demeaning, good for gauging input requirements not for measuring outcomes (pers. comm., 23 January 2014).

Jon now prefers points to gaps, balancing hybrid economies to find the 'bliss point' (Altman 2010), where the market, state and customary economies happily meet.

It involves allowing 'the option for voluntary exclusion [from the mainstream economy and society] as a strategic choice' (Altman 2009: 14). Such voluntary exclusion would be no picnic and 'will never statistically close the gap' (Altman 2009: 11), but would succeed in valuing diversity.

I would need another paper to explore what the White anti-racists I studied might make of the bliss point of Indigenous development, if they were able to find it. I suspect, however, that they would continue to be troubled by the problem of distinguishing between the choice of difference and the trap of disadvantage. While Jon has worried all his career that attempts to close the gap ignore the choice to be different, some anti-racists would be equally concerned that perpetuating difference undermines the capacity to access mainstream education and employment opportunities, and that White desires to uphold difference are more to do with 'the choices of the West dropped into an Indigenous cultural substrate', as Murray Garde put it.[2]

We see this debate played out in relation to customary environmental management: de Rijke et al. (this volume) question whether environmental management is 'customary' if it involves helicopters and weed killers and is no different to the work a non-Indigenous environmental manager would do. What draws my attention is not

---

2   Murray Garde quoted from the conference presentation: Cooke P, Garde M, Guymala T and Yibarbuk D (2014). *Contemporary customary economy, attribution of value and the management of Warddeken Indigenous Protected Area*, presented at Engaging Indigenous Economy: Debating Diverse Approaches Conference, The Australian National University, Canberra, 4 September.

whether the work of Caring for Country programs is sufficiently different to earn the 'customary' descriptor, but why the question is so crucial. Depending on the answer, customary land management is either a bliss point or a Trojan horse for neoliberal environmentality (Agrawal 2005).

Jokes aside, the debates that Jon has so passionately contributed to for nearly 40 years are deadly serious. My insight in 1996 that the struggle for Indigenous social justice is the primary struggle of this country still drives my work, and it is a challenge but also a pleasure to work in a field where the stakes are so high and the issues so important. In this field where passionate debate sometimes spills into acrimony, the generosity Jon brings to academia is highly appreciated. I will finish with an anecdote that illustrates this generosity. He took it very well when, in a prominent 2008 article, I essentially used him as a straw man to stand in for a purely 'orientalist' approach that rejected remedialism (Kowal 2008). In retrospect it would have been more accurate to say he advocated for some 'pendulum swinging' back towards orientalism and away from the extreme remedialism of neoliberal intervention (Altman 2009). Rather than being annoyed that I called him an orientalist, he joked that he is actually an oriental, having been born in Haifa. He has been wonderfully supportive of my work, most recently bestowing on me the gift of a book title: *Trapped in the gap*. We are all still trapped in the gap—Aboriginal and Torres Strait Islander people most of all, but also those who try to close gaps, and those like us who pick apart logics and effects of intervention. I am glad Jon is trapped there with us.

References

Agrawal A (2005). *Environmentality: technologies of government and the making of subjects*, Duke University Press, Durham, NC.

Altman JC (1991). Conclusion. In Altman JC (ed.), *Aboriginal employment equity by the year 2000*, CAEPR Research Monograph No. 2, Centre for Aboriginal Economic Policy Research, The Australian National University, Canberra.

Altman JC (2007). *The Howard government's Northern Territory Intervention: are neo-paternalism and Indigenous development compatible?* Topical Issue 16/2007, Centre for Aboriginal Economic Policy Research, The Australian National University, Canberra.

Altman JC (2009). Beyond closing the gap: valuing diversity in Indigenous Australia. Working Paper 54, Centre for Aboriginal Economic and Policy Research, The Australian National University, Canberra.

Altman JC (2010). What future for remote Indigenous Australia? Economic hybridity and the neoliberal turn. In Altman JC & Hinkson M (eds), *Culture crisis: anthropology and politics in Aboriginal Australia*, UNSW Press, Sydney.

Altman JC & Nieuwenhuysen JP (1979). *The economic status of Australian Aborigines*, Cambridge University Press, Cambridge.

Altman JC & Rowse T (2005). Indigenous Affairs. In Saunders P & Walter J (eds), *Ideas and influence: social science and public policy in Australia*, UNSW Press, Sydney.

Altman JC & Sanders W (1991). *From exclusion to dependence: Aborigines and the welfare state in Australia*. Discussion Paper 1, Centre for Aboriginal Economic Policy Research, The Australian National University, Canberra.

Cooke P, Garde M, Guymala T and Yibarbuk D (2014). *Contemporary customary economy, attribution of value and the management of Warddeken Indigenous Protected Area*, presented at Engaging Indigenous Economy: Debating Diverse Approaches Conference, The Australian National University, Canberra, 4 September.

Kowal E (2008). The politics of the gap: Indigenous Australians, liberal multiculturalism and the end of the self-determination era. *American Anthropologist* 110(3):338–48.

Kowal E (2015). *Trapped in the gap: doing good in Indigenous Australia*, Berghahn, New York & London.

Pearson N (2007). White guilt, victimhood and the quest for a radical centre. *Griffith Review* 16:1–39.

15

Neoliberal rhetoric and guardian state outcomes in Aboriginal land reform

Leon Terrill

Introduction

When the *Forrest Review* was released in August 2014, few people would have been surprised to find that it included several recommendations with respect to land tenure reform in Aboriginal communities (Forrest 2014: 58–60). This was the latest instalment in an ongoing public dialogue about Aboriginal land reform in Australia. It is a discussion that began in earnest a little over a decade ago and has continued (at times quietly, at times prominently) throughout the period since. Since 2006, it has been accompanied by several sets of reforms: township leases, five-year leases, housing precinct leases, 'secure tenure' policies and, most recently, legislation to allow 'ordinary freehold title' in 34 Aboriginal and Torres Strait Islander communities in Queensland.

In this chapter, I argue that while public dialogue about the reforms has been dominated by neoliberal rhetoric the reforms themselves are, for the most part, better characterised in terms of guardianship or paternalism. I will also argue that this has been a form of *neoliberal* paternalism. This means that references to neoliberalism are not entirely misplaced, however it is paternalism that is the more defining element of the reforms. The reason this matters is because neoliberalism suggests the introduction of markets where those markets will have the disciplining effect of encouraging the development of individual motivation and resilience; whereas neoliberal paternalism instead describes how the government itself takes on the task of disciplining individuals, as part of a project of preparing those individuals to become capable market agents. The difference, which is significant, is with respect to the role played by governments.

I finish the chapter by asking two questions: What is the significance of the disjuncture between language and practice? And who should play the role of guardian with respect to land administration in Aboriginal communities?

Debate about Aboriginal land reform in Australia

A short chapter cannot authoritatively reproduce a decade-long debate. Instead, a representative sample of quotes is provided here that embody the dominant themes of the debate, particularly as they were articulated by those in favour of reform.[1]

The first quote is from a discussion paper by Noel Pearson and Lara Kostakidis-Lianos (2004). The authors argue that a 'key structural problem faced by many Indigenous people, particularly those living in remote communities, is the fact that they live in a welfare economy outside the mainstream Australian (real) economy'. They identify several reasons for this, but emphasise that this 'isolation is cemented … by specifically Indigenous landholding structures' (Pearson & Kostakidis-Lianos 2004: 1). Without being prescriptive, they argue that changes to land ownership are needed to allow Indigenous people in those communities to participate more fully in the 'real economy'.

---

1   For brevity I omit reference to statements about secure tenure, which were favoured by the Rudd–Gillard Labor governments but appeared to have been dropped by the Abbott Coalition Government.

Echoing similar themes, later that year Warren Mundine announced that Indigenous Australians 'need to move away from communal land ownership and non-profit community-based businesses and take up home ownership, economic land development and profit-making businesses' (quoted in Metherell 2004). Mundine's comments were widely reported and provoked a number of responses, including a statement of endorsement by Prime Minister John Howard (Bradfield 2005: 3). The following April, Howard announced that his government planned to introduce reforms to enable individual ownership, for the reason that '[h]aving title to something is the key to your sense of individuality, it's the key to your capacity to achieve, and to care for your family' and that he didn't 'believe that indigenous Australians should be treated differently in this respect' (quoted in Grattan 2005). Here the formative role of property ownership is made explicit. The Prime Minister saw land reform not just as an avenue for economic development, but also as a means of altering the norms and behaviours of people living in Aboriginal communities. As Michelle Grattan (2005) said at the time, the Prime Minister appeared to be 'bent on taking the white picket fence to remote Aboriginal Australia'.

The Australian newspaper editorialised in favour of the reforms on several occasions. They described how there was a 'revolution under way in thinking about black land rights in Australia', which had been given 'tangible shape in the Howard Government's plan … to allow individuals to privately own what is now communal property' (*The Australian* 2005). They characterised this as 'the most determined effort yet to create an enterprise culture within Aboriginal communities', again referring to a change of culture.

More recently, current Minister for Indigenous Affairs Senator Nigel Scullion (2014) argued that:

> Land tenure reform is not about benefiting government and it is not about giving government control of the land.
>
> It is about giving Aboriginal people the same opportunities and responsibilities as other Australians to own their own homes, and leverage their land assets to generate wealth for the benefit of themselves, their families and their community.

I return to this statement below, to argue that it misrepresents the impact of recent reforms.

Neoliberal themes

These and related statements suggest that the role of land reform is to bring Aboriginal communities into the mainstream economy, not just to enable greater wealth creation but so that the introduction of markets might alter community norms by creating the incentives for individual endeavour and fostering an 'enterprise culture'. There are some bold assumptions being made here about the role of existing tenure arrangements in preventing economic development, but that is not the focus of this chapter. Instead, I wish to clarify what these statements suggest about the role of governments.

To borrow from a related context, the theme here is very much along the lines of 'normalise, exit'. These statements suggest that the role of government is to enable markets, or to remove barriers to the entry of markets, and to then get out of the way and allow those markets to do their work, to have their impact both in terms of wealth formation and norm development. Below I contrast this with the reforms themselves.

The reforms

As it is not possible here to describe all of the recent reforms—which include the five-year leases, 'secure tenure' policies, permit reforms, and changes to leasing in Queensland—I am going to concentrate on the Australian Government's flagship reform, which is township leasing in the Northern Territory.

To understand what township leases do it is necessary to begin with the situation before they were introduced. Previously, most infrastructure in communities on Aboriginal land was allocated under *informal arrangements*. That is, there were very few leases formalising the relationship between the Aboriginal landowners and the occupiers of each individual lot. For example, while the local council was the sole occupier of buildings such as council offices, workshops and staff accommodation, its rights to do so were informal rather than legal. While this might sound precarious, and it did have flaws, it appears that these informal arrangements were relatively stable and for several decades provided the basis for land use in communities on Aboriginal land.

What a township lease does is to *formalise* these tenure arrangements through a two-step process (Terrill 2014). The first step is that the entire community is leased to a statutory body called the Executive Director of Township Leasing (EDTL). This is the township lease and it is in the nature of a head lease. The next step is that the EDTL grants a sublease to each and every occupier, so that their right to occupy is made formal.

What differentiates township leasing from other formalising models is the role of the EDTL. That is, the function of a township lease is not just to formalise tenure through the grant of subleases, but to put the EDTL in charge of the process for doing so, rather than community residents or traditional owners or some other persons. This is of course an ongoing role. Once subleases have been granted, they must then be administered and ultimately renewed.

Wurrumiyanga

The first township lease was granted over the community of Wurrumiyanga (formerly Nguiu) in 2007. By now almost all lots within the community have been subleased, and I have been studying the way in which subleases have been granted. A key point is that township leasing has not led to the creation of a market in subleases. There are several reasons for this, one of which is the terms of the subleases themselves. While there is some variation, a typical sublease runs for about 20 years, is subject to ongoing rent, contains a long list of restrictions on use, and can only be transferred with the consent of the EDTL (which cannot be unreasonably withheld).

There are a small number of exceptions, the most notable being the grant of 16 home ownership subleases. These truly are in a marketable form (although to date there is no record of any being traded). This is because they run for much longer—up to 99 years—and are not subject to ongoing rent. They represent value, whereas most other subleases, with their ongoing rental obligation, have been described as arguably being 'a business liability rather than an asset' (Beadman 2010: 76).

The 16 home ownership subleases also represent a tiny fraction of all residential housing in the community. The other approximately 281 houses have instead been subleased long-term to Territory

Housing (Watson 2010: 9). This is because since 2007 the Australian Government has required that all residential housing in Indigenous communities be leased or subleased to the relevant State or Territory housing department. Previously, housing in Indigenous communities was a form of community housing managed by bodies called Indigenous Community Housing Organisations or ICHOs. As a result of these reforms it is now public housing, controlled and managed by the mainstream government housing body. This has been a far more widespread reform than the very limited introduction of home ownership.

Beyond the limited introduction of home ownership, which after all does not require a community-wide leasing scheme, there is no market in subleases in any of the existing township lease communities. They are not being bought and sold for value or at a market price because they are more like a liability than an asset. And contrary to what the Minister has suggested (Scullion 2014), those subleases are not a form of property that can be leveraged to create wealth. Instead, the main economic impact of township leasing has been a significant increase in the amount of rent being paid by occupiers such as enterprises and service providers. Most of this rent will ultimately be passed on to the traditional owners for that land.

If I were to make one comment on this as an economic model it would be to say that Hernando de Soto (2001) would not be happy. This is not capital creating in the sense he envisages. Nor is it coherently neoliberal in any meaningful sense. There is no market and the most widespread 'price', which is the amount of rent paid on subleases, is unilaterally set by the EDTL.

Neoliberal or paternal?

The reason I argue that it is misleading to simply describe these reforms as neoliberal is because that term suggests the introduction of markets, with markets then playing a formative role in the development of individuals and of society. This is made explicit in some of the quotes described above, however that is not what has happened under recent reforms.

They are better characterised as what Soss et al. (2011) refer to as 'neoliberal paternalism'. They describe how:

> ... neoliberalism and paternalism converge on a distinctive agenda for poverty governance. Together, they define a strong state-led effort to bring discipline to the lives of the poor so that they can become competent actors who recognize and act on their own interests as freely choosing agents of the market (Soss et al. 2011: 27).

Australians are already familiar with this approach being used and advocated in the context of welfare reform. For example, the *Forrest review* recommends the introduction of a cashless welfare card to protect people who are at 'risk of making poor, short-term purchase decisions' and to 'assist individual responsibility by eliminating spending on alcohol, gambling, and instruments that can be converted to cash like gift cards' (Forrest 2014: 102, 104). State-led discipline is required in the short-term so that individuals can make better decisions in the long-term.

I suggest that neoliberal paternalism also describes many, though not all, of the recent land reforms.[2] It is not that the government is enabling markets and allowing those markets to have their impact on individuals. It is that governments have taken on the role themselves of disciplining individuals. With respect to housing, I have found a rare quote in which this role is made explicit with respect to the broader housing reforms described above:

> Tenants are required to sign up to, and adhere to, normal tenancy agreements—an important lever to rebuild positive community values and behaviour. These reforms will also see tenants required to pay regular and standardised rent and meet care of property requirements. This is part of developing the personal responsibility and individual financial resilience and discipline that is also required to purchase and pay off a home (Australian Government 2010: 14).

---

2   Most notably, recent Queensland legislation to allow partitioning of Indigenous land might more aptly be described as neoliberal, see the *Aboriginal and Torres Strait Islander Land (Providing Freehold) and Other Legislation Amendment Act 2014* (Qld). That legislation raises a number of issues that are not addressed here.

In other words, the state has inserted itself into housing tenure arrangements so as to provide a higher level of discipline, which will in turn enable individuals to better meet the responsibilities of being a 'competent actor', more capable of purchasing their own home.

This raises a number of important questions, including the question of how well governments are equipped to take on this disciplining role, particularly in the context of Aboriginal communities. Those questions are elided when debate is instead conducted as if governments were introducing mainstream forms of property and then getting out of the way.

What is the significance of this disjuncture?

Such a significant disjuncture between language and practice cannot be accidental. One reason for it appears to be reluctance on the part of governments to publicly admit to their new, more intrusive role. This is apparent in the recent quote from the Minister for Indigenous Affairs (Scullion 2014), in which he states that land tenure reform 'is not about benefiting government and it is not about giving government control of the land'. I agree that land tenure reform is not about benefiting government, however the statement that it is not about giving government control over land is patently incorrect.

So why is the Minister reticent to admit this? I am yet to find a satisfactory answer to this. It is partly explained by the fact that this new, expanded role for government is at odds with some views of what liberalism and neoliberalism should entail. Tellingly, the Centre for Independent Studies, a neoliberal think tank, has criticised township leases for the fact that they are held by the government and not by the community. They argue that 'governments should step back and enable communities to decide how to lease their land' (Hudson 2009: vii).

It is also notable that when the *Forrest review* refers to paternalism it ascribes a negative value to the term. It argues that '[i]n a nutshell, it's time to end the paternalism, to expect able first Australians to stand on their own feet and become independent' (Forrest 2014: 3). Australian governments have often expressed similar sentiments. Yet there is a tension between this and governments taking on a new and greater role in the management of Aboriginal communities. Resolving this tension requires an evolved set of theory and messaging that the government may not yet have developed.

It could be argued that it is simply more politically expedient for the government to promote land reform using the language of individual autonomy. However it is not just the government who employs this language, its use has been widespread. It does not appear that this has been manufactured to conceal an alternative agenda. It is more likely that the confusion is genuine, and that it reflects something significant.

Who should play the guardianship role?

Criticism of the Australian Government's new and more paternalistic approach to land tenure reform takes on a different hue when it is accepted that there might be a genuine need for *someone* to play a guardianship role with respect to some aspects of land administration in Aboriginal communities. I would argue that one of the reasons the Australian Government has opted for a more controlled approach to subleasing on township leases is because it was aware of the dangers inherent in removing all regulation. Due to the particular social and economic circumstances of remote communities, a community-wide, free market in subleases could be harmful. There is arguably value in retaining some centralised control over allocation.

If it were not the government, who should have this control? Who should manage the grant of leases or subleases to business and service providers? Who should set the amount of rent? If there is a closed market, such as for home ownership, who should decide whether someone is in or out? Who should manage the allocation of social housing? Some of these questions bring into play the relationship between traditional owners and (other) Aboriginal residents. They also raise issues around governance and the need to prevent situations of exploitation and nepotism.

In light of this, it appears that governments currently have an almost reflexive tendency to take the role of decision making upon themselves. There are real issues with this. But even in someone else's hands, I would argue that certain of these decisions are likely to entail a certain amount of guardianship. As Sanders (2009) has made clear, guardianship is not simply or always a retrograde concept. It is 'a *persistent idea* in Australian Indigenous policy' (Sanders 2009: 11, original emphasis), albeit one with a very troubling history. Nevertheless, its ongoing role cannot be ignored or dismissed out of hand, including with respect to land reform.

References

The Australian (2005). Editorial: Black revolution: economic engagement is the path to prosperity. *The Australian* 6 October:18.

Australian Government (2010). *Indigenous home ownership issues paper*, Department of Families, Housing, Community Services and Indigenous Affairs, Canberra.

Beadman B (2010). *Northern Territory Coordinator General for Remote Services: Report #2 December 2009 to May 2010*, Northern Territory Government, Darwin.

Bradfield S (2005). White picket fence or Trojan horse? The debate over communal ownership of Indigenous land and individual wealth creation, *Land, Rights, Laws: Issues of Native Title* 3(3), Native Title Research Unit, Australian Institute of Aboriginal and Torres Strait Islander Studies, Canberra.

de Soto H (2001). *The mystery of capital: why capitalism triumphs in the west and fails everywhere else*, Black Swan, London.

Forrest A (2014). *The Forrest review: creating parity*, Commonwealth of Australia, Canberra.

Grattan M (2005). Howard tilts at title fight. *The Sunday Age* (Melbourne) 10 April:17.

Hudson S (2009). *From rhetoric to reality: can 99-year leases lead to homeownership for Indigenous communities?* Policy Monograph 92, Centre for Independent Studies, St Leonards NSW.

Metherell M (2004). Land system holds us back, says Mundine. *The Sydney Morning Herald* (Sydney) 7 December:6.

Pearson N & Kostakidis-Lianos L (2004). Building Indigenous capital: removing obstacles to participation in the real economy, Cape York Institute, Cairns.

Sanders W (2009). *Ideology, evidence and competing principles in Australian Indigenous affairs: from Brough to Rudd via Pearson and the NTER*, Discussion Paper 289, Centre for Aboriginal Economic Policy Research, The Australian National University, Canberra.

Scullion N (2014). Land reform for the future. *Koori Mail* 26 March.

Soss J, Fording R & Schram S (2011). *Disciplining the poor: neoliberal paternalism and the persistent power of race*, University of Chicago Press, Chicago.

Terrill L (2014). What is Township Leasing? Indigenous Law Centre Research Brief, July, Indigenous Law Centre, UNSW, Sydney.

Watson P (2010). *Executive Director of Township Leasing Annual Report 2009–2010*, Australian Government, Canberra.

Part 3: Land, Housing and Entrepreneurship: Altman Applied

16

Dealings in native title and statutory Aboriginal land rights lands in Australia: What land tenure reform is needed?

Ed Wensing

Introduction

The current debate about Indigenous land tenure reform is skewed toward a neoliberal market view of private home ownership and capital accumulation at the expense of communal forms of tenure. I come at these issues from a very different perspective and background. As a land use planner, land administration and land tenure have been an integral part of my professional life since the early 1970s.

In 2011, I was lead researcher in a study undertaken for the Western Australian Department of Indigenous Affairs on whether the Aboriginal Lands Trust estate in Western Australia could be transferred to Aboriginal people within the existing land tenure system (SGS Economics and Planning 2012). The study found that there was:

- a low level of understanding among Aboriginal people of what 'home ownership' means and the implications of becoming a home owner;
- a high level of misunderstanding among Aboriginal people of the Crown's land tenure system and misapprehension about the need for change;

- a high level of mistrust among Aboriginal people and native title holders because governments are notorious for continually changing their policies and positions.

The study also found that native title holders are reluctant to surrender their native title rights and interests in exchange for a form of tenure of which they have little or no understanding and which they regard as inferior to customary land rights. But none of this is new to Aboriginal people.

With my professional land use planning and land administration background, two larger questions arose for me from this study:

- Why do native title holders have to surrender and agree to the permanent extinguishment of their customary rights and interests in order to participate in the modern economy?
- Why is it not possible for customary rights and interests to be accommodated in conventional land tenure systems in a way that would enable the customary rights holders to engage in the modern economy on their lands, on their terms and without having to surrender and extinguish their native title rights and interests forever?

These two questions made me think more deeply about what Aboriginal land tenure reform is needed and they are the focus of my PhD research.[1] This chapter provides some preliminary insights and arguments.

My starting position is that the current basis for admitting Aboriginal land rights into the Anglo-Australian framework of land law and tenure continues the dispossession of colonialism, only this time under the guise of inalienability and extinguishment. Under the new native title regime, the Crown has a monopoly power to extinguish customary rights and interests. Many statutory Aboriginal land rights regimes in Australia also severely restrict dealings in land held in Aboriginal ownership. I postulate that it is time to puncture some legal orthodoxies relating to property and dealings in land.

---

1   The focus of this paper is on mainland Australia. Consequently, the term Aboriginal is used except where the context makes it necessary to refer to Aboriginal and Torres Strait Islander people or Indigenous peoples.

A wider context

Issues of land tenure reform must be viewed in a much wider context and Jon Altman (2014) has done this by looking at what he calls the Indigenous land titling 'revolution'.

Fig. 16.1 shows the extent of dispossession and re-titling of Aboriginal and Torres Strait Islander people's interests in land from 1788 to the present. As Altman (2014: 3) notes:

> In 1788 Indigenous nations possessed the entire continent. Then during a prolonged period of land grab from 1788 to the late 1960s Indigenous peoples were dispossessed. But then, from the late 1960s, there has been an extraordinary period of rapid legal repossession and restitution that is ongoing. This has not occurred as part of some coherent policy framework, but rather as a somewhat ad hoc land titling 'revolution' driven intermittently by political, social justice and judicial imperatives.

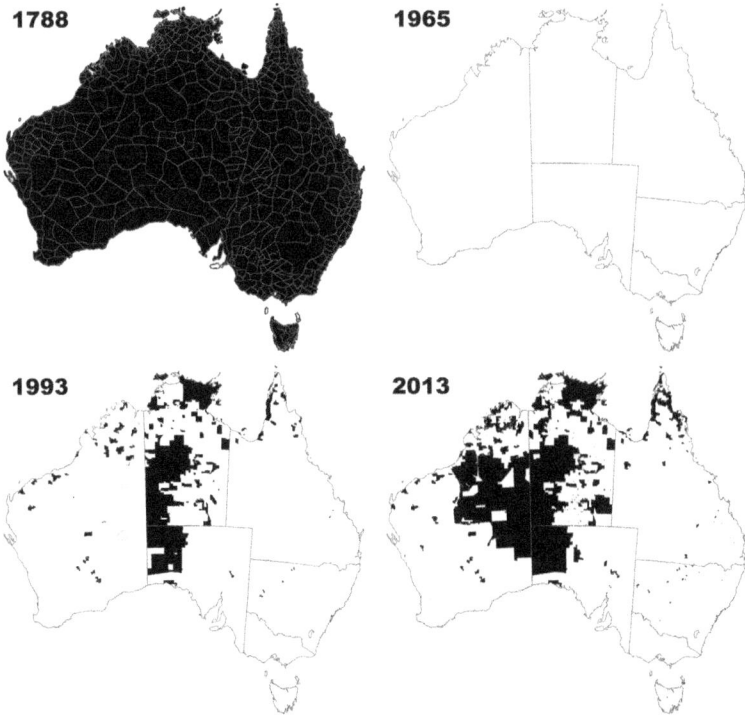

Fig. 16.1 A snapshot of Indigenous-held land from 1788 to 2013
Source: Altman (2014)

The land titling revolution includes a range of land rights grants, purchases, native title determinations and areas subject to Indigenous land use agreements or other joint management arrangements. Altman has recently mapped these land titles (Altman 2012, 2014) and they total around 2.5 million km² or roughly 33 per cent of terrestrial Australia (Fig. 16.2).² This includes land held under general land legislation that allows governments to create reserves, freehold title or leases for the benefit of Aboriginal or Torres Strait Islander people. It also covers statutory land rights regimes which generally grant an inalienable freehold title to traditional owners (who are identified in accordance with traditional laws and customs and are communal land holders) or to Aboriginal or Torres Strait Islander residents of a discrete community. Finally, it includes land held under the *Native Title Act 1993* (Cwlth) (NTA) which provides for the recognition of the communal group or individual rights and interests of native title holders under their traditional laws and customs in relation to their land or waters.

Altman (2014: 7) also highlights that most Aboriginal and Torres Strait Islander Australians do not live on Aboriginal titled land (Fig. 16.3), estimating that less than 100,000 do so from a total Aboriginal and Torres Strait Islander population of 660,00. He also notes that it is not clear how many living on Aboriginal lands are traditional owners (see Edelman 2009) or how many traditional owners live off their lands. By correlating population with land held under land rights or exclusive possession native title, Altman (2014: 7) estimates that over 80 per cent of the population in these locations is Aboriginal or Torres Strait Islander compared with a national proportion of just on 3 per cent. Altman also argues, hypothetically, that if all native title claims were successful, as much as 70 per cent of Australia could be under some form of Aboriginal title and as much as 40 per cent of the Aboriginal and Torres Strait Islander population could be resident on those lands.

---

2   Fig. 16.2 provides information on land titling under three tenures: land claimed or automatically scheduled under land rights law, an estimated 969,000 km²; 92 determinations of exclusive possession under native title law totalling 752,000 km²; and 142 determinations of non-exclusive possession under native title law totalling 825,000 km². The last category often provides a weak form of property right that needs to be shared with other interests, most commonly commercial rangeland pastoralism.

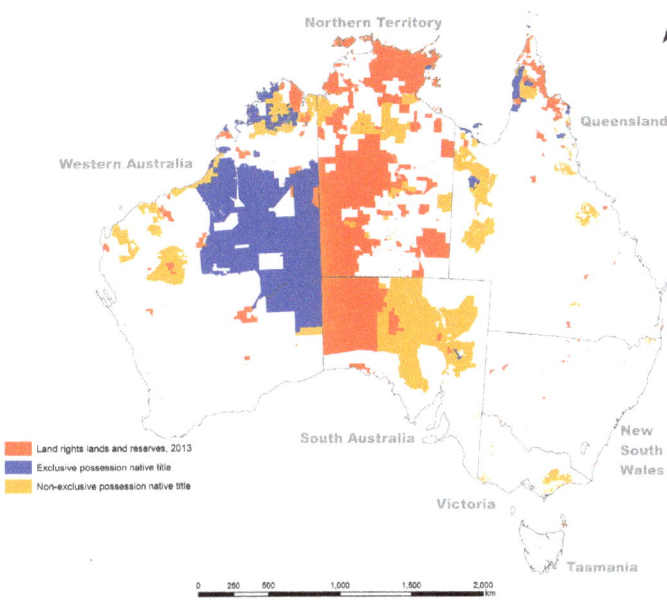

Fig. 16.2 Indigenous land titling under three tenures

Source: Altman (2014)

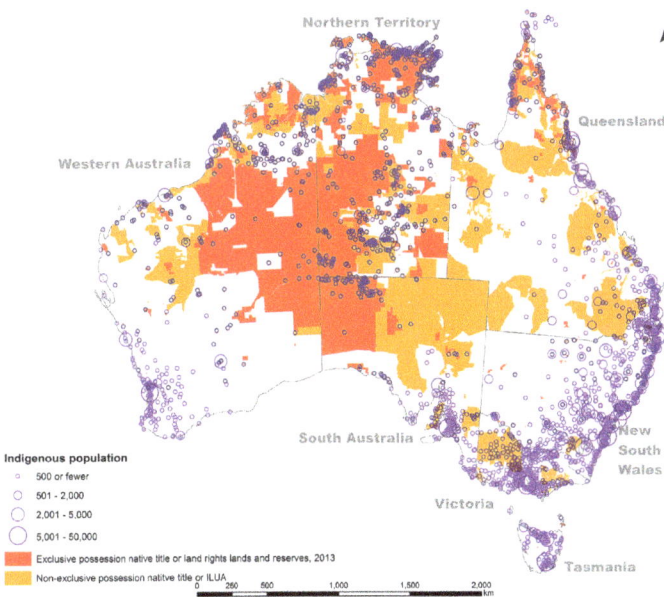

Fig. 16.3 Distribution of Indigenous population from the 2011 Census and Indigenous land titles in 2013

Source: Altman (2014)

Dealings in native title lands

Land granted or reserved for the benefit of Aboriginal and Torres Strait Islander people under statutory land rights regimes does not extinguish native title rights and interests (*Pareroultja v Tickner* 1993). Therefore dealings in Aboriginal communally owned land, or land reserved for the use and benefit of Aboriginal people, must also take into account the native title rights and interests for the dealings to be valid.[3]

Land subject to native title rights and interests is inalienable. Under the NTA, native title rights and interests can only be surrendered to the Crown. Further, a native title determination does not give native title holders any power or authority to grant subsidiary interests, including leases. Native title is also statutorily protected from debt recovery processes and is therefore unusable as security against a loan (Wensing & Taylor 2012: 22; Wensing 2013).

The extent to which a prescribed body corporate (PBC) or registered native title body corporate (RNTBC) is able to assign leases over land subject to native title rights and interests is also constrained by s. 56(5) of the NTA. This states that the native title rights and interests held by a body corporate are not able to be 'assigned, restrained, garnisheed, seized or sold' or 'made subject to any charge or interest … as a result of the incurring, creation or enforcement of any debt or other liability of the body corporate', including 'any act done by the body corporate'. Section 56(5) is a reflection of what is regarded as the common law position on native title set out in *Mabo (No. 2)*. It understands native title as a form of property subject to the Crown's radical title and therefore outside the real property system originating from the Crown. Native title cannot be transferred to anybody but the Crown. If that is the position, native title cannot subsist with the creation of a freehold title, lease or any sublease exercised pursuant to a lease (by native title holders or otherwise).

---

3   Dealing is the legal process through which land is bought and sold or otherwise transferred, also known as conveyancing. This involves the preparation of hard copy documents or records as evidence of a land transaction between parties.

The NTA alters the common law by enacting the non-extinguishment principle and applying it to specified future acts. The reality is that in striking contrast to other citizens, native title holders cannot enter the market to realise the value of their property rights by leasing, mortgaging or selling them, because the Crown has a monopoly over the acquisition and extinguishment of those rights (Gover 2012). Nevertheless, Gover (2012) asserts that governments have a moral obligation, if not a fiduciary duty, 'to act "reasonably, honourably and in good faith" in dealings with Aboriginal and Torres Strait Islander peoples and to make "informed decisions" where their interests are at stake'. The complexity of dealings in native title land should not be underestimated, as discussed in more detail elsewhere (Wensing & Taylor 2012: 22–7).

Dealings in statutory Aboriginal and Torres Strait Islander land rights lands

There are 23 different Aboriginal and Torres Strait Islander land rights statutes operating across Australia in addition to the NTA. The form of title under these statutory Aboriginal land rights regimes differs within and between jurisdictions, but titles are generally an estate in fee simple or freehold. These different statutory forms of title differ in whether the landholder can sell, lease, mortgage or dispose of their land. Table 16.1 is a comparative analysis of the statutory Aboriginal and Torres Strait Islander land rights regimes which lists the different statutes and includes details of the landowner, form of title, and whether private sale, leasing or subleasing, or mortgaging is permitted.[4]

---

4   The original source for this analysis was the Aboriginal and Torres Strait Islander Social Justice Commissioner's *Native title report 2005* (Calma 2006). However, since that time several jurisdictions have made significant amendments to their legislation or introduced new legislation. As stated in the *Native title report 2005*, to ascertain particular details in the different jurisdictions, a closer analysis of the strengths, weaknesses and workability of the existing arrangements is required.

The ability of title holders to deal in the land varies within and between jurisdictions. In most cases the land is inalienable and cannot be sold, transferred or otherwise dealt with, except in accordance with the provisions of the relevant legislation. Only in very few cases are there no statutory restrictions on dealings in the land.

Table 16.1 shows that in most cases land is not able to be sold on the open market, but in 20 instances a legislative basis already exists in all jurisdictions (with conditions attached) that enables leasehold interests to be created. In 15 instances this includes the ability to use the leasehold interest as security for a mortgage.

In response to the Commonwealth's and COAG's Aboriginal land tenure reform agenda of the last decade, only Queensland has enacted specific legislation that enables Aboriginal and Torres Strait Islander lands to be made freehold land and then traded in the open market. South Australia, by contrast, has recently endowed its existing Aboriginal Lands Trust with greater statutory independence and the ability to buy additional land on the open market and to undertake economic development on Trust land for the benefit of Aboriginal people. The Trust can also dispose of Trust land by transfer or grant of fee simple, but it can only do so if it is in accordance with a resolution of both Houses of Parliament and any requirements under the NTA have been satisfied.

From the perspectives of both economic engagement and social justice, perhaps the ideal situation is a 'no' in the sale column, and a 'yes' in the leasing and mortgaging columns. This would protect the underlying tenure of Aboriginal ownership, while also allowing use of the land as equity or security for finance. Fifteen of the 23 existing statutory land rights regimes show that this is possible. However, land rights land is also subject to native title rights and interests which, as discussed above and shown in the first row of Table 16.1, do not enable sale, lease or mortgage.

Table 16.1 Summary of dealing provisions in the NTA and the statutory Aboriginal and Torres Strait Islander land rights regimes around Australia (as at November 2014)

	Statute	Landowner	Form of Title	Is private sale permitted?	Is Leasing or subleasing permitted?	Is Mortgaging permitted?
CTH	*Native Title Act 1993* (Cth)	Common law holders as determined by the Federal Court of Australia, held in trust by a registered native title body corporate	Recognition of the communal, group or individual rights and interests in accordance with s.223 of the NTA.	No	No	No
ACT	*Aboriginal Land Grant (Jervis Bay Territory) Act 1986* (Cth)	Community Council	Vested in the Council & compulsory lease back to Commonwealth as National Park	No	Yes	Yes
NSW	*Aboriginal Land Rights Act 1983* (NSW)	Local Aboriginal Land Councils or NSW Aboriginal Land Council (NSWALC)	Freehold (except in Western Division – leasehold)	Yes, subject to NSWALC approval	Yes subject to NSWALC approval	Yes subject to NSWALC approval
NSW	*National Parks and Wildlife Act 1974* (NSW)	Local Aboriginal Land Councils or NSW Aboriginal Land Council (NSWALC)	Freehold & compulsory lease to NSW Govt as National Park	No	No	No
NT	*Aboriginal Land Rights (Northern Territory) Act 1976* (Cth)	Aboriginal Land Trusts-consisting of Aboriginal people resident in the regional Land Council area	Inalienable freehold title	No	Yes of leasehold interest	Yes of leasehold interest
NT	*Pastoral Land Act 1992* (NT)	Aboriginal Association	Restricted freehold	No	Yes, with restrictions	Yes, with restrictions

	Statute	Landowner	Form of Title	Is private sale permitted?	Is Leasing or subleasing permitted?	Is Mortgaging permitted?
QLD	Aboriginal and Torres Strait Islander Land (Providing Freehold) Act 2014 (Qld)	Specified Aboriginal or Torres Strait Islander people	Freehold	Yes, but subject to conditions	Yes	Yes
QLD	Aboriginal Land Act 1991 (Qld)	RNTBCs, Trustees or Aboriginal people	Inalienable freehold or leasehold	No	Yes	No
QLD	Torres Strait Islander Land Act 1991 (Qld)	RNTBCs, Trustees or Torres Strait Islander people	Inalienable freehold or leasehold	No	Yes	No
QLD	Aborigines and Torres Strait Islanders (Land Holding) Act 1985 (Qld)	Specified Aboriginal or Torres Strait Islander people	Leasehold	Transferable, but not sale	Yes	Yes, subject to conditions
QLD	Land Act 1994 (Qld)	Trustee	Reserve or fee simple in trust	No	Yes	No
SA	Aboriginal Lands Trust Act 2014 (SA)	Aboriginal Lands Trust	Freehold or leasehold or any other titles it purchases	Yes, but must have support of Parliament	Yes, subject to conditions	Yes, subject to conditions
SA	Anangu Pitjantjatjara Yankunytjatjara Land Rights Act 1981 (SA)	Anangu Pitjantjatjara body corporate representing all TOs	Inalienable freehold – vested in perpetuity	No	Yes, subject to conditions	No
SA	Maralinga Tjarutja Land Rights Act 1984 (SA)	Maralinga Tjarutja body corporate representing all TOs	Inalienable freehold – vested in perpetuity	No	Yes, subject to conditions	No
TAS	Aboriginal Land Rights Act 1995 (Tas)	State-wide Aboriginal Land Council	Inalienable freehold – vested in perpetuity	No	Yes	Yes on lease or licence
VIC	Aboriginal Lands Act 1970 (Vic)	Aboriginal Trust	Inalienable Freehold – vested in perpetuity	No	Yes, subject to conditions	Yes

	Statute	Landowner	Form of Title	Is private sale permitted?	Is Leasing or subleasing permitted?	Is Mortgaging permitted?
VIC	*Aboriginal Lands (Aborigines' Advancement League) (Watt Street, Northcote) Act 1982 (Vic)*	Aborigines Advancement League Inc.	Crown grant, unspecified	No	Yes	Yes
VIC	*Aboriginal Lands Act 1991 (Vic)*	Specified Aboriginal corporations	Conditional fee simple	No	No	No
VIC	*Aboriginal Land (Lake Condah and Framlingham Forest) Act 1987 (Cth) (at the request of the Vic G't)*	Specified Aboriginal corporations	Freehold	No	Yes	Yes
VIC	*Aboriginal Land (Northcote Land) Act 1989 (Vic)*	Aborigines Advancement League Inc.	Conditional freehold	No	Yes	Yes
VIC	*Traditional Owner Settlement Act 2010 (Vic)*	Traditional Owner groups	Inalienable fee simple	No	No	No
WA	*Aboriginal Affairs Planning Authority Act 1972 (WA)*	Aboriginal Lands Trust	Crown Reserve for the 'use and benefit of Aboriginal inhabitants'.	No	Yes, subject to conditions	Yes, subject to conditions
WA	*Land Administration Act 1997 (WA)*	Aboriginal person or approved Aboriginal corporation	Conditional freehold or lease. & Crown reserves for the 'use and benefit of Aboriginal inhabitants'.	No	Yes, subject to conditions	Yes, subject to conditions

Source: Author's research

What land tenure reforms are needed?

I have long stated that I believe there are two elements to *Mabo (No. 2)* (Wensing 1999). In substance, the judgement recognised that Eddie Mabo and others on behalf of the Meriam People of the Murray Islands in the Torres Strait had prior and continuing occupation and ownership of the Murray Islands. In essence, the judgement found that Aboriginal and Torres Strait Islander law and culture is recognised by the common law of Australia. As a consequence, there are now effectively two systems of land law in Australia, one deriving from colonisation, the other from prior traditional ownership of Australia by Aboriginal and Torres Strait Islander people. These conceptions flag some critical changes to the way we need to think about land tenure.

Aboriginal people have never ceded their lands and Australia has never dealt fairly with the Aboriginal and Torres Strait Islander people of Australia about the loss of their lands. We can no longer deny that at the root of all property in land for settler Australians were acts of dispossession of Aboriginal people, acts of theft for which no one has ever been held responsible (Kerruish & Purdy 1998). This denial of the existence of prior Aboriginal ownership of Australia has become an international embarrassment. It is no longer tolerable that we continue constructing legal orthodoxies that suit the settler state. For example, the provisions in the NTA declaring that the extinguishment of native title has occurred (partly or wholly) will not make the laws and customs of Aboriginal and Torres Strait Islander people disappear.

As Robert French and Graeme Neate have both stated, the term 'extinguishment' is just a metaphor for placing limits upon the extent to which recognition will be accorded to Aboriginal and Torres Strait Islander peoples under Australian law (French J in *The Lardil* case 2001; Neate 2002: 118). Regardless of judicial or legislative status, Aboriginal and Torres Strait Islander people will always retain their special relationship with and responsibility for land and sea country (Rose 1996; Dodson 1998: 209).

Given the many constraints around native title, it is reasonable to ask whether native title holders are feeling somewhat frustrated or disillusioned because they are not able to use their property rights to engage in the modern economy on their terms when opportunities arise and without having to surrender and permanently extinguish their hard won native title rights and interests. Smith (2001: 2) likens this to replacing 'the historical fiction of *terra nullius* with the legal fiction of extinguishment'. Little wonder that some commentators see native title as a 'dodgy conveyance' (Ring 2006).

It is time to 'puncture some legal orthodoxies' relating to property and land tenure (McHugh 2011). Let me finish with a few suggestions.

Real change has to happen inside the Crown's land tenure system. Let's turn the legal principles of property relations, inalienability and extinguishment on their proverbial heads. Let's develop a form of leasehold which will allow the native title holders to determine the terms and conditions for development on their lands so they can partake in the risks and benefits arising from land development and resource exploitation.

McAvoy (2014) believes that all Aboriginal and Torres Strait Islander people should aspire to ownership of their lands, planning control, self-determination, economic independence, and full compensation. My similar advice to native title holding groups is to make the most of any opportunity to reform state/territory land tenure systems, otherwise the opportunity will be lost for many decades and possibly generations to come. Use this opportunity to:

- make the most of being able to revive Aboriginal and Torres Strait Islander law and custom;
- take ownership of customary land in the strongest form of tenure possible;
- control uses of Aboriginal and Torres Strait Islander lands through planning regimes;
- be in control of your own future and destiny (self-determination);
- become economically independent; and
- seek full compensation for any loss, diminution or extinguishment of native title rights and interests.

Otherwise the essence of Aboriginal and Torres Strait Islander community life and culture will disappear.

I hope, like Jon Altman, I have challenged you to think differently about these important issues relating to property, inalienability, extinguishment and non-extinguishment of customary Indigenous rights to land.

References

Cases

Mabo v the State of Queensland [No. 2] (1992) 175 CLR1.

Pareroultja v Tickner (1993) 117 ALR 206.

The Lardil, Kaiadilt, Yangkaal and Gangalidda Peoples v State of Queensland (2001) FCA 414.

Reports and other documents

Altman JC (2012). People on country as alternate development. In Altman JC & Kerins S (eds), *People on country, vital landscapes, Indigenous futures*, The Federation Press, Sydney.

Altman JC (2014). The political ecology and political economy of the Indigenous titling 'revolution' in Australia. *Maori Law Review* March.

Calma T (2006). *Native Title Report 2005*, Australian Human Rights Commission, Sydney.

Dodson M (1998). *Six years of native title: extinguishment of native title*, public lecture at the University of New South Wales (UNSW), Native title: facts, fallacies and the future, University Symposium, Sydney, 30 May.

Edelmen D (2009). *Native title settlements and the meaning of the term 'Traditional Owners'*, paper presented to the National Native Title Conference, Melbourne, 4 June.

Gover K (2012). A matter of trust: what we can learn from the Treaty of Waitangi. *The Conversation* 6 February.

Kerruish V & Purdy J (1998). He 'look' honest: Big White Thief. *Law Text Culture* 4:146–71.

McAvoy T (2014). *An Assembly of First Nations and a Treaty*, paper presented to the National Native Title Conference, Coffs Harbour, NSW, 4–5 June.

McHugh PG (2011). *Aboriginal title: the modern jurisprudence of tribal land rights*, Oxford University Press, Oxford.

Neate G (2002). Indigenous land rights and native title in Queensland: a decade in review. *Griffith Law Review* 11(1):90.

Ring G (2006). Native title and the seven-year itch. *Online Opinion* 21 September.

Rose DB (1996). *Nourishing terrains: Australian Aboriginal views of landscape and wilderness*, Australian Heritage Commission, Canberra.

SGS Economics and Planning (2012). *Living on our lands*, a study undertaken for the Department of Indigenous Affairs, unpublished, Government of Western Australia, Perth.

Smith D (2001). *Valuing native title: Aboriginal, statutory and policy discourses about compensation*, Discussion Paper 222, Centre for Aboriginal Economic Policy Research, The Australian National University, Canberra.

Wensing E (1999). *Comparing native title and Anglo-Australian land law: two different timelines, two different cultures and two different laws*, Discussion Paper 25, The Australia Institute, Canberra.

Wensing E (2013). *Indigenous land tenure reforms: implications for land use planning*, paper presented to the Planning Institute of Australia National Congress, Canberra, 25–27 March.

Wensing E & Taylor J (2012). *Secure tenure for home ownership and economic development on land subject to native title*, Discussion Paper 31, Australian Institute of Aboriginal and Torres Strait Islander Studies, Canberra.

17

Exploring hybridity in housing: Lessons for appropriate tenure choices and policy

Louise Crabtree

Introduction

Housing for Aboriginal and Torres Strait Islander peoples is an ongoing focus of public policy, which recently has been oriented towards the twin objectives of transitioning community housing into arrangements mirroring public housing, and the creation of mortgagee home ownership. Within this policy landscape, this contribution reflects on research that is concerned with exploring perpetually affordable housing and community benefit in diverse contexts.

The research rests on a combination of radical democracy, complexity theory, and work on diverse or hybrid economies. These frameworks offer a coherent suite of considerations focused on diversity and contextuality with regard to community governance, knowledge, and economic articulations. These considerations are relevant as they allow for engaging with diverse community and organisational objectives and capacities within coherent guiding principles and research heuristics. Exploring these frameworks within housing provision has led to engagement with the community land trust (CLT) sectors in the United States of America and the United Kingdom. Both sectors are concerned with substantial and ongoing community input into the provision of diverse housing options that respond effectively to community need; as such, both sectors are characterised by the dual objectives of community benefit and perpetually affordable housing (Crabtree et al. 2012).

The research documented here was undertaken through the second of two consecutive projects supported by the Australian Housing and Urban Research Institute (AHURI). It focused on the relevance and articulation of housing based on community benefit and perpetual affordability for Aboriginal and Torres Strait Islander housing in New South Wales (NSW) and the Northern Territory (NT). To address the question in two differing contexts, the specific research tasks were developed according to local objectives and concerns. The projects worked with Aboriginal community organisations under endorsement of their executives, with research methods developed with organisational staff in light of executive direction. In both jurisdictions, organisational staff members were involved in and/ or responsible for discrete research tasks, enabling appropriate data collection and interpretation. The protocols, case studies, methods and outputs of the projects were guided, reviewed and endorsed by two Indigenous Advisory Groups, one per jurisdiction.

Fostering housing diversity and discussion

The iterative and contextual methods created a diverse range of research outputs alongside the core AHURI research report. In NSW these were a renewable, inheritable 99-year lease between the community organisation and individual households; financial modelling based on an indicative lease price and local household data; and a decision-making tool to help other organisations think through whether they need or want to diversify the housing options they offer their residents. These outputs were the result of the partner organisation's desire to create a housing tenure option that acted like mortgagee home ownership without exposing the household or the community organisation to unacceptable risks. Hence the price point for the lease was set according to local Aboriginal residents' incomes and capacity to sustain a moderate mortgage, and the lease had a tailor-made, two-year initial period created to act as a 'testing of the waters' for both the resident and the organisation. This allowed a period for gauging the household's financial capacity and both parties' general satisfaction with the arrangement prior to the resident seeking and committing to the financial obligation of a mortgage. The use of a long-term lease ensures the underlying title remains with the community organisation, providing a buffer against loss of the house from the community should the resident be unable to sustain their tenancy. This was based on member communities' previous experience with home ownership schemes that had led to a loss of housing stock from the sector to the open market.

In the NT the research generated a survey of Town Camp residents' experiences of governance and housing before and since the Australian Government's Northern Territory Emergency Response (the Intervention), and aspirations for the future; a housing terminology brochure for residents; schematic diagrams of Camp governance before and after the Intervention; and a legal review of the issues emerging from consideration of long-term leases between households and their relevant housing organisation, whether an Aboriginal Corporation or a Housing Association. This suite of outcomes was generated by a sense that any discussion of tenure must first pay heed to prior and ongoing community experience, governance and expertise, and be built on communities' knowledge and aspiration for the future. The subsequent survey of 150 households across the relevant communities revealed a primary desire to see community governance and control reinvigorated.

Echoing previous research such as that of Memmott et al. (2009), issues such as community, stability, dignity and autonomy featured far more prominently in Town Camp residents' comments than did expectations of capital gain through housing. However, the latter remains a core federal housing policy objective and rationale regarding Aboriginal and Torres Strait Islander home ownership (FaHCSIA 2010). The potential community impact of excising individual housing lots from community control to enable mortgagee home ownership for selected households was a frequently raised concern amongst residents, and one that was felt not to have been acknowledged or addressed by current government policy imperatives. Moreover, there was much confusion created by a policy focus on 'ownership' when many households and communities already feel a sense of ownership due to their current perpetual community leases from government, multigenerational residency, and the presence of traditional owners amongst many communities. This confusion was the trigger for the creation of a housing terminology brochure that community researchers drafted and provided to residents after the survey, to inform discussion and help residents and communities develop a position in response to policy. As with the NSW case study, the retention of underlying title by relevant Aboriginal community entities was a primary concern.

Core principles emerging from diversity

The core concerns of the two case studies were brought together to develop appropriate overarching outputs. The first of these was a decision-making tool developed initially in and for the NSW context in collaboration with the NSW partner, but also endorsed by the NT Advisory Group as of use to communities in that jurisdiction. The tool broke the decision-making process down into a series of eight questions, with each corresponding to a series of talking points, relevant extant documents, and cross-references to related sections of both the tool and the Australian Community Land Trust Manual (Crabtree et al. 2013). The steps are:

1. Who can decide?
2. Community and household aspirations
3. Is a new program needed?
4. Organisation health check
5. Current stock characteristics
6. New program elements
7. Policy, tenure and legal settings
8. Design objectives and costs.

Building on the two case studies, a tenure model was described which could capture core principles without prescribing a particular legal arrangement. The principles of the model are:

1. Retention of an interest in the property by the relevant Indigenous organisation.
2. Determination and implementation of an appropriate legal agreement according to context and aspirations.

3. Inclusion of an upfront price and ongoing administration fee set according to aspirations, capacity and objectives.
4. Articulation of repairs and maintenance, inheritance, use, etc. in the legal agreement.
5. Articulation of any equity treatment at termination of the agreement in the legal agreement.

This is a core contribution of the research, as it provides a coherent framework for enabling operational diversity; in this, tenure is the tool or outcome of a community process, not an objective in and of itself. This allows for a diversity of operational objectives and legal forms, including resident equity input if desired and appropriate. A single organisation might offer a range of options within its portfolio, addressing bottlenecks in local housing created by a lack of appropriate housing choices. Further, the same basic legal arrangement, such as a long-term lease between a community organisation and a household, could be amended to provide a diversity of arrangements with regard to equity, repairs and maintenance, and other such considerations. To help illustrate this, the research team created a tenure spectrum diagram showing the axes along which an organisation might like to arrange its operational parameters (see Fig. 17.1). As part of this, the team tried to start moving the language away from 'renting' or 'owning' as these terms are too simplistic to capture the nuance of how many communities experience their residency, and convey problematic associations regarding the underlying relationships or economic arrangements tied up in housing tenure. The terms adopted for the purpose of the diagram were non-equity, limited-equity and market-equity; however, more appropriate language might emerge over time.

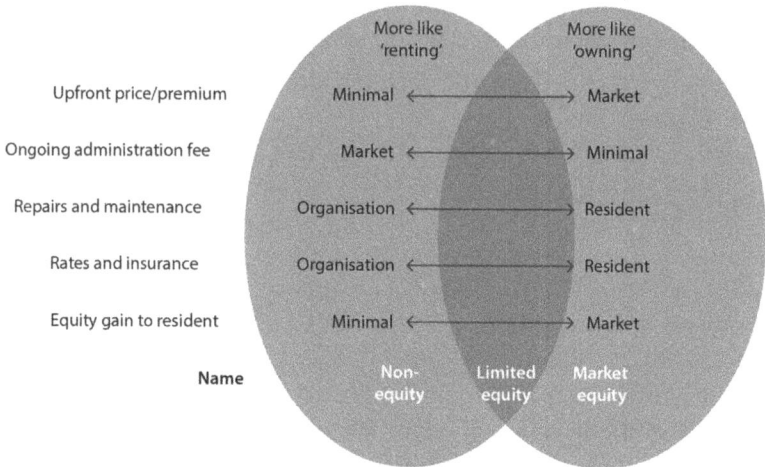

Fig. 17.1 A spectrum of housing options according to key variables
Source: Crabtree et al. (2015: 6)

Implications for process and policy

Both jurisdictions highlighted the need and relevance for accessible and streamlined processes for lodging an expression of interest or applying to buy housing, as community organisations felt that current processes and policies (where these exist) were unclear. As with the outputs described above, it was seen to be important that any such process reflect community consideration. Fagan (2012) documented an expression of interest process currently being facilitated by the government in the context of Section 19A leases amongst selected communities in the NT. That process could present a relevant example for communities wishing to lease directly to their households, and could be similarly supported by government if this was a policy imperative.

The models outlined above highlight numerous avenues for policy support, where this supports the functions and objectives of the model, rather than asserting or assuming a particular tenure form. In addition to government support of an appropriate expression of interest or application process, the model highlights the need for an accessible information service; various forms of funding; organisational training or capacity building; appropriate governance arrangements; appropriate asset management strategies; and termination of subleases to government where these are in place, or similarly the removal of any caveats found to be impediments (see Crabtree et al. 2015 for fuller discussion of policy implications). In these, the determination of 'appropriate' must occur in genuine discussion with community, rather than in deference to top-down economic efficiency measures. The Papakāinga housing toolkit developed by Tauranga City Council (2013) to facilitate Māori housing in the Auckland region is a relevant example, as it consciously highlights the strengthening of the overall efficacy of the process and outcomes though building knowledge at each step (see Fig. 17.2). This is a core lesson for policy making in this space in Australia.

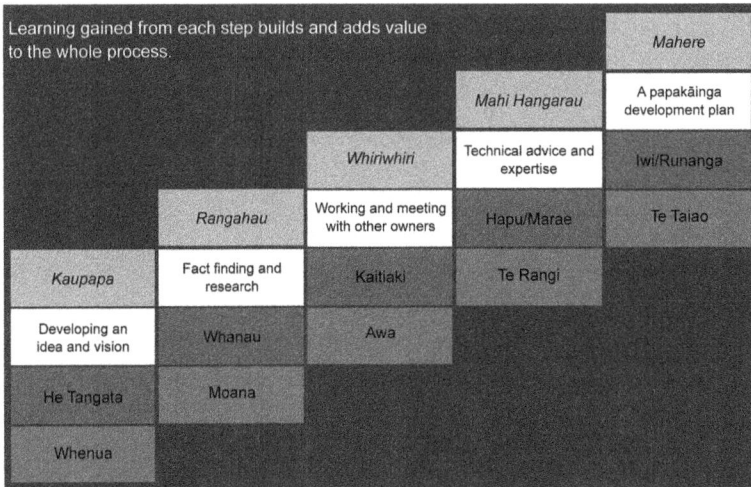

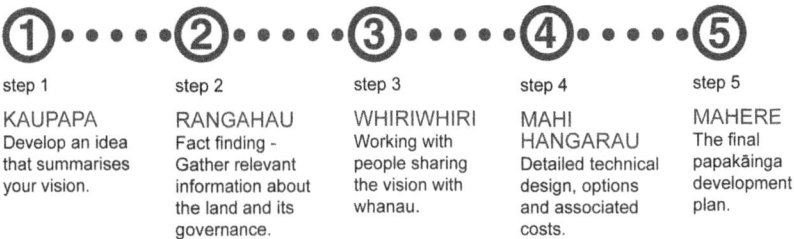

Fig. 17.2 Steps in the Tauranga Papakāinga housing toolkit

Source: Tauranga City Council (2013: 2, 4), with Joint Agency Group members: Tauranga City Council, Western Bay of Plenty District Council, Environment Bay of Plenty, Housing New Zealand Corporation, Te Puni Kōkiri, and, the Waikato Maniapoto and the Waiariki District Māori Land Courts.

The current policy landscape is dominated by the twin objectives of moving Aboriginal and Torres Strait Islander housing into line with public housing, and the promotion of mortgagee home ownership on Aboriginal and Torres Strait Islander lands. On the latter, FaHCSIA's (2010: 18) core concern was:

> How can Government achieve the right balance between facilitating home ownership for Indigenous Australians as an economic opportunity and supporting home ownership as a means to help build individual and social responsibility?

That policy question highlights two potentially troubling assumptions or expectations. First is the assumption that home ownership will lead to economic development; in the case of communities that can experience low and unstable employment levels, and that may wish to restrict the pool of eligible buyers to community members or other appropriate individuals, this seems a misguided proposition. In such situations, the potential for either capital gains through ownership and resale, or business development on the basis of securitisation would seem low, and lending against housing in such situations would seem risky. It would seem that rather than exposing households and communities to risk and possible asset loss, economic development would best be pursued through appropriate economic development, education, community development and employment strategies rather than through tenure reform. Second is the assertion of tenure reform as a disciplinary measure, implying an inherent deficit of responsibility amongst communities, requiring as its remedy the promotion of a neoliberal citizen engaged in market-based forms of housing. In such policy formulations, there is no focus on strengthening culture and community, promoting health, fostering stability, or any of the other functions of housing. Moreover, such blanket approaches allow no room for the diversity of Aboriginal and Torres Strait Islander communities' and households' objectives for housing and communities, which may or may not align with federal policy objectives.

There is significant, ironic contradiction between the policy imperatives for Aboriginal and Torres Strait Islander housing and those for the broader housing sector. In direct contrast to the Aboriginal and Torres Strait Islander housing sector, the broader affordable housing sector is witnessing policy movement *towards* community housing providers as the primary delivery mechanism. Similarly, while the Aboriginal and

Torres Strait Islander sector is subject to manoeuvres towards market-based mortgagee home ownership, the broader housing market is seeing investigation of various intermediate tenure options, in which equity and obligations are shared between the resident and either the government or a community housing provider. These models of shared equity home ownership (e.g. Regional Development Australia 2014) have the potential to provide submarket ownership opportunities, and ideally avoid the levels of mortgage stress and arrears generated overseas by predatory mortgage lending practices amongst marginal communities. Indeed, foreclosure studies of the community land trust sector in the United States of America have shown foreclosure rates below that of the open market during the mortgage crisis, while housing low- to moderate-income households (National CLT Network 2008; Misak 2009; Thaden 2010, 2011).

Perhaps the most interesting model of shared equity housing is Michael Stone's (2009) 'resident-saver' model, which is based on housing built by the government being held by a cooperative or mutual housing association. As with all cooperative housing, ownership of a share in the cooperative confers the right to reside in one of the cooperative's housing units—let's say, a house on community land. Shares carry a nominal value, say, a dollar, and the resident pays an administration fee to the cooperative to cover any ongoing costs such as maintenance. This is similar to how cooperative rental housing currently operates. The twist is that on top of the administration fee, the resident pays an additional regular amount which is deposited in an affiliated investment vehicle, such that the total of this and the administration fee is no more than 30 per cent of the gross household income. If and when the resident decides to leave, their equity return is the return on that investment (see Fig. 17.3).

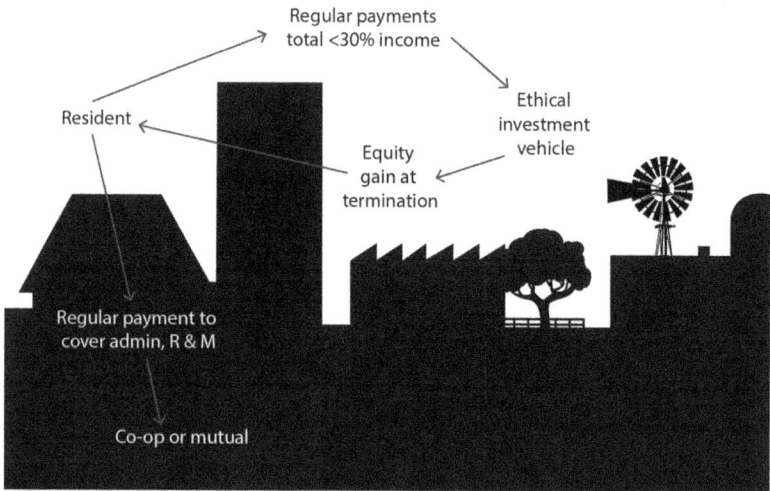

Fig. 17.3 Author's schematic of Stone's (2009) 'resident-saver' model
Source: Author

This might be a highly appropriate model for Aboriginal and Torres Strait Islander communities, as it dislocates any equity investment and housing security from each other, and does not demand equity investment to secure long-term tenure; rather investment is an option for households if and as they have capacity. This creates an avenue for equity to be directed into appropriate community enterprises, which can operate at any scale. Further, the existence of a cooperative or mutual means that the resident's right to—and eligibility for—housing is not tied to an individual home, but rather to a unit within the organisation's stock, which can change. As allocations within the organisation's stock are made by the organisation, current mismatches between community housing allocation protocols and government allocation processes can be ameliorated, or hopefully avoided altogether. While currently a hypothetical model, this might be worth consideration for communities, and by policymakers with regard to the development of appropriate support mechanisms.

There are already innovative housing and investment activities emerging, such as the Kariyarra Mugarinya Joint Venture aiming to make housing available to resources companies through long-term leases, and channel the income to the development of affordable housing for community members (YMAC 2011, Massey 2012). There are also communities developing rent-to-buy schemes. However without appropriate controls, those might not provide the ongoing community role that many communities wish to see, and may ultimately lead to assets and land being lost from community or broader Aboriginal and Torres Strait Islander ownership. Given there is existing interest in diversifying tenure and enabling hybrid forms to underpin appropriate community stability and development, it would seem timely to explore and explain the mechanisms that can be developed to do so.

Reflections: Recognising and enabling hybridity

At a more conceptual level, models such as Stone's are interesting, as they start to identify and unpack the social and economic functions of housing tenure, and separate and allocate these amongst the multiple stakeholders involved in the creation and enactment of property. These multiple parties are hidden in dominant models of tenure, which default to either a singular owner, a precarious private renter, or a dysfunctional tenant of the state. All of these are simplistic erasures of the vast socioeconomic arrangements that make property comprehensible, or tenure possible. Erasing or denying diversity severely limits the options available or the relationships that can be articulated through tenure. Engaging with the relationality of property and fostering subsequent diversity in tenure raises the question of how this can be enabled by an appropriate, supportive policy framework. This requires a focus on principles rather than forms which, while requiring an awareness of and sensitivity to nuance, is possible. Such conceptualisations of tenure resonate with Altman's (2007, 2008, 2009) focus on hybridity, as they focus on models discussed elsewhere in the housing literature as 'intermediate' tenures (e.g. Whitehead & Monk 2011), that are seen to lie between owning and renting. Fig. 17.4 provides a possible reading of the intermediate tenure space.

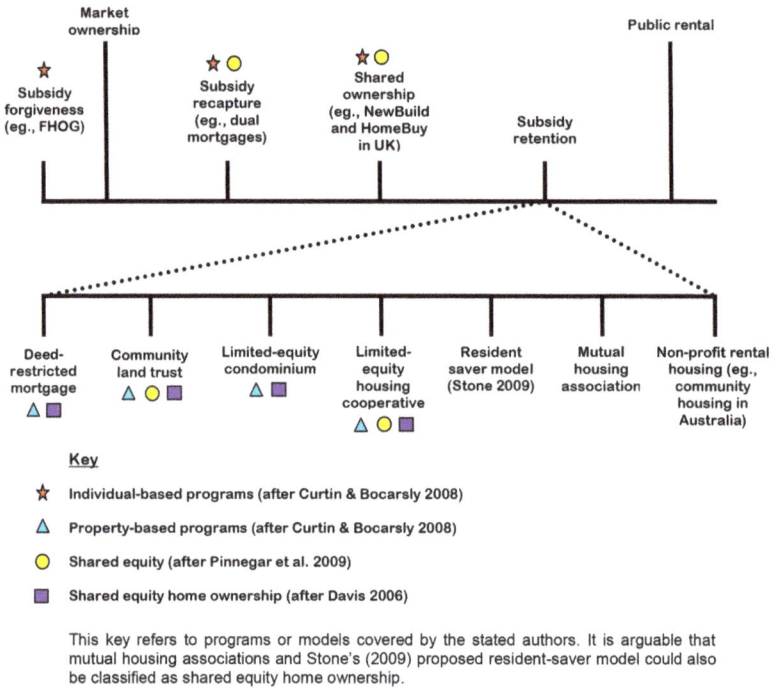

Fig. 17.4 Spectrum of housing tenure models across the US, UK and Australia

Source: Crabtree et al. (2012)

Further, much recent work in legal geography is revealing and exploring the actual complexity of property, highlighting the critical relevance of this in work to appropriately identify, recognise, and empower First Nations' property relations (e.g. Blomley 2004, 2013, 2014). This can be seen as the translation of concerns for difference-based policy (e.g. Sanders 2010, Crabtree 2014), flexibility and self-determination (e.g. Altman et al. 2005) into legal property articulations. This has the potential to create tenures that reflect diverse community and household aspirations, which may or may not align with extant tenure forms. However, the point is not the resultant tenure form, but the deployment of an understanding of property as an articulation of diverse and hybrid social and material relations. Focusing on the relationality of property in such ways has the potential not only to enable diverse, appropriate tenures for Aboriginal and Torres Strait

Islander communities, but also to develop tenure diversity across the broader housing system, which can speak to ongoing struggles for affordable and appropriate housing (Crabtree et al. 2012).

References

Altman JC (2007). In the name of the market? In Altman JC & Hinkson M (eds), *Coercive reconciliation: stabilise, normalise, exit Aboriginal Australia*, Arena Publications Association, Melbourne.

Altman JC (2008). *Submission to the Northern Territory Emergency Response Review*, Topical Issue 10, Centre for Aboriginal Economic Policy Research, The Australian National University, Canberra.

Altman JC (2009). *Beyond closing the gap: valuing diversity in Indigenous Australia*, Working Paper 54, Centre for Aboriginal Economic Policy Research, The Australian National University, Canberra.

Altman JC, Gray MC & Levitus R (2005). *Policy issues for the Community Development Employment Projects scheme in rural and remote Australia*, Discussion Paper 271, Centre for Aboriginal Economic Policy Research, The Australian National University, Canberra.

Blomley N (2004). *Unsettling the city: urban land and the politics of property*, Routledge, New York.

Blomley N (2013). Performing property: making the world. *Canadian Journal of Law and Jurisprudence* XXVI(I):23–48.

Blomley N (2014). The ties that blind: making fee simple in the British Columbia treaty process. *Transactions of the Institute of British Geographers* 40(2):168–79.

Crabtree L. (2014). Community land trusts and Indigenous housing in Australia: exploring difference-based policy and appropriate housing, *Housing Studies* 29(6):743–59.

Crabtree L, Blunden H, Phibbs P, Sappideen C, Mortimer D, Shahib-Smith A & Chung L (2013). *The Australian community land trust manual*, University of Western Sydney, Sydney.

Crabtree L, Phibbs P, Milligan V & Blunden H (2012). Principles and practices of an affordable housing community land trust model, Research Paper, Australian Housing and Urban Research Institute, Melbourne.

Crabtree L, Moore N, Phibbs P, Blunden H & Sappideen C (2015). *Community land trusts and Indigenous communities: from strategies to outcomes*, Final Report No. 239, Australian Housing and Urban Research Institute, Melbourne.

Fagan M (2012). *Towards privately financed property on Indigenous land in the Northern Territory*, Final report of the Access to Finance on Indigenous land in the Northern Territory Project, prepared for the Department of Business, Northern Territory Government, Darwin.

FaHCSIA (Department of Families, Housing, Community Services and Indigenous Affairs) (2010). *Indigenous home ownership issues paper*, FaHCSIA, Canberra.

Massey A (2012). Joint venture aims to bring homes to market. *North West Telegraph* 12 December.

Memmott P, Moran M, Birdsall-Jones C, Fantin S, Kreutz A, Godwin J, Burgess A, Thomson L, & Sheppard L (2009). *Indigenous home-ownership on communal title lands*, AHURI Final Report No. 139, Australian Housing and Urban Research Institute, Melbourne.

Misak M (2009). *National Community Land Trust Network 2008 foreclosure survey: report October 26, 2009*, National Community Land Trust Network, Portland OR.

National CLT Network (2008). *2007 CLT Network foreclosure survey*, National Community Land Trust Network, Portland OR.

Regional Development Australia (2014). *Doors to ownership: a business case and guidelines for a shared homeownership scheme with NSW community housing associations*, Regional Development Australia, Sydney.

Sanders W (2010). Ideology, evidence and competing principles in Australian Indigenous affairs: from Brough to Rudd via Pearson and the NTER. *Australian Journal of Social Issues* 45(3):307–31.

Stone M (2009). *Housing and the financial crisis*, paper presented to National Housing Researchers' Conference, Sydney, August 7–9.

Tauranga City Council (2013). *Te Keteparaha Mo Nga Papakāinga. Māori Housing Toolkit*, Tauranga City Council, Tauranga NZ.

Thaden E (2010). *Outperforming the market: making sense of the low rates of delinquencies and foreclosures in community land trusts*, National Community Land Trust Network, Portland OR.

Thaden E (2011). *Stable home ownership in a turbulent economy: delinquencies and foreclosures remain low in community land trusts*, Lincoln Institute of Land Policy, Cambridge.

Whitehead C & Monk S (2011). Affordable home ownership after the crisis: England as a demonstration project. *International Journal of Housing Markets and Analysis* 4(4):326–40.

YMAC (2011). *Kariyarra Joint Venture Corporation in land development deal*, YMAC Blog, July 28, Yamatji Marlpa Aboriginal Corporation, Perth.

The political economy of the Aboriginals Benefit Account: Relevance of the 1985 Altman review 30 years on

David P Pollack

Introduction

This paper examines the 1985 Altman review of the Aboriginals Benefit Trust Account (ABTA) and evaluates the relevance of key recommendations and findings 30 years on.[1] It focuses on three key issues raised in the review:

- Are Aboriginals Benefit Account (ABA) payments public moneys or Aboriginal private moneys?[2]
- Should Mining Withholding Tax (MWT) be levied on ABA payments?
- Should the ABA be an autonomous statutory body?

---

1   In 1999 the Aboriginals Benefit Trust Account (ABTA) was renamed the Aboriginals Benefit Account (ABA).

2   The Act specified 'payments' from the ABA. Many authors use different terms such as 'ABA moneys' and 'ABA grants' when referring to the variety of types of payments that originate from the account.

I will argue that these questions are as relevant today as they were in 1985, noting that the current ABA has many ambiguous and problematic policy legacies but also the potential to be an important player in Northern Territory Aboriginal development. While the policy of self-management is now passed, the concept of converting the current ABA to a statutory authority is worthy of fresh consideration in the context of more recent policy developments, significant increases in ABA income, and other changing circumstances.

Background

The idea of paying royalties to Aboriginal people affected by mining has a long history in the Northern Territory. In the 1950s, the then Minister for Territories, Paul Hasluck, oversaw the drafting of an ordinance to permit mining on Aboriginal reserves with royalties being paid into an Aborigines Benefits Trust Fund (ABTF) (see Altman (1983) for an analysis of this regime).

The *Aboriginal Land Rights (Northern Territory) Act 1976* (Cwlth) (ALRA) established the ABTA to replace the ABTF and continued the practice of directing mining royalties from Aboriginal land to Aboriginal people and their institutions, although the method of payment was somewhat different. Instead of miners paying royalties direct to the ABTA, the royalties were directed to the Commonwealth and Northern Territory governments. Uranium royalties were paid to the Commonwealth while all other types of mineral royalties were paid to the new Northern Territory Government established in 1978. The Commonwealth would then calculate the total payments to both governments and pay an equivalent amount into the ABTA. Thus was created the notion of 'mining royalty equivalents' (MREs).

Through this arrangement the Commonwealth was maintaining the practice of paying mining royalties from Aboriginal land to Aboriginal people and also giving the fledging self-governing Northern Territory a source of revenue from mining similar to that in the states. The cost of the arrangement was born entirely by the Commonwealth, with payments to the ABTA coming from the Consolidated Revenue Fund (CRF). This arrangement was maintained in 1997 when the Aboriginals Benefit Trust Account was renamed the Aboriginals Benefit Reserve and in 1999 when it became the ABA. The regime continues to the current day despite changes by various governments to broader financial management aspects of policy.

The ALRA financial framework and the 1985 Altman review

Jon Altman was engaged by the Department of Aboriginal Affairs (DAA) in 1984 to undertake a review of the then ABTA and related financial matters under ALRA.[3] The review was undertaken with the assistance of a working party which consisted of representatives from the Central and Northern Land Councils, the DAA, and the ABTA Advisory Committee (Altman 1985: xi). The ALRA financial framework under review had three key institutions, the Land Councils, Royalty Associations and the ABTA, plus a corresponding 40/30/30 formula for disbursement of MREs.

The Northern and Central Land Councils were established in 1973. In 1976 under ALRA they were given statutory responsibilities to represent and consult with Aboriginal traditional owners on land claims, land management and all related land matters. Under subsection 64(1) of ALRA, the Land Councils were to receive 40 per cent of MREs for the administration of these statutory responsibilities. The possibility of supplementary payments of MREs to Land Councils was contemplated under subsection 64(7) and ultimate approval of Land Council budgets lay with the Commonwealth Minister under section 34. In 1978, the Tiwi Land Council was established, creating a third entity of this type by the time of the Altman review.

The second type of key institution was Aboriginal bodies known as Royalty Associations, comprising traditional owners and residents of areas affected by mining. These organisations would receive 30 per cent of MREs pursuant to subsection 63(3) as some indeterminate form of compensation or recompense for mining occurring on Aboriginal land in their geographic vicinity.

---

3   The context of the ABTA review was a recommendation from Justice Toohey's *Seven Years On* report of the ALRA in 1983. Toohey recommended a special review of the financial aspects of the ALRA be established. The review commenced in 1984 and the recommendations were published in 1985.

The third institution of the ALRA financial framework was the ABTA and the associated ABTA Advisory Committee established under section 65. While all MREs would pass through the ABTA on their way to the Land Councils and Royalty Associations, it was the final 30 per cent of MREs over which this Committee had an advisory role to the Minister for Aboriginal Affairs. Under subsection 64(4) this last 30 per cent could be spent on grants for the 'benefit of Aboriginal people living in the Northern Territory', but it could also be applied to supplement the budgets of Land Councils, to meet the running costs of the ABTA, or be invested. The Advisory Committee at the time of the Altman review consisted of seven Aboriginal Territorians. There was a ministerially appointed Chairperson, three members nominated by the Northern Land Council, two by the Central Land Council, and one by the Tiwi Land Council.

The primary task of the 1985 Altman review was to report against two broad terms of reference:

1. Conduct a general review of the role, structure, functions and operations of the ABTA and the Trust Advisory Committee.
2. Examine the nature and extent of the benefits derived by Aboriginal groups and communities from subsection 64(4) payments to date.

There were 14 sub-points for consideration under the first term of reference. These included the status of the ABTA under the Audit Act, policies and guidelines for payments (grants) from the ABTA under subsection 64(4) and their relationship to payments from other grant providers, the role and composition of the Advisory Committee, and the administrative structure of the ABA. One term of reference specifically asked whether the ALRA should be amended to guarantee that 'no less than 30 per cent' of MREs was used for payments under subsection 64(4) (Altman 1985: v–vi).

The Altman review made over 70 recommendations and other findings in response to these terms of reference. Over 40 per cent of the recommendations were implemented or partly implemented, in the years following the review. Examples of recommendations implemented included:

- an increase in size of the ABTA Committee;
- committee representation based on population;

- development of ABTA procedures and management documentation;
- improved investment management;
- a separate annual report for the ABTA;
- annual reports for the Land Councils; and
- changes to the administration and staffing of the ABTA.

The rest of this paper focuses on recommendations which were not implemented and still have relevance today. These relate to whether MREs are 'public' or 'Aboriginal moneys', the related issue of levying a withholding tax on MREs, and the proposal for an autonomous ABTA.

Public or Aboriginal moneys?

In the first chapter of the review report, Altman raised the important issue of whether MREs are public or Aboriginal moneys. This is a fundamental issue for administration and accountability regimes. If the MREs are Aboriginal moneys, then a case can be made for Aboriginal organisations to administer their disbursement. If they are public moneys, then they should be controlled by officers of the Australian Public Service and have accountability measures in line with other mainstream Commonwealth grants (Altman 1985: 11).

Altman (1985: 8) noted that the one important principle that divided the working party during the review was the nature of the MRE payments to the ABTA. All representatives of Aboriginal organisations held the view that MREs were Aboriginal moneys. The bureaucratic view expressed by DAA members was that MREs are public moneys.

Altman (1985: 9) explains the Aboriginal moneys position:

> In the letters patent that established the Aboriginal Land Rights Commission in 1973, the Federal Government instructed Justice Woodward to vest full land and mineral rights to the Aboriginal inhabitants of the NT. However, Woodward recommended that ownership of minerals and petroleum on Aboriginal lands should remain the property of the Crown. Woodward did recommend that Aboriginal interests should have full rights to royalties on Aboriginal land. This compromise has been widely interpreted by Aboriginal organisations and individuals in the NT to mean that while the minerals do not belong to Aboriginal interests, the royalties do. Prior to the granting of land rights, royalties raised on Aboriginal reserves

were transferred to Aboriginal interests, yet the land was Crown land. After the granting of land rights, it is not surprising that Aboriginal control of these moneys was assumed to have increased—after all, they are now levied on Aboriginal land.

On the other hand, DAA officers in the working party pointed to the fact that the ABTA has its origins in the CRF (Altman 1985: 11). As such the moneys are public, despite the fact that they are raised on Aboriginal land. Further, the division and payment of these MREs is at the discretion of the Minister and as public monies it is a requirement that these be controlled by officers of the Australian Public Service.

In his review, Altman (1985: 11) noted the variable accountability regimes applying to the Land Councils and Royalty Associations from the ABTA payments. Land Council moneys were treated as public moneys, while Royalty Association were effectively treated as private moneys. Payments under subsection 64(4) seemed to be treated somewhere in the middle, with lots of accountability requirements during the application process, but somewhat relaxed acquittal procedures after grants had been made (Altman 1985: 12, 164). The Altman review (1985: 29, 187) was strongly of the view that the ALRA should be amended to guarantee that 'at least 30 per cent' of MREs are paid out as subsection 64(4) grants and that supplementary funding for Land Councils, if needed, come from outside the ABTA.

The 1985 Altman review acknowledges that in law ABTA moneys are public, but also demonstrates how some elements of disbursements have lesser accountability requirements acknowledging some moral and practical concessions towards these being private Aboriginal moneys. In later writings (e.g. Altman & Pollack 1998, 1999; Altman 1999), Altman remains equivocal on these issues and hence open to the view that ABTA moneys are less than fully public.

Mining Withholding Tax critique

The Review working party was unanimous in its belief that the levying of MWT on MREs was iniquitous (Altman 1985: 229).

Altman (1985: 229) recounts amendment of the *Income Tax Assessment Act 1936* (Cwlth) (ITA Act) in 1979 'to include special provisions for taxation of payments made in respect of mining operations on

Aboriginal land'. The rate of taxation was specified in the *Income Tax (Mining Withholding Tax) Act 1979* (Cwlth) passed at the same time.[4] Section 23AE of the ITA Act provided that the assessable income of Aboriginal people and Aboriginal organisations shall not include amounts received as mining payments as these payments would be taxed under the MWT. In short, the MWT is levied at source and is considered a final tax.

Altman (1985: 229–34) described the MWT as confused and unclear and as having inequities in its application:

- ABTA moneys are subject to tax but ABTF moneys are not;
- MREs are subject to MWT but negotiated royalties are not;
- grants from the ABTA are taxed but grants made by government agencies are not;
- Land Councils are taxed but other Commonwealth statutory authorities are not;
- uranium royalties paid to Aboriginal interests are taxed while uranium payments to the Northern Territory government are not.

Altman (1985: 233) noted that the withholding tax on MREs fuelled the debate about 'whether these moneys are public or Aboriginal'. It seemed that for 'financial accountability purposes', these moneys were 'regarded by the Commonwealth as public'; 'but for taxation purposes they are regarded as Aboriginal'. He also noted that there was 'limited scope' for MREs to 'be paid to individuals', as this could occur primarily from the 30 per cent directed through Royalty Associations to people in areas directly affected by mining (Altman 1985: 231). He concluded that this limited amount of MREs 'paid to individuals' should attract income tax and that 'wider Aboriginal interests' were 'paying an enormous price' for the assumption that these individual recipients of MREs might not lodge tax returns (Altman 1985: 233).

Subsequent reviews of and commentaries on this tax regime have also been critical. Crough (1989) regarded it as discriminatory and an unnecessary and inequitable impost. Reeves (1998: 364) advocated

---

4   In 1978 the then treasurer John Howard introduced a Mining Withholding Tax (MWT) of 6 per cent on all payments out of the ABA by amending the *Income Tax Assessment Act 1936* (Cwlth). Over time the rate has been reduced to 4 per cent.

removal of any possibility of individual payments from MREs, which would mean that the justification for the withholding tax would then disappear.

Martin and Tran-Nam (2012) saw the MWT as inequitable and demonstrated that some Aboriginal people or organisations receiving MREs may be subject to double taxing. They regarded the MWT as simple but as imposing many inequities. Further, they argued that the MWT is potentially inconsistent with more recent income tax principles and other income tax laws.

An autonomous ABA?

Altman (1985: xii) distinguished between the 'clearing house' functions of the ABTA in which money was handed on to Land Councils and Royalty Associations and the discretionary 'granting operations' under subsection 64(4). Focusing on the latter, the Altman review envisaged the possibility of a new autonomous ABTA established as a statutory authority. Altman stated that 'there was general agreement among the working party that the ABTA should become autonomous from the DAA and that as a longer term objective, complete Aboriginal control of the ABTA is essential' (Altman 1985: xi). However, the 1985 Altman review also acknowledged 'current realities' which made it 'less than fair to suddenly pass all responsibilities to ... an all-Aboriginal committee' (Altman 1985: xi).

In 1998 the Reeves Review also picked up on the idea of an autonomous ABTA but did so in the context of a proposal to break up the Central and Northern Land Councils and create 18 regional land councils. Reeves proposed a Northern Territory Aboriginal Council (NTAC) which would fund the regional councils. The role of the ABTA was to be absorbed into the NTAC including its grant functions. The NTAC would also absorb the Indigenous programs run in the Territory by the Commonwealth and Northern Territory governments, and NTAC would be the only Native Title Representative Body in the Territory. Altman (1999) was critical of this model, as too were others and a subsequent parliamentary committee (Altman & Pollack 1999: 11). None of these proposals were taken up by the Commonwealth.

While the Reeves Review was the last major review of the ALRA, and the last to propose an autonomous body, the idea of an autonomous self-managing ABA has continually been the aspiration of current and past ABA Advisory Committees.

Changes since the 1985 review

There have been many changes over the last 30 years that have impacted or potentially impacted on ABA policy and operations. These include a change from policies of Indigenous self-management and self-determination to the more recent neoliberal and neopaternal policy approach. Despite these significant shifts in policy orientation, there has been little change to ABA policy and operations.

Some significant amendments to the ALRA were made in 2006 and 2007, which had some impact on the ABA financial framework: one was the repeal of subsection 64(1), meaning that Land Councils would no longer be allocated 40 per cent of MREs. Instead, the allocation was to be based on ministerial discretion, thus ending the original 40/30/30 regime for MREs. Another amendment was the introduction of a new leasing regime and the Executive Director of Township Leasing. This leasing scheme was designed to be self-financing, with costs paid from the ABA (including acquisition and administration costs) (Terrill 2010a, 2010b).

These amendments demonstrate the position of more recent governments on the ABA, reaffirming the official legal position that MREs are public moneys. Rather than moving towards the ABA being a more autonomous entity managing Aboriginal moneys within the ALRA framework, the Commonwealth is in fact exercising more control over the purse strings and functions of the ABA in the Northern Territory.

Conclusion

The payment of mining royalties and their equivalents to Aboriginal people and their institutions in the Northern Territory has a long history and has proved to be a resilient policy. Despite new directions in Indigenous Affairs, the MRE regime has been sustained for almost 40 years with only incremental change.

The relevance of the Altman review's recommendations after 30 years is clear. Ambiguities and shortcomings identified in the 1985 review remain today:

- the issue of whether ABA moneys are public or Aboriginal remains unresolved; and
- the Mining Withholding Tax remains an inequitable tax but continues to be levied on MREs.

As Altman and Pollack (1999: 18) note, these issues have bedevilled policymakers and reviewers since the enactment of the ALRA in 1976. A review of the current ABA would only re-emphasise the findings of the Altman review 30 years ago and raise questions as to why there has not been change to these policy shortcomings.

There is considerable merit in re-examining the proposal for an autonomous statutory ABA. The size of the ABA reserve was $402,129,000 at 30 June 2013.[5] This means that a self-managing, self-funded Aboriginal institution based on the reserve could be an important player in Aboriginal development in the Northern Territory. Should such an autonomous body be established, the existing ALRA legislation could be used to clarify the intent of the application of MREs and ensure that they are clearly directed to benefits for Aboriginal Territorians.

References

Altman JC (1983). *Aborigines and mining royalties in the Northern Territory*, Australian Institute of Aboriginal Studies, Canberra.

---

5   In 2011–12 the account had an investment portfolio of $418,994,000.

Altman JC (1985). *Report on the review of the Aboriginals Benefit Trust Account (and related financial matters) in the Northern Territory land rights legislation*, Australian Government Publishing Service, Canberra.

Altman JC (1999). The proposed restructure of the financial framework of the Land Rights Act: a critique of Reeves. In Altman JC, Morphy F & Rowse T (eds), *Land rights at risk? Evaluations of the Reeves Report*, CAEPR Research Monograph No. 14, Centre for Aboriginal Economic Policy Research, The Australian National University, Canberra.

Altman JC & Pollack DP (1998). *Financial aspects of Aboriginal land rights in the Northern Territory*, Discussion Paper 168, Centre for Aboriginal Economic Policy Research, The Australian National University, Canberra.

Altman JC & Pollack D (1999). *Reforming the Northern Territory Land Rights Act's financial framework: a more logical and more workable model*, Working Paper 5, Centre for Aboriginal Economic Policy Research, The Australian National University, Canberra.

Crough G (1989). *Report on the Aboriginals Benefit Trust Account*, unpublished report prepared for the Minister for Aboriginal Affairs, Economic and Social Policy Unit, University of Sydney, Sydney.

Martin F & Tran-Nam B (2012). The Mining Withholding Tax under Division 11C of the Income Tax Assessment Act 1936: it may be simple but is it equitable? *Australian Tax Forum* 27(1):149–74.

Reeves J (1998). *Building on land rights for the next generation: the review of the Aboriginal Land Rights (Northern Territory) Act 1976*, 2nd edn, Aboriginal and Torres Strait Islander Commission, Canberra.

Terrill L (2010a). Indigenous land reform: an economic or bureaucratic reform? *Indigenous Law Bulletin* 7(17):3–7.

Terrill L (2010b). *Indigenous Land Reform: what is the real aim of reforms?*, paper delivered at the National Native Title Conference, 7 September.

19

The work of rights: The nature of native title labour

Pamela McGrath

Australia's native title regime is, by any measure, a significant social phenomenon. In the two decades since the *Native Title Act 1993* (Cwlth) (NTA) was passed into law, thousands of Aboriginal and Torres Strait Islander people and their advocates have actively pursued many hundreds of native title claims; at time of writing, 243 of these had been successful (National Native Title Tribunal 2014a). Collectively, these cover more than 2 million square kilometres (25 per cent) of the total Australian land mass (National Native Title Tribunal 2014b). And yet, despite the increasing numbers of Registered Native Title Bodies Corporate (RNTBCs) established to manage native title business on behalf of rights holders, there is a remarkable lack of research into how voluntary or obligatory participation in, or exclusion from, the regime impacts the lives of both Indigenous and non-Indigenous people.[1]

---

1   At the time of writing there were 132 RNTBCs (Australian Institute of Aboriginal and Torres Strait Islander Studies 2014). As outlined by McGrath et al. (2013: 27), 'When a group of Aboriginal or Torres Strait Islander people succeed in having their native title recognised in a Federal Court determination, they are required to nominate a body corporate to hold and manage (as trustee) or manage (as agent) their native title rights and interests. These corporations are known as Prescribed Bodies Corporate (PBCs) because they have prescribed characteristics under the NTA [*Native Title Act 1993* (Cwlth)], including that they are incorporated under the *Corporations (Aboriginal and Torres Strait Islander) Act 2006* (Cwlth) (the CATSI Act). Once registered by the National Native Title Tribunal (NNTT), as required by the NTA, they are technically known as Registered Native Title Bodies Corporate (RNTBCs)'.

This paper reports on the preliminary findings of a case study that aims to address some of the deficiencies in existing accounts of the social impacts of native title, particularly in the area of labour and economic activity. The case study involved reviewing the native title activities of a Western Australian traditional owner group over a 15-year period, from around the time that their claim was first lodged in the late 1990s, to its determination 10 years later and including a five-year period of post-determination activities.

The various legal and policy assemblages of the native title regime together enable a complex and unique form of political economy that requires the labour of a wide range of specialist and non-specialist participants. There is a growing body of research about the potential or otherwise of native title agreements to improve the economic circumstances of Indigenous Australians (see for example O'Faircheallaigh 2004, 2007; Langton & Mazel 2012). But to date there has been very little attention paid to the labour implications of agreement making processes themselves, let alone any of the many other kinds of corporate activities associated with native title governance.

With the average resolution time for native title claims at one point reaching 13 years, the work of native title begins long before a determination is even made.[2] But the work of native title doesn't stop once native title has been recognised. Along with the facilitation and management of future acts, the 'core' post-determination activities of RNTBCs include basic governance and compliance activities such as convening meetings of members and directors; maintaining accounts and corporate records; managing and distributing benefits to members; consulting members on major decisions; and annual reporting of finances and membership to the Office of the Registrar of Indigenous Corporations (ORIC) (Deloitte Access Economics 2014: 75). Depending on where RNTBCs are located, they might also undertake cultural heritage and land management activities; enterprise development;

---

2   The 2014 *Social justice and native title report* provides statistics from the Federal Court of Australia that indicate a significant reduction in the median time for resolution of applications determined in 2013–14 compared to previous years, from an average of 12 years and 11 months in June 2013 to an average of two years and six months as at 30 June 2014 (Gooda 2014: 77).

service delivery; and political advocacy (Deloitte Access Economics 2014: 74). Some of these activities will be mandated by state or commonwealth legislation.

Significant to understanding the nature of the labour associated with RNTBCs is the fact that these corporations are not actually necessary to enabling the exercise of native title rights by the members of the native title group, who have already proven in court that they have their own body of laws and customs for governing rights in land. Rather, as conceptualised by Rowley (1972) and rearticulated by Levitus (2009), as Aboriginal organisations RNTBCs are a kind of carapace: 'simultaneously a transactional boundary and a point of articulation between external agencies and an Aboriginal domain' (Levitus 2009: 75). They are necessary to the effective operation of the native title system because they provide an interface for negotiation between Indigenous and non-Indigenous interests in land.

Recently there has been broad reporting of the fact that the vast majority of RNTBCs are poorly resourced to undertake the onerous work of managing and governing their native title (see Bauman et al. 2013, Deloitte Access Economics 2014). But there is little quantitative data available to illustrate the actual time and social effort such work involves. Nor are there any comprehensive ethnographic accounts of the character of native title labour and how it is being incorporated into contemporary Indigenous lifeworlds.

Working in collaboration with the Nyangumarta people of the east Pilbara through their RNTBC Nyangumarta Warrarn Aboriginal Corporation (NWAC), and the regional Native Title Representative Body (NTRB), Yamatji Marlpa Aboriginal Corporation (YMAC), this case study aims to address this gap. The preliminary findings reported here are based on data collected through an extensive review of legal and research files to capture information about the number and nature of native title related activities (e.g. meetings, surveys, field trips) and the number and identities of the individuals who participated in them over a 15-year period between 1999 and 2014. This has enabled an estimation of Nyangumarta people's investment of time on native title-related activities (measured in people days), and social effort (measured by number of external relationships).

What emerges is a picture of a complex, dynamic and outwardly focused corporate domain that requires a lot of labour, much of it unpaid. This labour simultaneously reinforces place-based social identity while increasing social visibility and engagements with Australian society more broadly, bringing people together in old ways for new purposes that are rarely intramural.

I readily admit to being a newcomer to economic anthropology and I am indebted to Jon Altman's early work on hunter-gatherer economies for helping me think through the applicability of a time allocation methodology to understanding native title work. While acknowledging the difficulties with attempting to define labour and equating 'time' with 'work effort' (Altman 1987: 72), I proceed reassured by Jon's proposition that time spent is nevertheless an important measure of labour significance (1987: 71).

The Nyangumarta people's country is located in the east Pilbara between the town of Port Hedland and the community of Bidyadanga. It brings together desert and coast, and includes the majestic Eighty Mile Beach. Nyangumarta first started organising towards recognition of their native title in the mid-1990s, but it wasn't until 11 years later in 2009 that they achieved a consent determination over 33,000 square kilometres of country. In 2012 they achieved further recognition of jointly held rights with their Karajarri neighbours over an additional 2,000 square kilometres.

Nyangumarta people have described their native title journey as *kaja karti marnti*, 'our long walk'.[3] In the words of senior woman Winne Coppin: 'It's been hard, going around talking, meeting, from the day one, start, till today [the day of their determination]' (YMAC 2010). Post-determination, the Nyangumarta group are responsible for the governance of two RNTBCs as well as a third Aboriginal corporation set up in 2003 in order to receive land previously held by the Aboriginal Lands Trust. They have initiated or been key partners in a number of community development and natural resource management projects including the Nyangumarta Ranger program, the Nyangumarta Warrarn Indigenous Protected Area, Eighty Mile Beach Marine Park, and the Kidson Track 4WD tourism route.

---

3   *Kaja Karti Marnti* is the title of a short film commissioned by YMAC in 2009 to document the long awaited Nyangumarta native title determination.

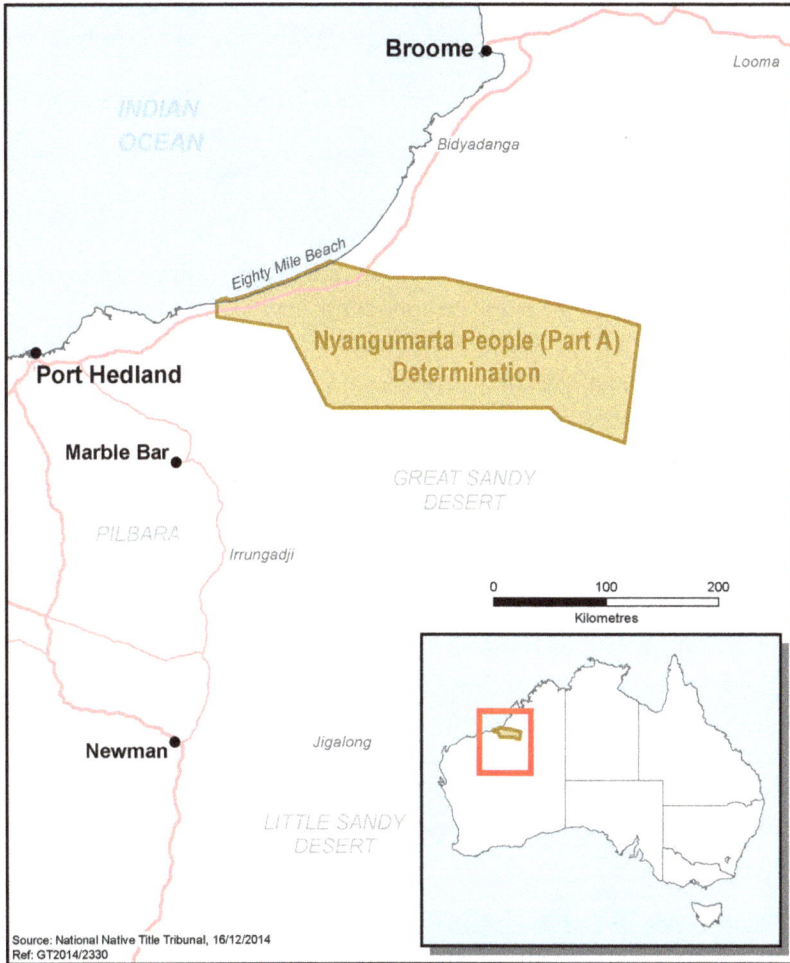

Fig. 19.1 Map of Nyangumarta native title determination area
Source: National Native Title Tribunal

When reflecting on the figures that follow, it is worth bearing in mind that the work of native title doesn't get any *less* demanding than this. The dataset does not include undocumented or informal activities (such as phone calls and emails, travel and family meetings) and it is very likely that some records relating to formal activities have been lost or overlooked.

In addition, the particular circumstances of the Nyangumarta have resulted in workloads that are comparatively much less than other native title groups in the region. Indeed, when speaking to others who have worked in the Pilbara about the possibility of collaborating with Nyangumarta on this project, the universal response was along the lines of, 'But they don't do very much!'

The reasons for this comparatively low labour burden are complex. First, during the period under review the Nyangumarta had stable leadership and experienced minimal conflict within the group. Second, their connection evidence was strong and their claim was determined via meditation rather than litigation. Third, there were only a few non-government respondents to their claim (including three pastoralists, the fishing industry and Telstra), and for most of the time they were negotiating with a relatively supportive WA State government. Fourth, even during the heady days of the Pilbara mining boom there were few future acts notified and no operational mines on Nyangumarta land. And finally, the Nyangumarta have been fortunate to have a number of long-term relationships with NTRB support staff and advisors, including a senior anthropologist who has worked with them since 2000.

All these factors reduce the amount of time people have to spend in meetings and on other activities in order to strategise, resolve disputes, educate outsiders and negotiate land access agreements, etc. Not all groups are so fortunate. On the other hand, NWAC has no independent source of income from mining agreements and relies entirely on small amounts of government funding, YMAC and volunteer labour to keep everything running.

Over the past 15 years, Nyangumarta people have spent a total of at least 2,728 days at almost 300 native title related events held over a total of 417 days (see Table 19.1). That is the equivalent of approximately seven and a half years of one person's time. Over 140 Nyangumarta people have been involved in these events, although the bulk of the work appears to have been undertaken by a core group of around 20 people, with the numbers of participants per event ranging from one to around 75.

The majority of this effort—58 per cent, or over 1,500 days' worth of Nyangumarta people's time—was spent in 146 meetings held over 175 days (see Table 19.1 and Fig. 19.2). Nyangumarta people spent a further 240 people days in 14 negotiation meetings in order to facilitate future acts. In addition to all these meetings, over these 15 years

Nyangumarta people spent a total of 122 people days taking part in 23 heritage surveys. Most future act related activities (13 meetings and 15 surveys) took place after the Nyangumarta people's native title rights were first recognised in 2009. All activities related to mediation occurred prior to their native title determination.

For the Pilbara, 23 surveys over 15 years is a very light future act load. To put it in perspective, in the 2012–13 financial year alone YMAC facilitated 787 future act notices and organised 247 heritage surveys comprising 1,428 days on behalf of the 25 or so groups the organisation represents (YMAC 2013: 42, 94). That is an average of about 12 surveys per group for a single year. YMAC has described the current level of future act heritage work as placing 'considerable pressure on the native title groups we represent, particularly Elders with extensive cultural knowledge and authority who are required to participate in multiple surveys, often for weeks at a time' (YMAC 2014: 2).

Table 19.1 Nyangumarta native title work by activity type, 1999–2014

Activity type	Total no. of events	Total days	Nyangumarta participation (days)	% of total time spent on native title activities
Meetings	146	175	1576	58%
Future act meetings	13	15	240	9%
Heritage surveys	23	66	122	5%
Native title research and legal testimony	79	110	360	13%
Mediations	23	23	336	12%
Other field research and workshops	7	28	94	3%
Total	292	417	2728	100%

Source: Author's research

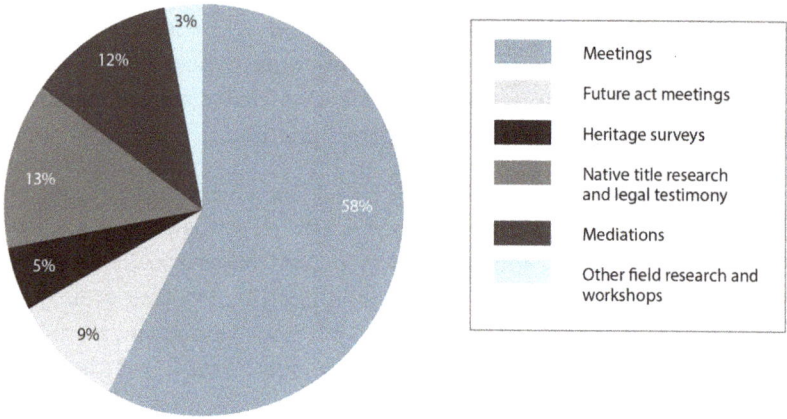

Fig. 19.2 Nyangumarta native title work by activity type (% of total time of Nyangumarta participation)

Source: Author's research

Of all the native title related activities listed above, only future act meetings and heritage surveys (14 per cent of total time spent on native title activities) provide any significant compensation or formal payment for people's involvement. At the time of writing in late 2014, the average daily rate paid to an Aboriginal native title representative for participation as an advisor on a future act heritage survey was reported to be around $500 per day (Norris O, pers. comm., 30 August 2014). Sitting fees for negotiation meetings vary between $300 and $500 per day. Although irregular and unpredictable, in a region where the unemployment rate for Indigenous Australians sits at around 14 per cent and the median weekly personal income at around $297 (Australian Bureau of Statistics 2013), this is significant income for an individual. However, my research suggests that the total amount paid to members of the group for their participation in such activities over the 15-year period was less than $250,000.

Turning to the social relations of native title work, the numbers and identities of the non-Nyangumarta people involved in Nyangumarta native title work during this period are significant: 345 non-Nyangumarta people from 91 different organisations were involved in the 292 documented events. They included 116 bureaucrats; 61 mining executives; at least 45 lawyers representing NTRBs, respondent parties and government; 20 anthropologists; 10 archaeologists; eight business owners; five hydrologists; and four geologists. Fig. 19.3 sets out the numbers of people involved by profession (note that most of the anthropologists and lawyers involved worked for government or NTRBs and are not represented as separate professions). Around two thirds of these people were men; among the Nyangumarta themselves, there were more or less equal numbers of men and women involved. And in contrast to the situation of the Nyangumarta, it is very likely that most of these 345 non-Nyangumarta people were paid for their time, via either a salary or a daily consultancy rate.

The quality and intensity of the relationships between Nyangumarta people and these professional outsiders varied, but the findings indicate that the vast majority were brief and singular encounters between strangers. Only in a few instances have these relationships endured beyond one or two meetings.

The 91 organisations involved in the documented events (see Fig. 19.4) included NTRBs (3), mining companies (27), Commonwealth, State and local government departments (29), research organisations/consultants (8), pastoralist companies (3) and tourism ventures (2). The number of people involved who represented NTRBs is particularly striking: 104 staff from only three organisations. This reflects not only the number of professional staff needed to support a native title claim but also the difficulties many NTRBs face retaining qualified and experienced staff (for more discussion of NTRB capacity see Martin 2004, Deloitte Access Economics 2014).

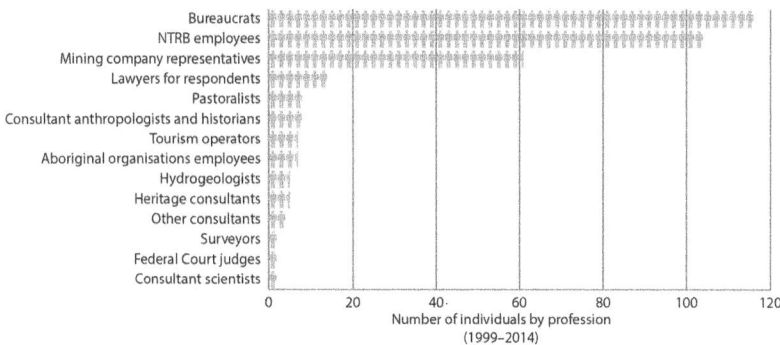

Fig. 19.3 Professions of non-Nyangumarta individuals involved in Nyangumarta native title activities, 1999–2014

Source: Author's research

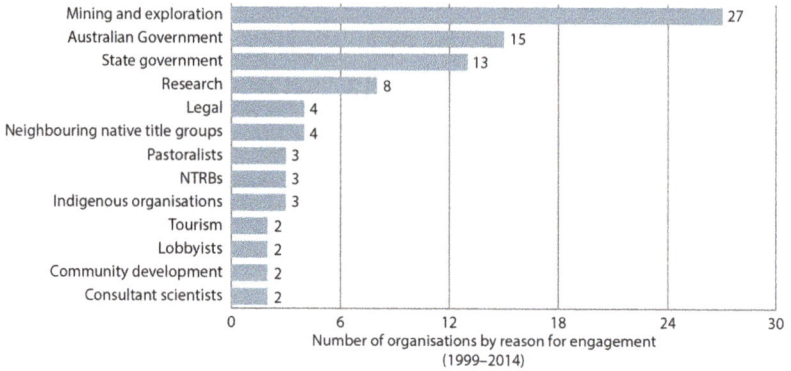

Fig. 19.4 Number of organisations involved in Nyangumarta native title activities by type, 1999–2014

Source: Author's research

Also notable are the numbers of people and agencies that Nyangumarta people have dealt with around land and sea management: at least 41 individuals from 11 agencies. This reflects the scale and complexity of the natural resource management projects that NWAC have been involved with, namely the Indigenous Protected Area and the Eighty Mile Beach Marine Park.

Finally, these figures point to the extent to which native title was born from and remains a project of government. Over 110 different representatives from just under 30 Commonwealth, State and local government departments have been in some way involved in the prosecution of the Nyangumarta native title claims and the post-determination management of their rights. The role of government in this space has been truly diverse, with representatives coming to the table as respondents, mediators, facilitators, researchers, proponents of future acts, funders, policymakers, and potential project partners. While the introduction of the NTA in 1993 certainly doesn't mark the beginning of the bureaucratisation of Indigenous people's lives, native title doesn't appear to have at all lessened the burden of being governed.

Overall, these findings give a very concrete sense of the enormous commitment of time and social effort that Aboriginal and Torres Strait Islander peoples are prepared to make in order to secure formal legal recognition of traditional rights and interests in land. More analysis is required to understand the specific demands of post-determination governance, and it is hoped that further case studies will help illustrate the diversity of native title work for groups in different areas of the country.

There remains much to be learned about Nyangumarta people's perspectives on *warrkam* (work). From interviews already conducted it is clear that native title work is very much seen as 'working for your people', and has been very empowering for Nyangumarta in many respects. But it comes at a cost, and those most heavily involved in the governance of NWAC at times find it challenging to balance this volunteer work with other family and professional commitments such as caring for elderly relatives or holding down a full-time job (Rose M, pers. comm., 3 June 2014).

Among other things, native title work has brought Nyangumarta people together in old ways for new purposes, leading to a strengthening of country group identity. It has rendered Nyangumarta people visible to outside interests and enabled them to insist on recognition of their traditional authority to an extent that was inconceivable only 20 years ago.

I am struck, however, by the frankness with which these figures illustrate the constant outwards orientation demanded by native title work; the unrelenting pulling of focus, resources and relationships away from Nyangumarta interests and aspirations towards those of others. This continuous outward orientation seems to me to be in clear tension with people's primary motivations for pursuing native title in the first place, and that is to achieve an easier and more frequent inward orientation, back towards country.

References

Altman JC (1987). *Hunter-gatherers today: an Aboriginal economy in north Australia*, Australian Institute of Aboriginal Studies, Canberra.

Australian Bureau of Statistics (2013). *2011 Census QuickStats: Aboriginal and Torres Strait Islander people—usual residents*, www. censusdata.abs.gov.au/census_services/getproduct/census/2011/ quickstat/IARE506001?opendocument&navpos=220.

Australian Institute of Aboriginal and Torres Strait Islander Studies (2014). *Registered Native Title Bodies Corporate summary*, www.aiatsis.gov.au/_files/ntru/rntbc/registered_native_title_bodies_corporate_summary_2014.pdf.

Bauman T, Strelein LM & Weir JK (2013). Navigating complexity: living with native title. In Bauman T, Strelein LM & Weir JK (eds), *Living with native title: the experiences of registered native title corporations*, Australian Institute of Aboriginal and Torres Strait Islander Studies, Canberra.

Deloitte Access Economics (2014), *Review of the roles and functions of native title organisations*, Deloitte Access Economics Pty Ltd, Kingston ACT.

Gooda M (2014). *Social Justice and Native Title Report 2014*, Aboriginal and Torres Strait Islander Social Justice Commissioner, Australian Human Rights Commission, Sydney.

Langton M & Mazel O (2012). The resource curse compared: Australian Aboriginal participation in the resource extraction industry and distribution of impacts. In Langton M & Longbottom J (eds), *Community futures, legal architecture: foundations for Indigenous peoples in the global mining* boom, Routledge, Oxon UK.

Levitus R (2009). Aboriginal organisations and development: the structural context. In Altman JC & Martin DF (eds), *Power, culture, economy: Indigenous Australians and mining*, CAEPR Research Monograph No. 30, ANU E Press, Canberra.

Martin D (2004). *Capacity of anthropologists in native title practice*, report to the National Native Title Tribunal, Anthropos Consulting Services, Canberra.

McGrath PF, Stacey C & Wiseman L (2013). An overview of the Registered Native Title Bodies Corporate regime. In Bauman T, Strelein LM & Weir JK (eds), *Living with native title: the experiences of registered native title corporations*, Australian Institute of Aboriginal and Torres Strait Islander Studies, Canberra.

National Native Title Tribunal (2014a). *Statistics: native title determinations*, www.nntt.gov.au/Pages/Statistics.aspx.

National Native Title Tribunal (2014b). *Determinations of native title (as at 30 September 2014)*, www.nntt.gov.au/Maps/Determinations_map.pdf.

O'Faircheallaigh C (2004). Evaluating agreements between Indigenous people and resource developers. In Langton M, Tehan M, Palmer L & Shain K (eds), *Honour among nations? Treaties and agreements with Indigenous peoples,* Melbourne University Press, Carlton.

O'Faircheallaigh C (2007). 'Unreasonable and extraordinary restraints': native title, markets and Australia's resources boom. *Australian Indigenous Law Review* 11(3):28–42.

Rowley C (1972). *Outcasts in White Australia*, Penguin Books, Harmondsworth.

YMAC (Yamatji Marlpa Aboriginal Corporation) (2010). *Kaja karti marnti [The long walk]*, video recording, vimeo.com/98205705.

YMAC (Yamatji Marlpa Aboriginal Corporation) (2013). *Annual Report 2013*, YMAC, Perth.

YMAC (Yamatji Marlpa Aboriginal Corporation) (2014). *Submission no. 034 to the Inquiry into non-financial barriers to mineral and energy resource exploration*, Productivity Commission, Canberra.

.

20

Indigenous small businesses in the Australian Indigenous economy

Jock Collins, Mark Morrison, Branka Krivokapic-Skoko, Rose Butler and PK Basu

Introduction

There are many pathways to Indigenous entrepreneurship in Australia: partnerships between corporate Australia and Indigenous corporations/communities; Indigenous community-owned enterprises; Indigenous social enterprises and cooperatives; and Indigenous private enterprises. One of the most significant developments in the Australian Indigenous economy over the last decade has been the increasing importance of Indigenous enterprises and Indigenous entrepreneurs. As Foley (2006) has persuasively argued, not all Indigenous enterprises are run by community organisations and they are not all in the outback. The majority of Indigenous enterprises are private enterprises. Analysing census data from 1991 and 2011, Hunter (2013) provided evidence that the number of Indigenous self-employed—the largest component of Indigenous entrepreneurship—almost tripled from 4,600 to 12,500. Indigenous entrepreneurs are also much more likely to employ Indigenous workers than other Australian enterprises (Hunter 2014: 16). For these reasons Indigenous entrepreneurship in Australia plays a growing role in the Indigenous economy within a framework of self-determination by providing jobs for Indigenous workers.

Jon Altman has pioneered research related to economic aspects of Indigenous lives in Australia and the Indigenous economy. His detailed understanding of the tourism and art industries is key to understanding contemporary Indigenous entrepreneurship in these industries, particularly in remote and regional areas. His work has identified new possibilities for the Indigenous economy opened up by the *Native Title Act 1993* (Cwlth). Altman outlined what he thought would be required as follows:

> New horizons and new opportunities suggest the need for new strategies and these are evident at the government, industry, and Indigenous communities levels ... The new strategies for Indigenous communities include using native title and land rights leverage to ensure greater participation in business, primarily through joint venturing. However, such new approaches require the development of appropriate Indigenous structures to overcome problems of external and internal accountability (2001a: 3).

In 2001 Altman introduced the concept of the hybrid economy which emphasised the importance of the interaction of three sectors (market, state and customary) in shaping the diverse and distinct forms of economic activity on Aboriginal land (Altman 2001b). Traditional economic models of Indigenous economic activity had focused on a two-sector model of the interaction of the market or private sector and state or public sector. However Altman argued that this ignored the economic importance of customary (non-market) social relations, obligations, practices and activities. While previously Indigenous culture was seen as detracting from, and a constraint on, Indigenous economic activity, Altman argued that positive externalities emerged and needed to be valued if we are to fully understand the Indigenous economy.

This paper aims to briefly reflect on Jon Altman's contribution to the field of Indigenous entrepreneurship in Australia through the lens of a recent study of Indigenous private and community-owned enterprise in mostly small businesses across urban, regional and remote Australia. It looks at some of the qualitative and quantitative findings of a three-year research project titled Determining the Factors

Influencing the Success of Private and Community-owned Indigenous Businesses across Remote, Regional and Urban Australia. Funded under the Australian Research Council (ARC) Linkage Grant scheme, the research project conducted interviews with, and collected surveys from, male and female Indigenous entrepreneurs across Australia. It provides the most comprehensive, contemporary insights into Indigenous entrepreneurship available in Australia.

The ARC Linkage Grant on Indigenous entrepreneurship in Australia

Qualitative fieldwork

The qualitative fieldwork in this research consisted of in-depth, semi-structured interviews with 38 Indigenous entrepreneurs across Australia using a purposive sampling approach of maximum variation sampling. There were 22 male and 16 female Indigenous entrepreneurs, as shown in Table 20.1. The sampling process was designed to include informants from urban, regional and remote Australia, and to include informants from a range of different industries.

Table 20.1 Gender of businesses across region: qualitative results

	Male		Female		Total	
	N	%	N	%	N	%
Urban	5	13%	11	29%	16	42%
Regional	15	39.5%	3	8%	18	47.5%
Remote	2	5.5%	2	5.5%	4	10.5%
Total	22	58%	16	42%	38	100%

Source: Authors' research

Quantitative fieldwork

The quantitative survey sample consisted of 324 businesses. Similar to the qualitative interview sample it was conducted in urban, regional and remote areas of all states and territories of Australia except Tasmania, and included both privately owned and community-owned enterprises (including cooperatives). Of the 324 businesses,

263 (82 per cent) were privately owned and 61 (18 per cent) were community/cooperatively owned. The geographic distribution of these businesses is shown in Table 20.2.

Table 20.2 Location of businesses across region and state: quantitative sample

	NSW	VIC	QLD	SA	WA	NT	ACT	Total
Urban	51 *44.7%*	27 *58.7%*	21 *37.5%*	9 *100%*	31 *57.4%*	23 *60.5%*	7 *4.1%*	169 *52.2%*
Regional	57 *50.0%*	19 *41.3%*	34 *60.7%*	0 *0%*	0 *0%*	0 *0%*	0 *0%*	110 *34.0%*
Remote	6 *5.3%*	0 *0%*	1 *1.8%*	0 *0%*	23 *42.6%*	15 *39.5%*	0 *0%*	45 *13.9%*
Total	114	46	56	9	54	38	7	324

Note: Column percentages are shown in italics
Source: Authors' research

Definitions of Indigenous entrepreneurship

Much of Altman's scholarship on the Indigenous economy relates to policy issues: what structures are most likely to deliver Indigenous peoples the greatest and most sustainable benefit. Altman (2001a) has stressed the need for governments to shape the horizon for Indigenous enterprises with a careful, differentiated and nuanced policy framework.

> In the Indigenous business domain alone there is an urgent need to differentiate forms of Indigenous enterprise, not only according to scale of enterprise (micro, small and medium categories). Indigenous enterprise should be differentiated into target populations (individuals or families, traditional owners or native title parties, communities or regions) and target objectives (socio-cultural, public good or commercial). Even such oversimplified differentiation does not lend itself to any easy-fit matrix because of enormous category overlap.

> ... Policy realism is essential in any consideration of enhancing Indigenous participation in the business sector. The diversity of circumstances of Indigenous Australians that are the result of the interplay of locational, cultural, structural, historic, political, and other factors will mean that any overarching policy framework or mix of government programs will need to be sufficiently flexible to match this diversity (Altman 2001a: 3–4).

One point of departure for policy in the area of Indigenous enterprises and entrepreneurship relates to the definition of Indigenous enterprises that is employed by policymakers. The most authoritative definition comes from Supply Nation, adopting the definition from Willmett (2009), which uses a majority equity definition of an Indigenous business where there is 'at least 51% owned by Indigenous Australians and the principal executive officer is an Indigenous Australian and the key decisions in the business are made by Indigenous Australians'. However as Foley (2005) and Foley and Hunter (2014) have pointed out, this definition is contestable because it excludes the 50:50 business partnership of an Indigenous and non-Indigenous couple (see Hunter 2013: 16–7). These definition issues are important because they decide which enterprises are able to participate in programs designed to support Indigenous entrepreneurship. Access to public and private sector procurement for Indigenous enterprises generally requires certification of an Indigenous enterprise by Supply Nation. The *Forrest Review* suggested that the definition of an Indigenous business (or, as the report calls them, first Australian firms) be changed to include 'those that have 25% or more first Australian ownership and management and can demonstrate significant first Australian employment outcomes' (Forrest 2014: 186).

Our fieldwork included a large number of Indigenous entrepreneurs who had a non-Indigenous spouse who was also a formal business partner or contributed substantially to the business. In our qualitative sample, nine out of 38 entrepreneurs (23.5 per cent) were in a business partnership with their spouse, and six of these spouses were non-Indigenous (Table 20.3). Seventeen entrepreneurs across the total sample of 38 (44.5 per cent) reported their spouse playing a central role in their business, whether as a formal partner or through recognised contributions. This included management, financial or technological support, childcare and emotional labour. For example, B1, a man in his 60s in regional New South Wales who sold a self-made industrial product globally, embedded the success of his business in his relationship with his wife.

Table 20.3 Role of spouse in the business (formal business partner and contributor to the business): qualitative results

Role of spouse in business	Business partner		Business contributor*		Partner or contributor	
	N	%	N	%	N	%
Indigenous spouse	3	8%	0	0	3	8%
Non-Indigenous spouse	6	16%	8	21%	14	37%%
Total	9	23.5%	8	21%	17	44.5%

Source: Authors' research

In our quantitative survey sample, 31.7 per cent of entrepreneurs who owned a business had a non-Indigenous spouse who was either a business partner or was actively involved in the business. If businesses surveyed were owned and controlled equally (50:50) by the Indigenous entrepreneurs and their non-Indigenous partner they fell outside the Supply Nation definition of what constitutes an Indigenous enterprise.

Contributions of Indigenous enterprises to the hybrid economy

Most Indigenous businesses in this research were micro and small businesses under private ownership. In our qualitative fieldwork we included only four Indigenous businesses in remote regions and only seven community businesses. We found that for these businesses, customary obligations and practices had only a marginal impact on their businesses. Moreover, for these businesses the state shaped business activities in the same way as for other small businesses in Australia. A significant number of Indigenous entrepreneurs cited public sector employment as part of their trajectory of entrepreneurship, however the market was the major factor shaping enterprise activity and success. This is not to say that Indigenous culture is not relevant to the dynamics of Indigenous private enterprises or to the lives of Indigenous entrepreneurs.

We sought to investigate the extent of community contribution by Indigenous entrepreneurs, and whether this differed across business type and location. Similar to previous literature, we found in our qualitative analysis that major contributions were the provision of employment (Antinori & Bray 2005, Manyara & Jones 2007, Torri 2010);

skill development and training, community development, cultural development and empowerment (Ketilson & MacPherson 2002, Manyara & Jones 2007, Memmott 2010, Torri 2010); and involvement in networks (Ketilson & MacPherson 2002, Manyara & Jones 2007). We also identified other contributions, notably providing a role model to younger people, challenging mainstream Australia's view of Indigenous Australians, the provision of goods and services to Indigenous communities, and donations to the Indigenous and non-Indigenous community.

Using the results from our quantitative survey, we examined whether the extent of these contributions differed across business type and location. Our findings suggest that privately owned businesses make contributions to their communities, but that this does not occur to the same extent as for community-owned or cooperatively owned businesses, as might be expected given the differing goals of the entrepreneurs running these two different types of businesses (Johannisson & Nilsson 1989, Peredo & Chrisman 2006) (Table 20.4). Nonetheless, many privately owned businesses still make significant noneconomic contributions to their communities, which are valuable.

Table 20.4 Community contributions of private, community and cooperatively owned businesses: quantitative results

Community contributions	Privately owned	Community owned	Co-operative
Volunteer time to be involved in local community events or activities not related to their business	67%	61%	90%
Been on management or organising committee	12%	19%	17%
Sponsor local sport teams or cultural events	54%	55%	70%
Provide discounted/free goods or services to Community Groups or Events:			
– Occasionally	36%	20%	0%
– Frequently	36%	57%	80%
Provide advice and support not paid for:			
– Occasionally	22%	20%	10%
– Frequently	56%	69%	80%
Seek to employ Indigenous people	62%	94%	100%
Give percentage of profits to community organisations and initiatives	17%	49%	40%
Act as positive role model for young people in community	89%	92%	90%

Source: Authors' research

Table 20.5 Community contributions of urban, regional and remote Indigenous businesses: quantitative results

Community contributions	Urban	Regional	Remote
Volunteer time to be involved in local community events or activities not related to their business	69%	70%	51%
Been on management or organising committee	17%	13%	4%
Sponsor local sport teams or cultural events	54%	56%	53%
Provide discounted/free goods or services to Community Groups or Events:			
– Occasionally	31%	37%	29%
– Frequently	42%	32%	51%
Provide advice and support not paid for:			
– Occasionally	24%	21%	13%
– Frequently	59%	58%	60%
Seek to employ Indigenous people	66%	71%	71%
Give percentage of profits to community organisations and initiatives	23%	23%	20%
Act as positive role model for young people in community	91%	90%	84%

Source: Authors' research

We examined whether contributions to community differed according to location (Table 20.5). Overall, the community contributions in remote areas appeared to be slightly lower than in urban or regional areas, and owners/managers in remote areas reported a lower than average level of satisfaction with their community contributions. Remote business owners and managers were also less aspirational in seeking to help future generations or change mainstream perceptions of Aboriginal people. This may relate to the capacity or capability of the businesses or the managers/owners; it is possible that less effective business practices and resources may limit the ability of remote businesses to contribute to their communities. If this is the case, it could provide a rationale for increased governmental support of Indigenous businesses in remote areas. These results demonstrate that the community contributions of Indigenous businesses are much broader than previously realised in the literature. This suggests a relatively large hybrid economy, as many contributions are made by a large proportion of businesses.

References

Altman JC (2001a). *Communities and business: three perspectives, 1998–2000*, Working Paper 9, Centre for Aboriginal Economic Policy Research, The Australian National University, Canberra.

Altman JC (2001b). *Sustainable development options on Aboriginal land: the hybrid economy in the 21st century*, Discussion Paper 226, Centre for Aboriginal Economic Policy Research, The Australian National University, Canberra.

Antinori C & Bray DB (2005). Community forest enterprises as entrepreneurial firms: economic and institutional perspectives from Mexico. *World Development* 33(9):1529–43.

Foley D (2005). Understanding Indigenous entrepreneurs: a case study analysis, PhD Thesis, University of Queensland, Brisbane.

Foley D (2006). *Indigenous Australian entrepreneurs: not all community organisations, not all in the outback*, Discussion Paper 279, Centre for Aboriginal Economic Policy Research, The Australian National University, Canberra.

Foley D & Hunter B (2014). *Indigenous entrepreneurship: establishing some definitions and theoretical perspectives*, 59th Annual International Council for Small Business World Conference, Dublin, 11–14 June:1–18.

Forrest A (2014). *The Forrest review: creating parity*, Commonwealth of Australia, Canberra.

Hunter B (2013). *Recent growth in Indigenous self-employed and entrepreneurs*, Working Paper 91, Centre for Aboriginal Economic Policy Research, The Australian National University, Canberra.

Hunter B (2014). *Indigenous employment and businesses: whose business is it to employ Indigenous workers?* Working Paper 95, Centre for Aboriginal Economic Policy Research, The Australian National University, Canberra.

Johannisson B & Nilsson A (1989). Community entrepreneurs: networking for local development. *Entrepreneurship and Regional Development* 1:3–19.

Ketilson LH & MacPherson I (2002). *A report on Aboriginal co-operatives in Canada: current situation and potential for growth*, BC Institute for Co-operative Studies, Vancouver.

Manyara G & Jones E (2007). Community-based tourism enterprise development in Kenya: an exploration of their potential as avenues of poverty reduction. *Journal of Sustainable Tourism* 15(6):628–44.

Memmott P (2010). *Demand-responsive services and culturally sustainable enterprise in remote Aboriginal settings: a case study of the Myuma Group*, Desert Knowledge CRC Report No. 63, Desert Knowledge CRC, Alice Springs.

Peredo AM & Chrisman JJ (2006). Toward a theory of community-based enterprise. *Academy of Management Review* 31(2):309–28.

Torri M (2010). Community-based enterprises: a promising basis towards an alternative entrepreneurial model for sustainability enhancing livelihoods and promoting socio-economic development in rural India. *Journal of Small Business and Entrepreneurship* 23(2):237–48.

Willmett N (2009). *Why we cannot wait: the urgent need for strategic Indigenous business sector development and Indigenous enterprise integration in Australia*, Churchill Fellowship Report, Winston Churchill Memorial Trust of Australia, Canberra.

Part 4: Personal Reflections

21

Reflections of a PhD student

Benedict Scambary

Within two weeks of arriving at the Centre for Aboriginal Economic Policy Research (CAEPR) in 2002 I found myself at a planning retreat at Charlottes Pass. As a new student of Jon Altman, I did not quite know what to expect and certainly did not know how to behave. I was a slightly angry and jaded refugee from the applied land rights and native title scene in the Northern Territory, and found myself immediately resentful of the perceived largesse of Canberra: its roads, its public buildings, its rules, its affluence, its power, its whiteness and, in particular, the number of Australian anthropologists based at ANU! What are they all doing in Canberra, I asked myself; why aren't they out in the bush?

At Charlottes Pass I learned that CAEPR was in crisis. A seven-year funding agreement with the Aboriginal and Torres Strait Islander Commission (ATSIC) had been reduced to three years. The discussion focused on the cooling of the relationship between CAEPR and ATSIC and the need to ensure that deliverables were generated and funding maintained. In my naivety I scoffed, 'what are you worried about?' The Northern Land Council (NLC) native title program, funded from the same bucket as I recall, could only secure one-year funding at best, and by the time the wheels of bureaucracy had turned, this only translated to five months' secure funding. This privileged relationship with government confused me.

In hindsight I think I also witnessed a pivotal moment at CAEPR, and a turning point in Indigenous policy. It's not something I fully understand, but the cooling of the relationship between ATSIC and CAEPR could possibly have signalled a shift in the relationship between the academy and the state more broadly, where funded research suddenly had to be accountable to the public purse by showing its support for the political ideology of the day. If that was the beginning, then to the outside observer, it certainly seems that we are seeing an advanced stage of that now.

There is no doubt that at that point Indigenous policy was changing— native title was hotly contested by governments in every Australian jurisdiction. *Cash langa finger*, or 'welfare autonomy', had moved to 'sit down money', and was transforming into 'welfare poison'. *Our right to take responsibility* quickly morphed into shared responsibility and mutual obligation. In 2007, the Intervention crashed through the cultural museums—the neoliberal conniption of the state, wreaking havoc on the Northern Territory, placing the blame firmly on Aboriginal people for the situation they found themselves in. All bets were off, all research was out the window, everything tried before had failed, and any criticism of the approach was to sanction paedophilia. This strategy by the state had the remarkable effect, it seems, of disarming the academy. The critique appeared to come from just a few, and Jon Altman was at the forefront.

During my time at CAEPR I witnessed the prodigious response of the organisation to these policy shifts under Jon's stewardship. The response was always reasoned, evidence-based, and exploratory in a way that sought to highlight the positives and negatives of an approach—to give credit where it was due, and to provide criticism where it was due. CAEPR engaged in rigorous, often multidisciplinary, research that could only be described as being in the public good. The ethos of the research appeared to me to be based on notions of equality, pragmatism, and fiscal responsibility.

These rapid shifts in Indigenous policy gave little time for reflection on the part of the policymakers and politicians. CAEPR research appeared to be uncomfortably ignored in favour of research based more on ideology than evidence. As the gulf between policy and the policy research of CAEPR widened, it seemed to me that Jon increasingly sought to use the media to get his message across. His research also became more action oriented, though arguably it always was. At the conference that led to this volume we heard of the influence of Jon's and CAEPR's research in the inclusion of aspects of cultural production in the first National Aboriginal and Torres Strait Islander Survey, the programs employing rangers in environmental services, the establishment of the Indigenous Governance Awards, and the Community Development Employment Projects (CDEP) scheme, to name a few. I would also add that CAEPR research on mining is acknowledged as being a key influence on RioTinto's $2 billion mining agreement in the Pilbara. In rebutting Nicolas Peterson, Jon succinctly describes the hybrid economy as a question, a model for talking to Aboriginal people to apply pushback on the relentless neoliberal project and a question that addresses the global issue of surplus labour (Altman, this volume).

Incredibly, Jon has managed to be responsive to policy shifts and an integral commentator on Indigenous policy for decades. Examples include responses to John Hewson's *Fightback!*, changes to CDEP, and the Northern Territory Intervention. While Jon has been characterised as a critic of government policy, I would argue that he has been frank and fearless through examination and analysis of the evidence available. While his opinion may differ from the status quo, he maintains a level of integrity in his scholarship that is true to his own values of fairness and equality.

Often Jon's commentary has been perceived as overly critical of new government initiatives, too idealistic and therefore too hard to warrant incorporation into mainstream policy initiatives. The level of retort undoubtedly reflects the level of discomfort that his critique creates for an often lazy, unimaginative and ill-informed bureaucracy, and let's not forget the politicians.

But it is this discomfort—sometimes annoyance—engendered in the debate around Indigenous policy that is in many ways the fundamental value of Jon's research. He seeks to hold accountable the bureaucrats, politicians and commentators who all too readily retreat to ideology as a basis for justifying and implementing punitive and disruptive policy initiatives—initiatives that ignore the reality of people's lives, that ignore the evidence of research, that favour market interests over those of the most disadvantaged. In arguing against the Intervention, *Stronger Futures*, and those who seek to portray

Indigenous disadvantage as resulting from the cultural prerogatives and choices of Aboriginal people, Jon has consistently highlighted the historic underspend on Indigenous citizenship rights. He takes issue with policy initiatives that grossly misrepresent the scale of the problem they are designed to address and consistently underestimate the resources required.

Nic Peterson (this volume) states that government and policymakers 'do not have the luxury of doing nothing', but it is apparent, as Peter Cooke has highlighted, that they do have the luxury to make an awful hash of doing something.[1] That is what is happening at the moment. In the Northern Territory as politicians call for the 'patriation of the Land Rights Act' to the Territory (because Canberra is too far away), policymakers are scrambling to reverse engineer the justification. Reforms in Aboriginal land tenure are placing a complex of leases and subleases on Aboriginal land so that the conditions for private home ownership can be created. This is being hailed a success, with 11 enquiries received from people at Gunbalanya, Yirrkala, Groote Eylandt and the Tiwi Islands. A matrix of stratification to assess the willingness of 'remote communities' to opt in or out is being applied to redirect government services in a way that is not too far removed from the limitations Nicolas Peterson (this volume) identifies of 'desirable long term dependencies'.

In returning to Canberra in 2014 for the Engaging Indigenous Economy Conference, I had a different perspective than back in 2002. Thanks to Jon, I have a better understanding of the power of research, and its relationship to power. The conference and this volume have highlighted the impacts of Jon Altman's research on Indigenous policy and academic thinking. But it is clear that Jon's research influence reaches beyond policy development and into the realm of empowerment of Aboriginal people, and that he has achieved an enormous amount in this regard. His research is frank and fearless, and is of its nature political. The academy still occupies a position of privilege, and to Jon's credit he has used that privilege to speak truth to power.

---

1   Peter Cooke spoke at the Engaging Indigenous Economy Conference as part of Cooke P, Garde M, Guymala T & Yibarbuk D (2014). *Contemporary customary economy, attribution of value and the management of Warddeken Indigenous Protected Area*, presentation at Engaging Indigenous Economy Conference: Debating Diverse Approaches, The Australian National University, Canberra, 4 September.

References

Cooke P, Garde M, Guymala T & Yibarbuk D (2014). *Contemporary customary economy, attribution of value and the management of Warddeken Indigenous Protected Area*, presentation at Engaging Indigenous economy conference: debating diverse approaches, The Australian National University, Canberra, 4 September.

22

Reflections of a senior colleague

John Nieuwenhuysen AM

It was a privilege and pleasure to be allowed to speak at the end of the remarkable conference, Engaging Indigenous Economy: Debating Diverse Approaches, and to offer a few reflections on the brilliant career of my friend, co-author and colleague of Melbourne University days, Professor Jon Altman.

Jon has worked on Indigenous development issues in Australia since 1976. He has made extremely important contributions which have been recognised in several ways, including a highly prestigious Australian Research Council (ARC) Professorial Fellowship and election as a Fellow of the Academy of Social Sciences in Australia. His role as foundation Director of the Centre for Aboriginal Economic Policy Research (CAEPR) at ANU between 1990 and 2010 has been inspiring and enormously productive. Jon has led the Centre by example and has combined the undoubted difficulties of gaining funds and ensuring the Centre's broad success with his own personal research, including many stints away from Canberra. In particular, Jon has worked for 30 years on 'People on Country' in the Top End, mainly in the Arnhem Land/Kakadu region.

Old men such as me are inclined to look back on their careers thinking of their mistakes and failures, of which there are many. But occasionally there is a bright moment in which a wise, even enlightened, action comes to the fore, and in my long working life, which lasted till the age of 75, there was one particular decision which proved extremely successful. That came in the mid-1970s when I was Chair of the Economics Department at the University of Melbourne, and we advertised a position of Senior Tutor. For this, an application was received by a then young man from the University of Auckland, Jon Altman. The department had a general rule that all applicants for positions should be seen in person. But, because Jon was outside Australia, a telephone interview was undertaken as a preliminary step. In the interview, Jon dazzled the committee with a rhetorically strong, clear, persuasive presentation. This was based on his fine, logical mind and wide knowledge and reading. And it led the committee to take the unprecedented decision to offer him the job without requiring his attendance at interview in person.

The decision proved an excellent one. Jon was a great tutor and a promising scholar. He had been at Melbourne less than a year when my own application for a grant of funds from the then Department of Aboriginal Affairs to do a study of the economic status of Aborigines succeeded. That grant was to finance a graduate research assistant for 1977, and I invited Jon to take the post. He did so, and as is often said, the rest is history. Jon worked assiduously and with great skill. He produced a manuscript that was completed in the year, and accepted for publication by Cambridge University Press. This 230-page volume, based on the 1971 Census, received considerable international notice and, 27 years later, in 2006, had an astonishing Cambridge reprint of the text as it stood.

After Melbourne, Jon went to ANU, where he undertook his PhD on hunter-gatherers in northern Australia—a thesis that was subsequently published as a book (Altman 1987).

From then on, Jon's publication list speaks for itself. It runs to over 30 pages, and totals nearly 400 items. The breadth of coverage is enormous, and the excellent annotation of the list by Annick Thomassin and Rose Butler (2014) is 109 pages long. In my many years of academic and research life, including a period on the ARC Panel on the Economic, Behavioural and Social Sciences Grants Committee, there are only a few scholars I have come across who can equal the inspirational imagination, volume, variety and quality of Jon's output.

Happily, while Jon describes himself as an economic anthropologist, he has not trodden the path of the mainstream economics profession. As John Kenneth Galbraith explained, the prime criterion for admission to the apex in the hierarchy of the profession is that one should speak in a language so technical and complicated that no one outside the top echelon can comprehend it. By contrast, Jon's work has been directly related to policy. His independent research has made a striking and consistent contribution to knowledge and analysis, and he has been a tireless warrior in debate resting upon well-founded information.

Unlike some scholars who labour only in narrow, specialised segments of their discipline, Jon has ranged extremely broadly and is indeed a Renaissance man in Indigenous studies. Even the most casual glance at Jon's publications list will bear this out. Almost every facet of Indigenous studies in Australia has a place in Jon's encyclopaedic interest and productive output. The annotated list of his works is, as I have already mentioned, evidence of Jon's truly prodigious energy and commitment.

From my knowledge of Jon, three especially noteworthy aspects of his contribution deserve to be highlighted. The first is his involvement in Parliamentary Standing Committee proceedings. For example, on page 27 of Jon's publication list alone, there are seven items mentioning his submissions to Senate and House of Representative Standing Committees on a variety of important Indigenous affairs topics. Second are Jon's skills in linking scholars with business for ARC research projects. In one, the Committee for Economic Development of Australia (CEDA), of which I was then CEO, combined with Rio Tinto and CAEPR as partners to create a very generously funded and successfully completed project relating to mining and Indigenous employment. In this work, PhD theses were part of the design. Third is Jon's great popularity as a speaker. This capacity enabled him to maintain a strong image for the centre in a number of fields. For example, I recall listening to Jon deliver the Kenneth Myer lecture at the Melbourne Museum to a packed audience on the subject of Indigenous art. I may observe, however, that Jon's speech itself on that occasion was not all that excited every member of the audience. I was seated behind two attractive young women whose whispers as Jon spoke included interchanges on the possible extent to which Jon might 'pump iron', to use their phrase, and how it was that a university professor could look and sound so vibrant and virile.

The Engaging Indigenous Economy Conference and this volume are a striking and well-deserved acknowledgement and celebration of Jon's wonderful contribution to Indigenous studies over nearly 40 years. In those decades, Jon has earned the right to declare, as Saint Paul did in his letter to his son Timothy, that he has fought the good fight and kept the faith. Jon's good fight has been for opportunity, equality and justice for Indigenous people in Australia. And he has waged this battle through keeping the faith for independent, fearless scholarly research that is exposed to a public debate in which Jon has been a persistently enlightened and reasonable but forceful voice. Jon is a man of scholarship, integrity, community, conscience and humanity. Australia, I believe, is a great beneficiary of his decision to come and work and live here.

A former New Zealand Prime Minister Mr Piggy Muldoon once famously said that the departure of New Zealanders to Australia raised the IQ of both countries. In Jon's case, his movement here was New Zealand's loss and Australia's gain.

Mr Muldoon also once said that Australia has 100 million sheep, 20 million of which considered themselves to be people. So we can only be grateful that Jon did not believe him.

I mentioned Saint Paul's reference to fighting the good fight and keeping the faith, and Jon's achievement of this. There was, however, a third part of his statement, namely that he had run his race to the finish. Many of us older folk rather like the quote that goes:

> How nice it is to stand upon the shore and see the waves in wild commotion,
>
> and enjoy it all the more because I am no longer on the ocean.

I do not think that Jon will align with that enjoyment. For I firmly believe that he still has an enormous amount of energy left in him and that—fortunately for Australia—Jon will continue his remarkable contribution for many years to come. So, we are all grateful for Jon's wonderful work and presence so far, and look forward to more to come.

References

Altman JC (1987). *Hunter-gatherers today: an Aboriginal economy in north Australia*, Australian Institute of Aboriginal Studies, Canberra.

Thomassin A & Butler R (2014). *Engaging Indigenous economy: a selected annotated bibliography of Jon Altman's writings, 1979–2014*, Working Paper 96, Centre for Aboriginal Economic Policy Research, The Australian National University, Canberra.

23

Self-reflections: 1977–2014[1]

Jon Altman

When you talk about retiring, one question people start asking is how did you get to work in this area and stay in it for so long? So let me answer this question briefly.

I came to Australia from New Zealand in 1976 as a young academic with a Master's degree in economics from the University of Auckland and a job as a senior tutor at the University of Melbourne. My chair of department and supervisor was John Nieuwenhuysen. I had previously migrated with my family from Israel via India to New Zealand, so I had some cultural complexity in my own mix of identities. I had also done some fieldwork for my Master's degree in Western Samoa, supervised by the late Conrad Blyth, an unusual economist with historic links to The Australian National University (ANU) who was a firm believer in primary data collection.

In Melbourne I met and befriended a young Aboriginal man from Alice Springs, Kumanjay Willis, who was studying law. He lit my short fuse for social justice as we hung out together and I shared some of his experiences of racism first-hand. A year later I got an opportunity to work on a project with John Nieuwenhuysen funded

---

1   This essay seeks to reflect as accurately as possible my closing comments to the Engaging Indigenous Economy Conference: Debating Diverse Approaches at The Australian National University on 5 September 2014.

by the Department of Aboriginal Affairs in Canberra on Aboriginal economic status. Our approach was institutional and formal (Altman & Nieuwenhuysen 1979). Kumanjay Willis's social justice fire expired in 1981, just four years later, when he killed himself. Mine has not abated.

I was challenged by anthropologists, mainly Nicolas Peterson, and encouraged by the late economist Fred Fisk to seek an understanding of Aboriginal development via the concept of 'embeddedness'—about how human economy and making a livelihood were embedded in the social and cultural—and to simultaneously question whether there was a universal *Homo economicus*, Western rational economic man, that was deeply embedded as a competing concept in dominant and conventional economic thinking.

My research beginnings in this area occurred in the early post-assimilation era. Australia was discovering that, counter to thinking in the 1960s evident in books like Donald Horne's *The Lucky Country* (published in 1964), Aboriginal societies had not been extinguished. Indeed, in many situations distinct Indigenous non-Western norms, values, beliefs, orientations and practices were alive and well, even if altered.

With some assistance from the late Anthony Forge, and his partner in scholarly innovation John Mulvaney, I was awarded, after some struggle, a scholarship to undertake a doctorate in anthropology at ANU from 1978. Nicolas Peterson and Howard Morphy were my supervisors.

I drove from Canberra to the Maningrida region to undertake participant observation fieldwork in May 1979. Carefully following the instructions of my guide, the late Ray Nulla, I got deeply embedded in the Mann River for three days (Fig. 23.1). My bogging occurred right next to Mumeka outstation, which was unoccupied at the time as all residents—members of the highly mobile Kuninjku community— were at a *Kunabibi* ceremony at Mimanyar.

Three months later I was welcomed as an apprentice member of the Kuninjku community at Mumeka under the tutelage of Anchor Kalumba and his family (Fig. 23.2). I learned all about embeddedness by living with people and engaging in their very human economy. This was the tropical savannah and I was poorly adapted to the local version of the mixed modern economy. Together with my classificatory Kuninjku kin we eked out a livelihood, me on my ANU scholarship being the most affluent at the outstation.

Fig. 23.1 Bogged in the Mann River Crossing, May 1979
Photo: Jon Altman Collection, courtesy of AIATSIS

Fig. 23.2 Anchor Kalumba at Mumeka, late 1979
Photo: Jon Altman Collection, courtesy of AIATSIS

I have never abandoned Mumeka and have been back there over 50 times. It is my second home even though I am neither Kurulk (a fictive land owner), nor Darngkolo (a fictive manager), but a Kardbam (a fictive affine).

I try to repay people there for my training and their hospitality at Mumeka by advocating for them and their very different way of living and by adhering to three long-held principles drawn from early training in philosophy and welfare economics. These principles are nicely summed up by Guy Standing (2014) in *A precariat charter: from denizens to citizens*:

- Security Difference Principle: a policy or institutional change is only socially just if it improves the security of the most insecure groups in society (among whom I count the Kuninjku);
- Paternalism Test Principle: a policy or institutional change is socially just if it does not impose controls on vulnerable groups that are not imposed on the most-free groups in society; and
- Dignified Work Principle: a policy or institutional change is only socially just if it promotes capacity to pursue work that is dignified and rewarding. This last principle explains in part my decades-long advocacy since 1977 for the Community Development Employment Projects (CDEP) scheme as a basic income institution.

Postdoctorally, from 1983 I spent seven years at the then Research School of Pacific Studies in the Department of Political and Social Change. I competed successfully for a job looking for either a North Korea or north Australia specialist. I am not sure how many applied. My supervisor was the late Jamie Mackie, an academic deeply committed to social justice and the abolition of the White Australia policy in the 1960s.

In the 1980s I had postdoctoral opportunities unimaginable today. In particular I chaired reviews of the Aboriginals Benefit Trust Account (discussed by David Pollack, this volume) and the Aboriginal arts and crafts 'industry' (discussed by Marianne Riphagen, this volume), both for the Australian Government.

In the former I made recommendations that resulted in technical tinkering but not in radical change or political empowerment. My recommendations in the second review were adopted, a little serendipitously, as the framework for Indigenous arts marketing support that remains today as the Indigenous Visual Art Industry Support program. Both resulted in at least some progressive legal and policy changes.

I was seduced by what seemed to be admirable state processes for policymaking: engage an academic to examine a complex policy issue at arm's length from government, collaborating and building consensus with Aboriginal and other stakeholders, to have influence with politicians via bureaucrats.

I made representations to the Miller Committee of Review of Aboriginal Employment and Training Programs in 1985 to establish a research centre to keep operating in this productive way. Among the members of the Committee was the late HC 'Nugget' Coombs.

From 1985–90 I battled hard for the Centre for Aboriginal Economic Policy Research (CAEPR) project. It was finally established by the Commonwealth Department of Aboriginal Affairs in its dying days to assist the embryonic Aboriginal and Torres Strait Islander Commission (ATSIC) with independent university-based research to implement the Aboriginal Employment Development Policy (AEDP). ATSIC backed CAEPR from 1990 to 2004, even if at times our research findings were extremely uncomfortable for it and the government.

On 7 May 1990 I gave a lecture at the then Commonwealth Department of Finance about recent reforms in Indigenous affairs. I asked if ATSIC was a bold attempt to swim against the mainstreaming tide and emerging 1980s neoliberal thinking and new public sector management. With hindsight I think it was, but ATSIC's goals to deliver some Indigenous-specific AEDP programs Australia-wide were aided by much grounded research from CAEPR.

In a nutshell, CAEPR's tasks were twofold:

- to advise on progress on the emerging grand national plan for convergence in outcomes for Indigenous and other Australians at a number of regional levels;
- to advise on how this might be facilitated and what it might look like in the continental and grounded diversity of Indigenous circumstances.

These two research and policy goals can be viewed from the twin disciplinary perspectives of economics and anthropology that were, and remain, in a healthy tension with each other (see Altman & Rowse 2005). Economics, with its focus on the quantitative and statistically abstract and theoretical, favours equality and sees difference as a negative indicator of inequality. Anthropology, with its focus on the qualitative, cultural and local, favours plurality and sees difference as a positive indicator of self-determination and choice.[2] This creative tension needs to be vigilantly kept in appropriate balance and it became a hallmark of CAEPR's research.

Our first workshop and first substantial publication *Aboriginal employment equity by the year 2000* (Altman 1991) told ATSIC and the Hawke government just what they did not want to hear: that the goal of statistical equality or sameness could not be delivered by 2000 as promised by then Prime Minister Bob Hawke. To use the words of Will Sanders (1991), it was a goal 'destined to fail'.

It is noteworthy that Indigenous Australians only became statistically visible after the 1967 Referendum, from the 1971 census onwards. Since then the self-identifying population has grown fivefold (Fig. 23.3).

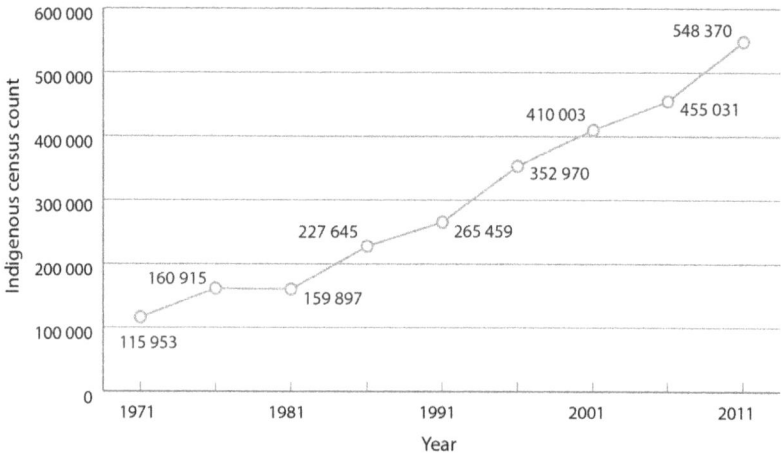

Fig. 23.3 Indigenous census count 1971–2011
Source: Author's research with Francis Markham using published ABS data

---

2   At the conference I joked in poor taste that if one goes directly to *abstracta* (or theory) without *concreta* (or empirics) you get *excreta*.

It is mainly from the 1990s that statistical picturing with all its Foucauldian implications has become a growth industry in Indigenous policy research. CAEPR initially held a monopoly in this area and has consistently tracked, reported and often critiqued the goals of statistical sameness, practical reconciliation, closing the gap, Indigenous advancement, and most recently 'parity'.

The evidence that gaps are not closing largely reflects colonial assumptions about what gaps are important and what is possible. Fig. 23.4 and Fig. 23.5 use five-yearly census data to show that, across a range of social and economic indicators, gaps have not closed nor reached parity in the last 40 years. Some are converging slowly, some are diverging, most will take decades to close if at all under current policy settings.

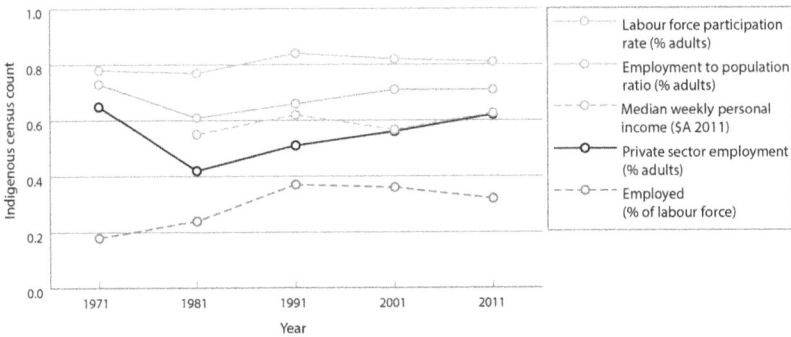

Fig. 23.4 Ratio of Indigenous to non-Indigenous employment and income outcomes, 1971–2011

Source: Author's research with Francis Markham using published ABS data

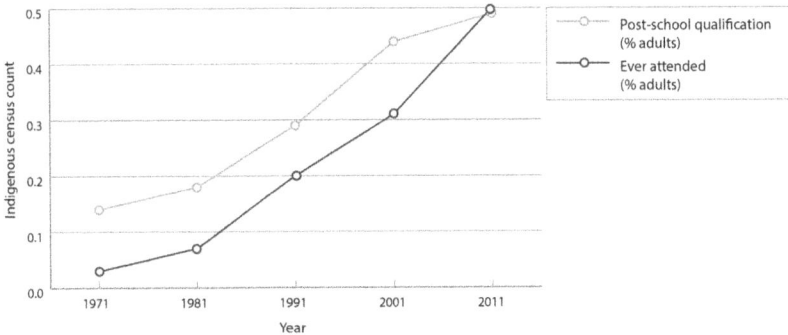

Fig. 23.5 Ratio of Indigenous to non-Indigenous educational outcomes, 1971–2011

Source: Author's research with Francis Markham using published ABS data

I have become increasingly critical of such statistical picturing. It is not that Indigenous subjective views are not canvassed and known, it is just that they are rarely reported or considered important in policy decision-making when they differ from the overarching goal of convergence. In special surveys like the National Aboriginal and Torres Strait Islander Social Survey, information collected on Indigenous views invariably emphasises that language, ceremony and connection to country are fundamental to their views of well-being. But such statistics are generally overlooked in favour of preconceived ideas about what matters.

From the 1970s to the present we have seen a massive change in land titling in Australia. When I started in this area in 1977 the *Aboriginal Land Rights (Northern Territory) Act 1976* (Cwlth) was just passed by the Fraser government. Today, 37 years on, 33 per cent of the Australian continent is under some form of diverse Indigenous tenure (Fig. 23.6).

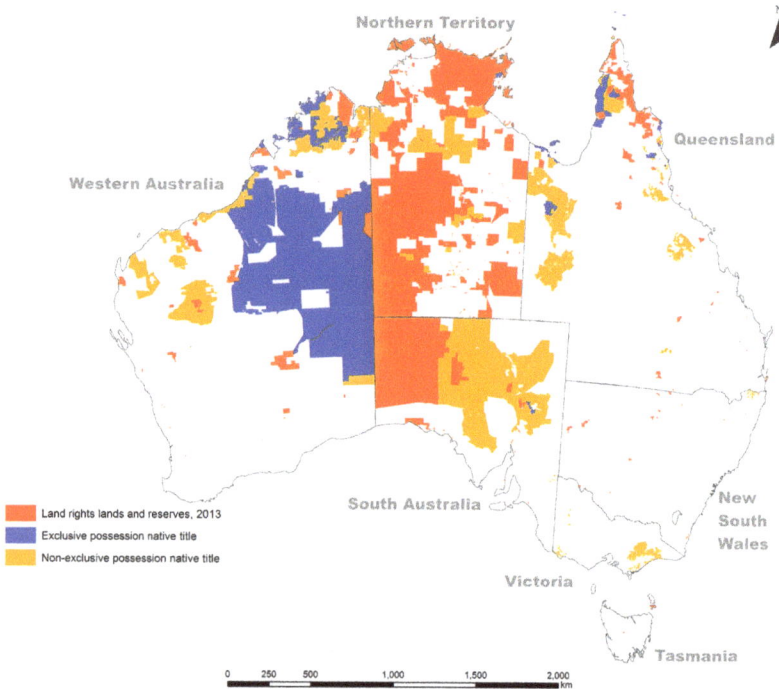

Fig. 23.6 Land rights and ownership under three tenures, 2014

Source: Author's research with Francis Markham using a variety of sources

However, one needs to add people to these forms of tenure and when this is done using 2011 census information, it is clear that most Indigenous titles are in very remote Australia. Most Indigenous people—over 80 per cent—reside elsewhere, and might be depicted as 'the invaded' (Fig. 23.7). There are over 1,000 discrete Indigenous communities, as they are called by the Australian Bureau of Statistics, on or near Indigenous land (Fig. 23.8).

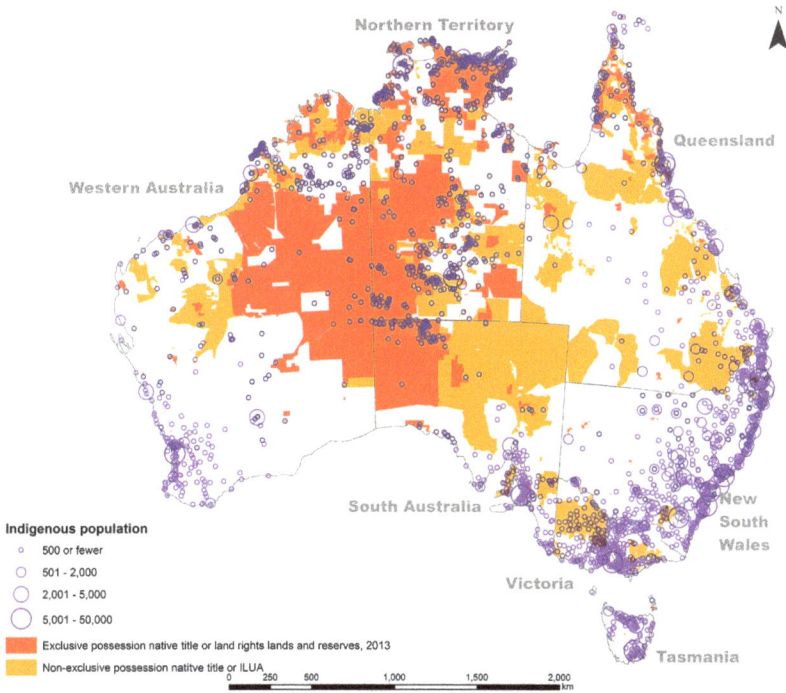

Fig. 23.7 Distribution of the Indigenous population, 2011
Source: Author's research with Francis Markham using a variety of sources

This mismatch between land, people and location is highly problematic for the project of sameness, but has seductive appeal for the project of difference or alterity.

This spatial picturing is challenging to vested capitalist and national interests that need continual access to the land for resource extraction. Kevin Bruyneel (2007), in *The third space of sovereignty*, notes that postcolonial possibility is opened up with land rights and then slammed shut by the settler state, especially if successful Indigenous enterprise is perceived as threatening the status quo.

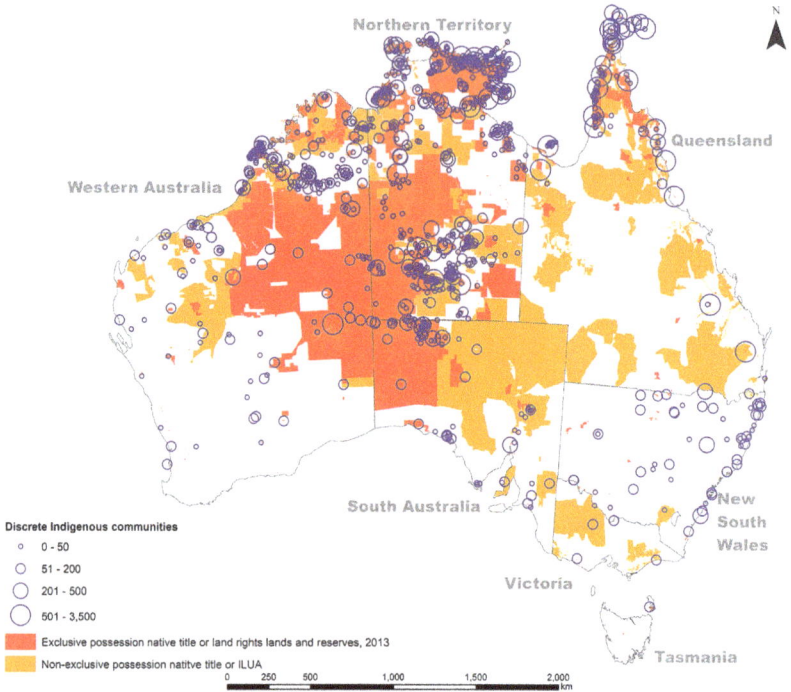

Fig. 23.8 Distribution of discrete Indigenous communities
Source: Author's research with Francis Markham using a variety of sources

In 2004 the dam burst on ATSIC after 14 years of holding neoliberalism at bay as a policy regime embedded in institutions, class and ethnic relations and ideological norms. ATSIC was blamed for the apparent failure of so-called self-determination to deliver parity in socioeconomic outcomes and cultural norms between Indigenous and other Australians. CAEPR in turn was regarded with suspicion by the new Indigenous policy regime and fiscally punished and politically marginalised for its research support of ATSIC.

In 2007 we saw the debacle of the Northern Territory 'National Emergency' Intervention which signalled a dramatic turn in approach in Indigenous policy—the imposition of guardian Leviathan with complete disregard for evidence-based research produced by CAEPR and other academics over many years. I took a decisive stance against the Intervention based on a personal re-evaluation of the altered nature of the state. This was a crucial turning point in my approach as a policy scholar—on the back of the Intervention I felt it was no longer possible to produce research in good faith that would be genuinely received by government at face value so as to influence policymaking decisions.

Since then, policy and its production has become more deeply confused and riddled with contradictions, relying less and less on evidence and increasingly on anecdote and ideology—a political consequence of history and culture wars. There has been a dilution in the role of the expert—unless the expert is supportive of the current dominant state project of improvement. There has also been a rapid increase in the number of research organisations and consulting firms willing and able to undertake research work to government-dictated agendas, as policy development has been commoditised and, in the name of competitive tendering, governments pick and choose. This has all made CAEPR's work more difficult, straining at times the need to balance a broad tripartite set of interest groups: Indigenous stakeholders in all their diversity, the policy community, and the academy. All need to be nourished while also kept at arm's length. This is a difficult juggling act.

The last four Australian governments have shifted the focus of Indigenous-specific policy interventions and expenditures to remote Australia, culminating in the current Indigenous Advancement Strategy, with all its evolutionary connotations. This is partly because remote communities are regarded as being both in greatest need and in need of greatest moral restructuring. They are also the most physically discrete and visible.

And yet their remoteness suggests that achieving parity in these places will be most difficult. In part because norms are most different; in part because market capitalism is most absent.

And so we see the deployment of more and more invasive and intensive and expensive technologies of government surveillance based on the behavioural assumption that remote Indigenous norms and practices can be readily replaced by assumed superior and usually imagined neoliberal norms and practices.

We see imaginative proposals to replicate southern development in the north and so provide precarious opportunity for Indigenous people in situ; or a need to attract or entice Indigenous people to take up diasporic living in the interests of their individual betterment and viability.

Simultaneously it is assumed that the process of parity is well under way in non-remote Australia, that the historical legacy of neglect, structural barriers like location, and the spectre of discrimination no longer matter. The playing field is assumed level and well-being is harshly judged as just a matter of individual agency, not sociopolitical structural factors and power relations. The evidence, and there is plenty of it, says something very different.

Paradoxically this path to parity, or imagined homotopia, a utopia of sameness, is being promoted just as Australia is entering a contrived Era of Austerity and just as the mining boom, proposed as a solution to fly in/fly out, orbiting or diasporic labour, is ending.

I have long held the view that we need to radically reform our current approach which is increasingly based on the imposition of neoliberal governmentality—the creation of inappropriate and punitive institutions to discipline—alongside policy and practice in the last decade that has looked to dilute and depoliticise, if not destroy outright, the community sector. At the same time it clings to some notion of capitalist economy for Indigenous Australia. This has recently re-emerged in the long-held discursive myth of 'developing the north'.

Today, in 2014, policy challenges are greater in my view than in 1977. There is a rhetorical narrative of inclusion but a hardened practice of conditionality—inclusion only on certain terms. I have become increasingly sceptical of:

- the capacity of the state to deliver normal, let alone appropriate, services to Indigenous communities without the community sector;
- the appropriateness and validity of hegemonic, deficit-focused indicators of success, failure and accountability, and
- the legitimacy of the state in the eyes of Indigenous land owners as it seeks to recolonise Indigenous spaces and jurisdictions.

CAEPR today is an embedded institution at ANU, but at a precarious time for the promotion of a healthy diversity of views about the question of Indigenous development. Yet it is a research centre that is needed more than ever in a political environment that is unsympathetic to evidence-based and grounded multidisciplinary research (despite all the political noise to the contrary). Government is more likely to be influenced by 'superstar' reviewers like Andrew Forrest, a narrow range of key Indigenous political actors, ideology of a particular hue, and an overarching state project to embed neoliberalism in Indigenous Australia.

I encourage my academic colleagues to retain the productive, interdisciplinary tension that has been a hallmark of CAEPR since 1990; to manage the creative tension evident in multiple accountabilities to Indigenous Australians; to scholarship inclusive of teaching; and to informing policymakers and the general public. In my view it is especially important not to lose sight of actually existing Indigenous economies and societies out there and, as privileged university researchers, to always speak truth to power—a luxury that funded Indigenous organisations, modern bureaucrats, and captured vested interests do not enjoy.

When you say you are 'retiring' you elicit two other responses beyond 'why did you start?' The first is an assertion, 'no you are not!' The second is a question, 'so what will you do next?' To answer the second, I borrow a phrase from my friends Chips Mackinolty and Therese Ritchie: 'Not Dead Yet' (see Fig. 23.9). In the immediate future I plan to move to the multidisciplinary Regulatory Institutions Network in the College of Asia and the Pacific to continue my research as a 'retired' academic.

Fig. 23.9 Poster from *Not Dead Yet: A Retrospective Exhibition* featuring the work of Therese Ritchie and Chips Mackinolty

Source: Reproduced with kind permission of the artists

I am keen to work on honing my social justice and theoretical arguments while engaging with global scholarship about governance and sustainability and gaining greater understanding of the workings of power so as to better challenge the hegemony of embedded neoliberalism. In my view, this hegemony is doing economic violence not just to many Indigenous Australians, but also to others experiencing precarity in Australian society.

I am especially keen to continue advocating for people at Mumeka and in the Maningrida region and elsewhere to ensure that alternatives are considered. I have tried to do this in the last decade with an emerging theory of economic hybridity deployed as a heuristic device aiming to fundamentally reframe development thinking to focus on actually existing livelihoods. I want to further develop this model that is neither prescriptive nor 'problem solving': it aims to ask still more questions about Indigenous development in Australia and to empower Indigenous people with pushback possibilities.

I realise that I am leaving CAEPR at a difficult time, caught between the pressures of the current university environment and the current Indigenous affairs environment. I wish all my academic colleagues well in their challenging endeavours and will be watching their progress with great collegial interest from just across the ANU campus.

Postscript

Much of my watching will be from Melbourne where I relocated in October 2015, going full circle after 40 years by returning to the Australian city where my research on Indigenous economic development began. I failed 'retirement' and will begin as a research professor at the Alfred Deakin Institute for Citizenship and Globalization at Deakin University in February 2016, exactly 40 years after I migrated to Australia. I will retain my links with the Regulatory Institutions Network at ANU and so will be able to gaze across the ANU campus on visits from time to time.

References

Altman JC (ed.) (1991). *Aboriginal employment equity by the year 2000*, CAEPR Research Monograph No. 2, Centre for Aboriginal Economic Policy Research, ANU, Canberra.

Altman JC & Nieuwenhuysen JP (1979). *The economic status of Australian Aborigines*, Cambridge University Press, Cambridge.

Altman JC & Rowse T (2005). Indigenous affairs. In Saunders P & Walter J (eds), *Ideas and influence: social science and public policy in Australia*, UNSW Press, Sydney.

Bruyneel K (2007). *The third space of sovereignty*, University of Minnesota Press, Minneapolis.

Sanders W (1991). Destined to fail: the Hawke Government's pursuit of statistical equality in employment and income status between Aborigines and other Australians by the year 2000 (or, a cautionary tale involving the new managerialism and social justice strategies), *Australian Aboriginal Studies* 2:13–8.

Standing G (2014). *A precariat charter: from denizens to citizens*, Bloomsbury Publishing, London.

CAEPR Research Monograph Series

1. *Aborigines in the economy: a select annotated bibliography of policy relevant research 1985–90,* LM Allen, JC Altman, and E Owen (with assistance from WS Arthur), 1991.

2. *Aboriginal employment equity by the year 2000,* JC Altman (ed.), published for the Academy of Social Sciences in Australia, 1991.

3. *A national survey of Indigenous Australians: options and implications,* JC Altman (ed.), 1992.

4. *Indigenous Australians in the economy: abstracts of research, 1991–92,* LM Roach and KA Probst, 1993.

5. *The relative economic status of Indigenous Australians, 1986–91,* J Taylor, 1993.

6. *Regional change in the economic status of Indigenous Australians, 1986–91,* J Taylor, 1993.

7. *Mabo and native title: origins and institutional implications,* W Sanders (ed.), 1994.

8. *The housing need of Indigenous Australians, 1991,* R Jones, 1994.

9. *Indigenous Australians in the economy: abstracts of research, 1993–94,* LM Roach and HJ Bek, 1995.

10. *The native title era: emerging issues for research, policy, and practice,* J Finlayson and DE Smith (eds), 1995.

11. *The 1994 National Aboriginal and Torres Strait Islander Survey: findings and future prospects,* JC Altman and J Taylor (eds), 1996.

12. *Fighting over country: anthropological perspectives,* DE Smith and J Finlayson (eds), 1997.

13. *Connections in native title: genealogies, kinship, and groups,* JD Finlayson, B Rigsby, and HJ Bek (eds), 1999.

14. *Land rights at risk? Evaluations of the Reeves report,* JC Altman, F Morphy, and T Rowse (eds), 1999.

15. *Unemployment payments, the activity test, and Indigenous Australians: understanding breach rates,* W Sanders, 1999.

16. *Why only one in three? The complex reasons for low Indigenous school retention,* RG Schwab, 1999.

17. *Indigenous families and the welfare system: two community case studies,* DE Smith (ed.), 2000.

18. *Ngukurr at the millennium: a baseline profile for social impact planning in south-east Arnhem Land,* J Taylor, J Bern, and KA Senior, 2000.

19. *Aboriginal nutrition and the Nyirranggulung Health Strategy in Jawoyn Country*, J Taylor and N Westbury, 2000.

20. *The Indigenous welfare economy and the CDEP Scheme*, F Morphy and W Sanders (eds), 2001.

21. *Health expenditure, income and health status among Indigenous and other Australians*, MC Gray, BH Hunter, and J Taylor, 2002.

22. *Making sense of the census: observations of the 2001 enumeration in remote Aboriginal Australia*, DF Martin, F Morphy, WG Sanders and J Taylor, 2002.

23. *Aboriginal population profiles for development planning in the northern East Kimberley*, J Taylor, 2003.

24. *Social indicators for Aboriginal governance: insights from the Thamarrurr region, Northern Territory*, J Taylor, 2004.

25. *Indigenous people and the Pilbara mining boom: a baseline for regional participation*, J Taylor and B Scambary, 2005.

26. *Assessing the evidence on Indigenous socioeconomic outcomes: a focus on the 2002 NATSISS*, BH Hunter (ed.), 2006.

27. *The social effects of native title: recognition, translation, coexistence*, BR Smith and F Morphy (eds), 2007.

28. *Agency, contingency and census process: observations of the 2006 Indigenous Enumeration Strategy in remote Aboriginal Australia*, F Morphy (ed.), 2008.

29. *Contested governance: culture, power and institutions in Indigenous Australia*, J Hunt, D Smith, S Garling and W Sanders (eds), 2008.

30. *Power, culture, economy: Indigenous Australians and mining*, J Altman and D Martin (eds), 2009.

31. *Demographic and socioeconomic outcomes across the Indigenous Australian lifecourse*, N Biddle and M Yap, 2010.

32. *Survey analysis for Indigenous policy in Australia: social science perspectives*, B Hunter and N Biddle (eds), 2012.

33. *My country, mine country: Indigenous people, mining and development contestation in remote Australia*, B Scambary, 2013.

34. *Indigenous Australians and the National Disability Insurance Scheme*, N Biddle, F Al-Yaman, M Gourley, M Gray, JR Bray, B Brady, LA Pham, E Williams, M Montaigne, 2014.

Centre for Aboriginal Economic Policy Research,
College of Arts and Social Sciences,
The Australian National University, Acton, ACT, 2601

Information on CAEPR Discussion Papers, Working Papers and Research Monographs (Nos 1–19) and abstracts and summaries of all CAEPR print publications and those published electronically can be found at the following website: caepr.anu.edu.au.

www.ingramcontent.com/pod-product-compliance
Lightning Source LLC
Chambersburg PA
CBHW050807270326
41926CB00026B/4591